THE LONG HAUL

Conversations with Southern Writers

William Parrill

UNIVERSITY
PRESS OF
AMERICA

Rn

Lanham • New York • London

SOUTHEASTERN
LOUISIANA
STATE UNIVERSITY

University Press of America® Inc.
4720 Boston Way
Lanham, Maryland 20706

3 Henrietta Street
London WC2E 8LU England

Library of Congress Cataloging-in-Publication Data

Parrill, William.
The long haul : conversations with southern writers /
by William Parrill.
p.   cm.
Includes bibliographical references.
1. American fiction—Southern States—History and criticism—Theory,
etc.   2. American fiction—20th century—History and criticism—
Theory, etc.   3. Novelists, American—Southern States—Interviews.
4. Novelists, American—20th century—Interviews.   5. Southern
States—Intellectual life—1865-   6. Southern States in literature.
7. Fiction—Authorship. I. Title.
PS261.P37   1993   813'.5409975—dc20   93–31587 CIP

ISBN 0–8191–9077–2 (cloth : alk. paper)
ISBN 0–8191–9078–0 (pbk. : alk. paper)

FTW
AFD 1614

From a distance the house looked intact but up closer Wendell could see it was a burnt-out shell. He did not know what caused the pang of melancholy that made him wonder about the family, what happened to them: they were nothing to him and his kind. But he did feel it and he did wonder as they turned onto a dirt track and passed the house and he heard Hal say, "Gone with the wind."

—Madison Jones, *Last Things*

For Sue, From Bill
"Till the Sun Dies"

Contents

Foreword

The Long Haul: Conversations With Southern Novelists is a series of conversations with important contemporary Southern novelists and with Lewis P. Simpson, long time co-editor of *The Southern Review* and an established authority on Southern literature.

The two long conversations with Professor Simpson place the post World War II Southern novel in the context of modern literature and of the classical Southern novel. Professor Simpson, who knew many of the giants of Southern literature, assesses the writers of the past and the possibilities of the future.

The volume includes conversations with some of the South's—and today's—most important novelists: Ernest Gaines (author of *The Autobiography of Miss Jane Pittman*), Madison Jones (*An Exile*), Shirley Ann Grau (*The Condor Passes*), David Madden (*Bijou*), the late John William Corrington (*Decoration Day*), and James Wilcox (*Modern Baptists*). A conversation with Vance Bourjaily (*The Man Who Knew Kennedy*), furnishes an outside perspective by a famed novelist who only recently moved to the South. Finally a chapter by the editor about his relationship with the late Walker Percy, *The Moviegoer*, concludes the volume.

The Long Haul is not a book of interviews in the conventional sense, but a group of carefully caculated responses on a number of important critical questions: Is the Southern novel still possible? Does the Southern literary response differ from that of other sections of the country? What are the economic difficulties facing the Southern novelist? How is the novelist to manage an often uneasy relationship with Hollywood and the academy? What part does religion play in the Southern novel of today? And perhaps most important of all: Does the Southern novel have a future?

The editor of *The Long Haul*, William Parrill, Professor of Communication and English at Southeastern Louisiana University, is a founding editor of *Louisiana Literature* and has writtern extensively on modern literature and film.

Introduction

Many people feel about Southern writing the way they feel about pornography: they do not know how to define it, but they know it when they see it. On closer examination, however, it is not always clear exactly what the phrase means. Does it mean books written by writers born and raised in the South, books written about the South, or books dealing with unique areas of Southern experience? Or does it mean books which deal with a declining, often feudalistic, and racist ideology which flourished both before and after the Civil War and expired as a viable literary entity with the death of William Faulkner? And if it still exists, has it been reduced from its former mythical greatness to mere local color, a Mardi Gras of the mind to attract trendy literary tourists?

The conversations in this book will hardly give answers to these questions, but they will provide a context in which to discuss them. They will provide strong, often divergent, opinions about the distinctiveness of Southern writing and its possibilities for survival in a rapidly changing world where the region's native culture is being relentlessly homogenized, and where a novelist is more likely to write about the year of the Stones tour than about the year of his first deer hunt.

Although some critics seem to think that Southern writing is in a state of decline and may be about to disappear completely—that is, to lose its identity as a recognizable entity and to merge into the general current of American literature—such a conclusion seems to me decidedly premature. If these interviews do nothing else, they testify to the vitality and validity of writing in the South during the postwar period, that is, during the period when implacable cultural forces began their steady, relentless attempt to make the South just like the rest of the country. They also testify to the continuing productivity, the often heated differences of opinion, the varied backgrounds, cultures, religious beliefs and ideologies, and above all the integrity of the writers, especially in their continuing respect for the story-telling tradition. They testify, in short, that Southern writing is in good hands.

I had originally intended to write a scholarly introduction to my collection of conversations or interviews, but the two long interviews with Lewis P.

Simpson, Emeritus Professor of English at Louisiana State University, long time
co-editor of *The Southern Review*, and acknowledged authority on Southern literature, has made my scholarship, which was likely to be shaky at best, superfluous.

I hope that the reader, even though he may have a particular interest in one
or the other of the novelists interviewed, will read the interviews with Professor
Simpson first. Simpson's roots stretch back to the frontier Texas background of his
youth, and his scholarly career covers virtually the entire postwar period. He has
devoted his life to the study of Southern literature, and his interviews furnish an
historical and ideological context for the people being interviewed. Many novelists have a deep, even a consuming, interest in history—John William Corrington,
for example was such a writer—but they tend to think of novels in in terms of
problem solving, of ways of achieving artistic goals. Like most creative people,
they tend to be intuitive rather than analytical, to go with their gut reactions rather
than with their minds. Here, the scholar and the critic can help in the analysis of
the historical background. He can furnish a disinterested but sympathetic voice.
And this is what I believe the conversations with Simpson do.

I admit that the admission of Vance Bourjaily may appear unjustified,
since all the other writers included here are Southern by birth, education and inclination. I have, however, included Bourjaily because I do not think that he has gotten anything like the recognition that he deserves. After a long career as a novelist
and a teacher of writing at Iowa, Bourjaily moved to Louisiana to become head of
the graduate writing program at Louisiana State University. Because of his interest
in jazz and the proximity of New Orleans, Bourjaily accepted a teaching job at a
time in his life when he might reasonably have been expected to retire and to
devote himself to writing.

Of all the writers included in this book, Bourjaily has had the longest
career. Originally a Scribners writer who began his career with the legendary
Maxwell Perkins, Bourjaily became established as one of the most important
young American novelists with the publication of John W. Aldridge's *After the
Lost Generation*. For a variety of reasons, however, Bourjaily's fame has not keep
pace with his merits, and although his later novels have received many favorable
reviews, his reputation has declined. Bourjaily has lived most of his life far from
New York, the center of literary power, and his stout adherence to traditional realism of the Fitzgerald mode has not helped his popularity in an age when non-tradi-
tional modes have become prestigious. Of late, however, Bourjaily's critical reputation has started to revive.

Bourjaily's novels are permeated with a sense of loss, of tragic waste, per-
haps best exemplified by the protagonist of *The Man Who Knew Kennedy*.
Bourjaily here hones in on the most glamorous myth of the sixties, that of the
Kennedys, and uses its brilliance to underscore the failure of his protagonist, Dave
Doremus. Bourjaily understands the American dream which goes wrong, the man
who seems to have everything but ends up with nothing. In hindsight, the novel,

which appeared in 1967, appears prophetic, and the blurring of the Kennedy myth which has occurred recently has only heightened the novel's almost unbearable poignancy. And Bourjaily's most recent novel, *Old Soldier*, published since my interview was finished, shows Bourjaily's continuing preoccupations with themes of love and honor developed against the background of a changing American society.

John William Corrington's tragic death in 1988 at a time when his reputation was growing and his works were for the first time beginning to reach a wide audience deprived American literature of a distinctive voice. The detective novels set in New Orleans which Corrington, with his wife Joyce, wrote during the last years of his life, are a distinct contribution to the genre, and the collection of short novels *All My Trials*, one of which was the basis for the televison film, *Decoration Day*, showed a sure command of style, technique and theme. *The Collected Stories of John William Corrington* (1990) includes all of Corrington's work in the shorter forms of fiction with the unfortunate exception of the novellas in *All My Trials* which could not be included if an already large volume were not to expand to a totally unwieldy bulk and price.

It may be some time before Corrington's contribution to American fiction can be fully assessed, but William Mills's introduction to *The Collected Stories* is a notable beginning.   Although Corrington wore his learning lightly, he had a formidable academic education with both a law degree and a Ph.D. in modern literature. He was certainly the most educated of the current generation of Southern writers, and his particular interests—Voegelin, Joyce, the law, Southern history, Catholicism—will require an equally learned critic.

But if Corrington were an intellectual, he was an unlikely one, and he prided himself on his red neck attitudes, and he may have been, as I accused him of being, the last of the unreconstructed Southerners. Indeed, his stories may turn out to be the last real justification of the Southerner's ferocious independence, and he may have been the last man to think that the wrong side won the Civil War. Like a number of the most important American novelists, Corrington did his best work in the short novel. The demands of the form curbed an expansiveness and exuberance which, I think, marred some of his novels. His short novels, particularly those dealing with the law, deserve a permanent place in American literature.

In her interview, Shirley Ann Grau says that the public likes only very young writers and very old writers, and that the period in between is a "long dry spell." The statement, however generally true, does not seem to apply to Grau's career. From the beginning, she has lacked neither critical nor popular recognition. Although she is hardly ancient, her first book appeared as long ago as 1955, and her career is already a long one. Grau, unlike Corrington, disdains the appelation, "Southern writer," but her early novels and stories often seem Southern with a vengeance; her more recent works,however, at least those published since *The Condor Passes* (1971), have been international in theme and subject matter.

Unfortunately, her pace of publication has slackened in recent years, but I suspect that she will yet produce major works, and that any current judgment is likely to be speculative at best.

The novels of Madison Jones have never lacked for critical recognition, but they have, unfortunately, never reached the wide readership enjoyed by some other novelists interviewed in this book. Even the film version of *An Exile*—called incongrously *I Walk the Line*, since that is exactly what the sheriff depicted in the novel did not do—failed to drum up much popularity either for it or for Jones's other novels. Although Jones himself is the mildest of men, his novels are violent tales of lust, murder and retribution set against the background of a changing South.

Written with a great economy of means, Jones's best novels move toward foreordained and tragic conclusions with powerful force. His masterpiece, *A Cry of Absence* (1971), grew out of the civil rights turmoil of the sixties, and Jones himself has said that during the early seventies, he felt abandoned by his materials. Jones is a novelist of the frontier and, recently, of the changing South of today, and his novels struggle to record that change.

Jones's most recent novel, *Last Things* (1989), deals with a young graduate student who becomes corrupted through involvement with the drug trade, but evil here, as elsewhere in Jones, is internal, and Wendell Corbin's fall is the result, not of external forces, but of tendencies inherent in his own character. Over the years, Jones has trimmed away the rhetorical richness of his earlier works. His novels have become progressively leaner and more spare, and he has developed a style of such simplicity that reviewers, who are not always the most careful of readers, have often regarded his recent works as rough drafts of violent stories rather than as, I believe them to be, compressed stories of great intensity which deal with often inadequate characters in situations of rapid change.

Ernest Gaines is Southern with a vengeance, but as a black novelist of the rural South, he might seem to be an anachronism were it not for the integrity with which he treats his subjects. The "quarters" of his youth are long vanished, but the examples of courage and fortitude and humanity which they furnish will continue to live in Gaines's novels and stories. Gaines has received numerous awards and presently holds what is in effect an endowed chair at the University of Southwestern Louisiana.

The Autobiography of Miss Jane Pittman and its attendant television version, one of the most highly rated programs ever shown on televison, gave Gaines an enormous audience, but the popularity of *Miss Jane*, which has sold as many copies as all of the author's other novels put together, has been a mixed blessing and has tended to obscure the full range of his achievement. For example, Gaines's darkest novel, *In My Father's House* (1978), has a powerful, tragic intensity far removed from the affirmations of *Miss Jane Pittman*. Set, like the rest of his novels and stories in the rural Southwestern Louisiana of Gaines's youth, *In*

My Father's House is a masterpiece of dramatic conciseness and will, I think, remain a thing apart: powerful, slightly painful to read, and universal in its humanity.

David Madden, who began publishing in the early 1960's, is more clearly a product of the oral tradition of backwoods Southern storytelling than any of the other novelists included in this book. Madden's novels and stories mimic the human voice, not only in the rhythms of speech, but also in his tendency to keep recasting his material in search of a more effective narrative form. The tendency is not only, as is the case of so many writers, toward expansion, but also sometimes toward concision, toward a more dramatically effective telling. Thus, Madden can chronicle the adventures of Lucius Hutchfield both in the short and dramatic *Brothers in Confidence* (1972) and in the long and expansive *Bijou* (1974), and then revise the earlier work for inclusion in *Pleasure Dome* (1979).

Madden has easily written more criticism than all of other novelists included in this book put together. His criticism is practical rather than theoretical—no deconstructionist speculations for him—but any critical assessment of Madden's work will have to take it into account. A consideration of the relationship between Madden's work, published and unpublished, and the writers he most admires—Wright Morris, the tough guy novelists of the thirties, and others not so well known—will be a fruitful enterprise for some ambitious graduate student of the future.

Jame Wilcox is the youngest novelist included in this book. Although he has already produced five books—his most recent, *Polite Sex* (1991), has appeared since my conversation was finished—he is still a young man, and considering his steady capacity for growth, it would be rash to predict his future development. He has already staked out a distinctive position among the younger Southern writers. Wilcox, who studied under Robert Penn Warren, has a keen sense of place and a nice eye for the eccentricities of character, but his literary models are as likely to be English as American, and it is no surprise to discover that he has a growing readership in England.

I had also scheduled an interview with Charles Willeford, former art student and writer of tough crime novels, but unfortunately he died of a heart attack before I was able to interview him. At his untimely death, Willeford, like John Corrington, was writing a series of detective novels which was just beginning to bring the fame which had eluded him earlier. I had long admired his work and had written strongly favorable reviews of *The Burnt Orange Heresy* and *Cockfighter* when they appeared, and we had enjoyed a brief correspondence. Willeford wrote that I had doubtless noticed the parallels between the actions of the protagonist of *Cockfighter* and Joyce's "silence, exile and cunning." (Of course, I had not.) Willeford's memoir of his military experiences, *Something About a Soldier*, and his hilarious spoof of modern art criticism, *The Burnt Orange Heresy*, have not received nearly the critical attention they deserve. Willeford had a remarkable capacity for growth and, at his death, was writing better than he ever had.

There are a number of other writers whom I wanted to interview but, for one reason or another, was unable to, sometimes through no fault but my own. Among them were two writers with large talents and often dominating positions in the lives of their fellow writers of the South: Cormac McCarthy and Walker Percy.

McCarthy is the great hidden talent of current fiction, a writer of great gifts and huge ambitions, a writer's writer. Anyone who doubts the admiration that McCarthy insipires can read what John William Corrington, no mean wordsmith himself, says about him in the interview in this book. The novels, *Outer Dark* and *Child of God*, and the television play *The Gardener's Son* are among the most beautifully written works of Southern literature, and I am sorry that, after a respectful correspondence, McCarthy declined my request for an interview. McCarthy's latest novel, *All the Pretty Horses* (1992), the first of a projected "Border Trilogy," is his most accessible novel and the first to reach a broad readership. If McCarthy's dark vision seems out of keeping with the bestseller lists, we should remember that all great writers—and I would certainly consider McCarthy in that group—eventually carry their readership with them.

Walker Percy was "King of the Cats" during the period when these interviews were conceived and carried out and other Southern novelists tended to define themselves by their often ambivalent attitudes toward him and his works. Although I did not do a written interview with Walker Percy, I interviewed him after the publication of *The Last Gentleman* in 1966, and I have included an account of that interview and of my limited relationship with this gifted and enigmatic man. I think that it is fair to say that Percy's fame transcended the merely literary and that he became a part of the Southern consciousness in a way no other writer has managed, at least since the death of Faulkner.

Of course, many of the dominant themes of these interviews would be typical of discussions with writers from any section of the country. These include, among others which the reader will pick out, the difficulty of making a living as a serious writer, a love-hate relationship between the writer and the academy, a covert glance—sometimes even a bold stare—in the direction of Hollywood, a respect for the integrity of the writing process, and the desire to communicate with a mass audience without lowering standards.

But there are also differences, the most important of which is, I think, a rejection of the popular culture in favor of a different set of values, if not always the values we might imagine. The Madison Jones who does not mention particular movie titles in a period novel because he does not want to "hold" the reader to a knowledge of them is not that far removed from the James Wilcox who derides the use of brand names in the novels of Brett Easton Ellis and others. If most of the Southern writers have by now pretty thoroughly rejected the old culture and values represented by William Alexander Percy and William Faulkner, it does not necessarily follow that they are quite ready to accept the new culture of consumerism.

The sense of place in Southern fiction is still quite strong, and while that sense is being steadily eroded, I do not believe that it will disappear, at least in the near future. The Southerner who wakes up in a mall may not know whether he is in Mississippi or Connecticut, but he is unlikely to confuse it with home. When James Wilcox says that he likes to hang out in malls to watch people and to listen to them, he is suggesting merely that the mall has taken the place of the front porch of the country store, and not that it has produced any fundamental change in the nature of Southern society.

At least one of the traditional themes of the Southern novel—that of racial conflict—is likely to disappear from the Southern novel, or at least to be presented in terms which are drastically altered. Of course, the relationship between the white man and the black man—Elizabeth Spencer's "the voice at the back door"—will continue to occupy the novelist, but the exchange is likely to be one of cultural equality, and not necessarily one in which the right and the wrong of a situation is readily apparent.

There remains to me only the task of telling how these conversations were done and what I hoped to accomplish.

To begin with, they are not real conversations: they are considered statements on the art of writing. They began with conversations, but they continued in writing and they ended in writing. My conversation was tape-recorded, edited and transcribed. It was then sent back to the writer for revision—and it received revision, in some cases a lot of it, in others less. In at least one instance, practically every word was changed. Then, depending upon how I felt about the success of the result, I either started the process over or settled for further minor revisions. In no case did the final product resemble what originally went into the tape recorder. Authors write: they are not necessarily more articulate than other educated people. Some, like the late John William Corrington, are extremely forceful and articulate in conversation; others are less so. But in all cases the interviews in this book represent considered judgments; they are not spur of the minute statements.

Unlike some interviewers, I have not attempted to suppress my own opinions. Without some interplay between two speakers, one does not have a conversation, but a monologue. This does not, of course, mean that the interviewer should express all points of disagreement with the writer, but it does mean that he should not be dishonest. If he does not respect the integrity of the writer enough to voice genuine disagreement, he ought to look for someone else to interview.

All the interviews included here are professional and not personal; they deal with the professional and only incidentally with the personal lives of the writers. But I will not deny that the relationship between the interviewer and the person being interviewed is to some small extent at least adversarial. Most novels begin in reality, usually with an incident which the novelist has experienced personally or which he knows about or with a person whom he knows. Just as Aragon based a character in his Napoleonic novel, *Holy Week*, on James Dean, so novelists of today have based characters, even in novels set in the past, on real people, sometimes members of their family, sometimes friends or acquaintances. Often for legitimate reasons the writer does not want the information known.

Furthermore, incidents from the past, from current events, or from the lives of his family are all grist for the novelist's mill. The incidents may be painful to family members or to others. Perhaps their use will offend someone, or perhaps the novelist simply does not want to show his hand. And if the writer is a serious one—and all of the people interviewed here are intensely serious—he certainly does not want to detract from the artistry of the story by talking about its source.

But literary gossip has only minor importance. If we have literary interests, we like to read about the models of Proust's novel—at least I do—but the originals are usually interesting only because they are part of a great novel and not for any other reason. The reader whose primary interest is extra-literary sources is advised to look elsewhere.

While it is important for an literary interviewer to be a good listener, it is more important for him to be well prepared. I think that the main reason the writers included in this book responded well to me is that in every case I read all, or substantially all, of their major works. It is difficult not to respond sympathetically to someone who is familiar with your novels and stories, even occasionally more familiar with them than you are, since he has read them more recently.

Generally those novelists who have spent a lot of time teaching remember their work better and are more articulate than those who have done little or no teaching. Students tend to read and ask questions and the writer prepares answers which he gives to the students and tends to repeat to interviewers. This is not necessarily an advantage. Unless the novelist, like Borges, gives the same interview over and over and the interviewer must perforce be satisfied with it, the interviewer must attempt to get beyond the formalized answers and seek a newer, if not always a more satisfactory response.

Does Southern literature have a future? The answer to the question depends largely upon what one thinks Southern literature is. In the sense that someone like Donald Davidson or Andrew Lytle might define the term, Southern literature is as dead as the dodo. The old South values are dead, and in retrospect *I'll Take My Stand* may be seen as merely a rear guard action, soon abandoned, at least as a practical course of action, by its most distinguished proponents. The war is over, finally and forever, slavery is gone, factories are everywhere, and malls spring like giant mushrooms out of the red clay soil.

But that does not quite mean that the South is becoming like everyplace else, and the novelists included in this book have a ferocious particularity of place and, to a lesser extent, of ideology. Place, family, oral tradition, the burden of history—these are the materials of the Southern novelist, and I will leave to others to sort out how much they are particular to a region and a people and how much they are currently property of the population and the country as a whole.

James Wilcox shows the Southern novel in transition, but then all good Southern writers do that at some point in their careers. While John William Corrington may have been the last of the unreconstructed Southerners, it does not follow that the Southern novel, which has had so long and illustrious a career, is on its deathbed. Within the past few months, the publication of new works by younger novelists—Donna Tartt's *The Secret History*, Sheilah Bosworth's *Slow Poison*, and Nancy Lemann's *Sportsman's Paradise*—as well as recent or soon to be published works by James Wilcox, Ernest Gaines, Anne Tyler, Cormac McCarthy, Gail Godwin, Ellen Gilchrist, Lee Smith, and others—argues a robust good health for the Southern novel.

The sense of place, the sound of the speaking voice, and the burdens of history are as present in Southern novelists today as in any period of the past. Those brave souls who forecast the imminent death of the Southern novel do so at their own peril.

Chapter 1
Scholarship in the South: A Conversation with Lewis P. Simpson

My interview with Lewis P. Simpson takes place in Baton Rouge at his office on the Louisiana State University campus. The English Department is on the second floor of Allen Hall, an aging and comfortable building named after the late governor of Louisiana, O. K. Allen. When I locate Professor Simpson, he greets me courteously and we walk to his office. Although recently retired, Professor Simpson continues as an advisory editor of *The Southern Review* and as an active scholar and critic. His door, marked with egalitarian plainness, "Mr. Simpson," does nothing to differentiate the distinguished author and long-time co-editor of *The Southern Review* from a lowly teaching assistant.

The office, like that of most teachers, is filled with an assortment of reading material, including scholarly magazines, review copies of books, and paperbacks of Faulkner, Warren and Percy used, I presume, as classroom texts. Photographs on the wall in front of the desk show a diverse group of distinguished Southern writers including Faulkner, Warren, Welty and others.

Professor Simpson's responses to my queries are thoughtful and softly spoken. He has the Southerner's—or the scholar's—habit of worrying over a question until he has included the information that satisfies him. Although most of the questions are long familiar to him—indeed, he has devoted a large portion of his life to answering some of them—his answers seem bright and new.

After the interview, we walk to the Faculty Club for lunch. There we discuss the Agrarians and the Fugitives, particularly Tate and Warren. At first the Augustan austerity of the one and the passion of the other seem far away, but as we speak, they become almost palpable presences. Some five hours after our conversation begins, we separate in front of the Union, I to see if my car has been impounded and he to return to his office.

WP: I believe that you were originally from Texas.

LS: Yes, I grew up in northwest Texas in a town called Jacksboro. It is the seat of Jack County. My father was a native Texan and my mother was a native of

Kentucky, but she had been brought to Texas at the age of three by her parents. Her father had decided to seek his fortune as a cotton farmer in the black land belt south of Fort Worth. In a way, the section of Texas I was brought up in west of Fort Worth was still semi-frontier country when I was a kid. I have thought about writing about it, but I have never done much except for a few unpublished poems and one short memoir, which I read at Nicholls State last year on the lecture program that Red Warren inaugurated several years ago, the Fletcher Lectures. James Olney wants to publish this in *The Southern Review* this fall. Northwest Texas is not a country like East Texas, which is more or less like Louisiana. It is not a country you associate with typical Southern themes. No Confederate soldiers stand in the town squares. It's ranching country, but when they discovered oil up there, it became heavily devoted to the oil industry. There were slaves there in ante-bellum times, but slavery was not really economically feasible beyond East Texas. The slaves in Jack County were mostly household servants, handymen, and so on. My paternal great-grandfather was a slave owner. Something of a Thomas Sutpen figure. He could neither read nor write but acquired a lot of land. Also operated one of the stations of the famous Butterfield Overland Stage. Converted all his cash into Confederate money when Secession came, but did not go belly up, still had land after the war. His name was Ham, a Scottish name. My paternal grandmother lived to be ninety-five years old, and I heard a lot of stories when I was a kid, about fighting with the Indians in particular. They were still fighting them up there in the 1870s. Today tourists go to Fort Richardson State Park just outside Jacksboro, where they see what is left of what was from 1867 to 1875 the largest Federal military post in America. Fort Richardson was one of several forts built to defend against the Indians, who were supposedly on reservations in Oklahoma, the Kiowas and Commanches notably, but they raided down into North Texas almost every full moon. There was pretty rough trouble, and they started to build a whole series of forts, but they actually built only a few. I was always aware of the old fort when I was growing up, and my grandmother had even lived there at one point. It was part of a kind of mixed heritage. When you look back at the records of the Civil War, you discover that secession in Texas was a very mixed thing. Sam Houston was a tremendous figure in Texas, and he was not in favor of secession. I've seen the voting records of the county that I was brought up in. The people who voted for secession included my great-grandfather, but they were a distinct minority. Of the fifty or sixty men who voted, the majority voted not to leave the Union, yet their allegiance when the fighting started was largely to the Confederacy. I was brought up in a world which was not the world of the deep South. The world of the West Texas South had its own qualities. My father's family had lived in Arkansas, and at one point they were burned out by the Yankees. My maternal grandfather and grandmother had come down to Texas after the war. As far as I know, they never owned any slaves although others in the family had slaves in Kentucky before coming to Texas after the war. In general, my family was on the edge of the old South heritage, and I was brought up as a "western Southerner." My father was a lawyer and an orator. His oratory was pretty much that of the old school.

WP: He had some pretensions as a writer, I believe.

LS: My father and his brother, who was somewhat younger, both got pretty good educations. My father had a varied career. He taught school for a while and even at one point attempted a weekly newspaper with another man for about six months in Jack County. I've never been able to find any whole copy of it and know it only as preserved in excerpts in a scrapbook. Apparently, my father kept most of his own contributions. The later files of the newspaper, the *Jack County News*, still exist. In those days newspapers, and especially country newspapers, frequently published stories and poems. My father wrote several stories and poems for the *News*; he also wrote various editorials, one or two militantly defensive of the South. He was young and they were not able to make any living out of the paper and they decided to sell out and to do other things. My father eventually managed to get to the University of Texas Law School, and to become a well-known lawyer in north Texas, although he never managed to make much money at it. He had a big family, and he bought and sold cattle some.

He had real literary interests especially as a young man. He became known as an orator. I managed to find a few of his addresses that he wrote out, and even one or two that were delivered in the courtroom, during the prosecution of criminal cases in particular. They represent typical Southern oratory. Lawyers of that time knew two things pretty well: Shakespeare and the Bible. Most of the Americans of that day thought of New England writers as the important American ones. My father had a copy of Longfellow's poems; on the flyleaf he wrote that he had begun to commit that book to memory on a certain date in 1893. Memorizing was a part of the educational process in those days, but whether he ever memorized it all or not, I don't know. (Laughs.) He had some sense of books, and his library, as small as it was, was by far the biggest in town. Among his books was a prized set of the *Library of Southern Literature*. This was edited by several Southerners and was published in the early part of the twentieth century. It's an amazing collection, mostly of sorry literature, except for Edgar Allan Poe.

WP: I was interested in what you had to say about literary talent being separated from oratory and public presentation.

LS: No, it wasn't that way, not in the South anyway, until the 1920s. As far as storytelling in general was concerned, the language was pretty colloquial. Most lawyers had several languages. When they were just among themselves talking, and I used to hear a good deal of that talk, they mostly told stories about the courtroom, and they told those in colloquial form. But as far as public address was concerned, there were certain prescribed literary rules. My father was a member of the debate team at the University of Texas and was apparently pretty successful. In those days, college debate was important, and he had kept a long account of a debate in New Orleans between Texas and Tulane. This was written up on a whole page of the *Times-Picayune*. The article singled out my father for the highest praise. Society respected the importance of oratory and of public address. We've completely lost that today.

WP: What sort of topics did they debate?

LS: They frequently debated general subjects of government and democracy. I've forgotten the exact topic being debated that night in New Orleans, but it was one of those topics relating to, as I recall, the education of women. It had a kind of feminist slant, but I don't recall exactly how it was worded. The irony was that all the debaters were men.

WP: What sort of reading did you do while you were in high school?

LS: At first, I read the books we had at home primarily. I read all kinds of stuff indiscriminately. My mother was a school teacher and she read a lot to us, and she encouraged us to read.

WP: Scott?

LS: I know that Scott was supposed to be the great writer of the South, but I don't remember reading him until I was in college. Well, maybe *Ivanhoe*. One set of books that was very influential on me was the so-called "authorized" edition of Mark Twain.

WP: I still have that set.

LS: I read all of those. My father also had a set of the complete works of Bret Harte, who was still pretty well-known. One summer I made it my job to read all the works of Bret Harte. I'm probably the only person who ever did it. Many of them were so slight that even a youngster couldn't take them too seriously. My father had a collection of Emerson's essays which he read sometimes even in later life. I remember that he said that Emerson always gave him a headache. (Laughs.) My mother had gone to the University of Texas, too, and she liked Thackeray and Dickens very much. I read the Bible a good deal, Shakespeare, books on the South, and in certain general collections like the *Harvard Classics*. All in all, it was pretty much of a mixed bag.

WP: Where did you go to college?

LS: I graduated from Jacksboro High School in the depths of the great depression. I didn't have any way to get to a four-year college at first. I went down to Arlington, Texas, where there was at that time what is now a branch of the University of Texas. It was then a branch of Texas A & M. It had about a thousand students, three hundred girls and seven hundred boys, and it was a military school, an ROTC school. Both the boys and girls wore uniforms at all times, but the girls weren't under military discipline. It was a pretty good community college.

WP: It was a two-year school?

LS: It was two years at that time. Thirty-five years or so ago, it became a four-year college. Now it probably has a good deal of graduate work. I was editor of the school newspaper there. Eventually, my father managed to get me a job at the state capitol in Austin. So after two years at Arlington I went to work for the Oil and Gas Division of the Texas Railroad Commission. I worked part time and went to school part time. I worked at least half a day and sometimes more than that and went to school in the time I had left. Those were the days when the big East Texas oil fields had come in, and the Oil and Gas Division was the biggest and the most complicated and the most corrupt division of the commission. I remember Lyndon Johnson and John Connolly and those guys when they were young around the capitol and all kinds of things that happened there. I eventually did get a B.A. and then an M.A. and eventually a Ph.D. All my degrees were from Texas.

WP: What was your major?

LS: Even at that time Texas had a pretty well-defined American lit program. An undergraduate could take a sort of major in American lit, which I did. At the M.A. level, I took medieval history under Frederick Duncalf, who was a great medieval historian. And then I got interested in Irish history and did a thesis on the playwright Sean O'Casey, who by that time had become fairly well-known. I got onto O'Casey simply by happenstance. I used to read a lot in the old Fort Worth Carnegie Library. I had two aunts who worked there. This was a most improbable library building. The old lady who ran it and started it with an apple barrel full of books had this peculiar sense that a library was also supposed to be partly a museum, and so she got all kinds of strange things in there including a Chinese rickshaw. She also had a World War I torpedo in the midst of a whole bunch of books that you could browse in. I used to go in and sit on the torpedo and read, and one afternoon in 1936 I picked up *Within the Gates* and read the whole thing sitting on the torpedo. (Laughs.) Finally I did write a master's thesis on O'Casey. At the same time, I never did really get committed to Irish literature. My chief interest was still American literature.

WP: Who were the avant-garde people who were admired at that time? Did you read James Branch Cabell? I know he's nearly forgotten now.

LS: Cabell was still pretty big in the thirties. I read *Jurgen* and *Figures of Earth*. He was considered a little wicked and somewhat daring to read. I read most of O'Neill's plays. He had become very popular.

WP: Dreiser?

LS: Not a great deal. *An American Tragedy*, of course. The university courses at that time basically didn't teach anything later than Thomas Hardy. The old Wood, Watt, Anderson book *From Beowulf to Thomas Hardy* was still the survey book. Some teachers would not go beyond Hardy in the novel.

WP: I had an old teacher at West Virginia University named John W. Draper—he was related to the nineteenth-century Draper—who wouldn't teach anything after 1798, but that seemed a little extreme.

LS: Yeah, that would. (Laughs.) I remember Leonidas Paine at Texas who stopped at Robert Frost and the First World War. I remember in the thirties, it was very hard to get writers like Hemingway and Faulkner on the list, but eventually you did begin to get courses in T. S. Eliot and some others by the end of the thirties.

WP: Nowadays I think we've gone to the other extreme.

LS: Yeah, anything goes. (Pauses.) I think the coming of the New Criticism had a great deal to do with the breaking down of the old philological tradition.

WP: What part do you think *Understanding Poetry* played in bringing that about?

LS: In the simplest sense it restored the sense of a direct relationship between the poem—the words, the images, and the music—and the reader of the poem. In this sense it was certainly not something "new" by way of an approach to understanding poetry. Anybody who had read Dr. Johnson knows this. But the Brooks and Warren approach tended to seem novel to American academics in its apparent lack of emphasis on the historical reconstruction of a poem. This was the approach that had come to be dominant in American universities with the disappearance of the Oxford-Cambridge classical model in the latter part of the nineteenth century and the elevation of the Germanic model, the Ph.D. system. If Cleanth and Red had gone through this system, there would have been no *Understanding Poetry*. But they both went to Oxford as Rhodes Scholars and got Oxford M.A.'s. I've discovered that when they came to LSU there was some opinion in the English Department that the virtuous and proper thing for them to do was to get their Ph.D.'s in order to be promoted, etc. Thank God they resisted the philological tyranny.

WP: What did you do your dissertation on?

LS: Well, I wasn't original enough to resist the system, but I kind of got in on something like the ground floor of a new structure in the system that had begun to be built with the development of so-called "programs in American Civilization." Today the term is "American Studies." This was an interdisciplinary approach, another kind of resistance to the philological tradition. I had the good luck at the University of Texas to study both under Henry Nash Smith and Theodore Hornberger. The result was that I came up with a dissertation with a title that sounds God-awful provincial—" The Age of Joseph Stevens Buckminster: The Boston-Cambridge Community, 1800-1815." It took a lot of time to see in this little world of the early American Republic the implication of the New England Renaissance to come, but the effort paid off. I learned a lot not only about New England culture but about the cultural meaning of the South. Later I picked up on the connection between New England and the South—which I now see as something like a tragic symbiosis—and made this over the years, so to speak, my subject.

WP: When did you get your Ph.D.?

LS: In 1948, and we moved over here that year, and I've been here ever since. It doesn't seem that long. That's one of the deceptions of getting old.

WP: You've spent a lot of time meditating on the history of the South, particularly on the relationship between the Southern literary tradition and the individual writer. How was it that the South managed to lose the war but to win the battle for minds that took place afterwards? How did the South pretty much manage to impose its view of reality on the country in the media? *The Birth of a Nation*, for example, is nothing but the perceived Southern view of reality.

LS: I think the reasons are very complicated and have never been truly fathomed. As far as *The Birth of a Nation* is concerned, I think it's a mistake to conclude that the segregationists were all Southerners. That's been proven totally false by the events of the past. *The Birth of a Nation* had a wide appeal. The Anglo-Saxon mystique of the white race is very strong in New England and elsewhere as well as in the South. Dixon and writers like that reflected the fears of many Americans. There was a real fear of other races exemplified not only by fear of the blacks but by the "yellow peril" as well. Dixon could write *The Clansman* and then have it immortalized in film because it expressed a widespread, accepted attitude. The Anglo-Saxon mystique has something to do, I think, with the acceptance of Southern writers after the Civil War. Of course, if Southern writers sold any books after the war, they were going to have to sell most of them in the North somewhere because there wasn't a large audience for them in the South and the Southerners didn't have money to buy them anyway.

WP: Why were Southern writers like Dixon so popular in the North?

LS: In addition to what I just said, I think part of the cause was the general American sense of nostalgia for a moonlight and magnolia South that never really existed except in the imagination, a world in which all the relationships between the whites and the blacks were somehow harmonious. So you have the popularity of movies about the South climaxed by *Gone With the Wind*. It became a big symbol in American culture and was celebrated by its anniversary just this past year. But *Gone With the Wind* is actually a pretty good novel with qualities that the film just ignored. When they filmed it, they pretty much omitted the realistic aspects of the novel and worked around the myth of the South and the Civil War.

WP: The new movie *Glory* is extremely interesting because it's the first movie since *Gone With the Wind* really to tackle that myth.

LS: My new book deals with the myth. When I started the book, I didn't mean for it to deal so much with Emerson. If you carefully read Emerson's journals as they have been now published, you'll discover a very different kind of Emerson from the one you might expect. He had a very racist attitude and at the same time was an abolitionist. In a way a racist Emerson is a much more plausible Emerson. Nobody seems to have quite got on to that, at least in the way I deal with it. The New England connection with the South began with a whole set of relationships going back to the English settlement and John Smith, who considered himself to be both the founder of Virginia and the founder of New England. Originally, all the area from Virginia northward was called Virginia. A real historical irony began to develop at that point in the relationship between the North and the South. You realize when you approach it from that point of view that New England nationalism was still strong in Emerson's mind. What Emerson really wanted to do was to preserve an imperialistic New England which might, after the Civil War, take over the whole country. Two republics actually came into existence when the Constitution was adopted in 1790 and continued down to the Civil War. The republic of the nation state, which we still live in, was born during the Civil War. Nobody on either side really wanted that to happen, but the issue was settled once it was decided that a state couldn't secede from the Union. The whole dynamic of the evolving nation state grew out of the struggle between Southern nationalism and New England nationalism.

WP: Daniel Aaron in his book on Civil War literature has pointed out that the people who might have been qualified to write the great Civil War novel never really served in the war. For that reason or for some other it doesn't seem to have gotten written. It's not like World War II or the Vietnam War, for example, where you have pretty direct literary attack on the material.

LS: I know Dan Aaron spent some years trying to get at that problem, and he has some rather startling things to say when discussing what American writers did during the war. Henry Adams went to England, William Dean Howells went to Italy, and so on. One thing that made this possible was that you didn't have the kind of conscription you had during World War I and II.

WP: It's interesting to speculate how Henry James's career might have been changed if he had served in the war.

LS: It is, and to speculate about other writers, too. James had an obscure injury that supposedly kept him out of the war. Emerson of course was a violent advocate of the war, but he very carefully managed to keep his own son out of it. Emerson was getting old during the war, and he began to suffer from senility. Thoreau died during the war, Hawthorne was accused of being a Southern sympathizer who thought that the South should be allowed to secede. He seemed to think that somehow the war would have to be won against the South and then the South must be let to go its own way. But he died during the war and of course he didn't write much about it.

WP: I think it's strange that there wasn't more literary absorption in the war.

LS: Some of the most interesting works written during the war are obscure and perhaps aren't ever going to be well-known. I've edited a series for some time for the LSU Press called the Library of Southern Civilization. We do primarily documents and reprints. We haven't emphasized fiction at all, but we do have some. Drew Faust has recently done an excellent introduction for a new edition of *Macaria, or the Altars of Sacrifice*. This novel was written right in the midst of the Civil War and it was published in Richmond on such sorry quality paper that the original edition is virtually unreadable.

WP: Who wrote it?

LS: It was written by a woman named Augusta Jane Evans who later married a man named Wilson. She wrote several very popular novels. *Altars of Sacrifice* was basically an effort to bring Southern women together in the war effort. The book is mostly about the proper attitudes for Confederate women; it is a war novel about the home front. So far as I know, Evans never participated in any activity which brought her close to the battlefield. There were books written about the Civil War, both North and South, which are unknown today, probably because they don't have the necessary artistic quality.

WP: I always thought that *The Children of Pride* and some of those non-fiction works come closer in some respects to capturing the times than do the fictional works.

LS: They do, they do. The novels that could have been written are in those letters. *The Children of Pride* is, so far as I know, almost the most remarkable collection of family letters in American history. Well, that might be saying a little too much, but it is a remarkable collection. They were written by people who were highly literate and deeply concerned about the souls of their slaves.

WP: And then there are the diaries and journals.

LS: Kate Stone, who lived on a plantation called Brokenburn in North Louisiana, kept a diary during the war. It was published by LSU several years ago under the title *Brokenburn*. Kate Stone had a pretty complete knowledge of what was going on. She was involved in the invasion of Louisiana and she saw the war close up. The family finally had to flee to Texas. The diary is very graphic and has something of the quality of a novel. A more substantial Civil War record was kept by Sarah Morgan of Baton Rouge. She later married a sort of British professional soldier who came over to fight for the South, a Colonel Dawson, but this was after the war. Baton Rouge, of course, was an occupied city during the war, and she kept a diary which was published by her son in 1904 under the title of *A Confederate Girl's Diary*. My friend Charles East, who is now associated with the University of Georgia Press, has just finished a complete transcription of the actual manuscript, which turns out to have been extensively altered by her son. The manuscript shows that, if Sarah Morgan had gone in a certain direction, she could have become a novelist of the war. There's also Mrs. Chestnutt's diary, which reflects the novelistic possibilities of the war. When C. Vann Woodward went back to look at her diary, which had always been known in Ben Ames Williams's edition, he discovered that the whole diary was really a very complicated problem. What Mrs. Chestnutt had done was to go back to what was really a rather stark diary which she had kept during the war and added and revised and in a sense made a novel out of it. At the same time, she had worked on other novelistic projects, and she had the mind of a novelist. It's only in records like the diaries, it seems, that you get the closest approach to some kind of actual on-the-scene sense of the war.

WP: I guess De Forrest is the best novelist of the war sort of by default.

LS: Of course. He was the Yankee who wrote *Miss Ravenal's Conversion From Secession to Loyalty*, and that is just about the best novel about the war published any time close to the time of the war. He has some remarkable realistic scenes of the war set in Louisiana, but there weren't many like him. The treatment of the war in novels seemed to come out largely in terms of romance and nostalgia. You have to go all the way past the war to Stephen Crane to get a great novel about it.

WP: And the question with Crane is whether he's really writing about the Civil War.

LS: It wasn't a war he knew. He had heard about it. In a way, he wasn't any closer to it than someone like Faulkner.

WP: Of course, Faulkner's treatment of the war is very indirect. But then that was his approach generally.

LS: Faulkner deliberately stayed away from the fighting. I don't think that appealed to him. He knew a lot about the war. I never did know Mr. Faulkner personally, but Shelby Foote, a friend of his, told me how he and Faulkner visited the battlefield at Chickamauga and, in order to see what difficulties the soldiers labored under, ran with heavy loads up a hill. They picked up logs and carried them up the hill. Faulkner was interested in strategies and battles, how men lived in battles, but he never really went into it in his novels.

WP: And we know that Shelby was interested in it since he wrote that great three-volume narrative history.

LS: That's true, but I think that Faulkner knew that writing about the Civil War had become a very specialized area, and he didn't want to compete with that kind of writing. Consequences were what interested him. *Absalom, Absalom!* is very much a novel about the Civil War, but there's little or nothing of the actual war in it.

WP: You mentioned Ben Ames Williams. He wrote two endless novels about the war.

LS: They say that no novel about the Civil War has ever lost money. (Laughs.) That's amazing when you think about how many there are. I think that by the time you got past the 1870s it was probably too late to get a novel with the sense of immediacy that Hemingway brings to the First World War. If Faulkner had actually been able to get into the First World War, which he tried to do, he might have been a different kind of writer. You would expect some kind of Hemingway to have come along in the 1870s, but he never appeared.

WP: The Southern writer has always been distinguished by a strong sense of place and of history, but when you look at the Southern writers today, and God knows there are a bunch of them out there, they all seem to have kept the sense of place and to have forgotten their sense of history. It's hard for me to think of any writer after the generation of William Styron who seems to be concerned with history much at all. The novels in some ways have a higher literary quality, but they seem to have gotten smaller.

LS: I think that it's the almost universal influence of writing schools. You have a great many writers who've achieved a certain competence in poetry and in fiction. The main focus is on the self rather than on society in the way of Dickens or Galsworthy or even Faulkner. Faulkner and Warren have a strong sense of history. And Styron came along soon enough to have that sense. But Southern writers in the 60s and 70s—you call them Southern, but it's hard to define them sometimes—don't really have much sense of history. Clyde Edgerton and James Wilcox and others write very interesting stories about people and family situations, but they lack the context of Faulkner and Warren, whose characters are involved in something much bigger than themselves, in the context of lives seen within the framework of history. That context does seem to have been seriously eroded in more recent fiction and poetry. T. S. Eliot is, of course, completely out now, and Eliot had a large public interest, and not just a private interest.

WP: But Eliot is not the only writer who's being rejected.

LS: Writers respond to their culture. Things began to change about the Second World War. You can see the ever-increasing emphasis on the self. I don't know if you've ever read Eric Vogelin, whose great work is called *Order in History*. He sees a kind of closing in the self which you can observe throughout modern times. Eliot struggles against this. In "Prufrock" he depicts a man closed in upon himself. Or take Allen Tate, whose most famous poem, "Ode to the Confederate Dead," attacks the idea that the autonomous self is the only thing that counts. The self is an endless theme, almost, it seems to me, the only theme during the last twenty-five or thirty years. (Pauses.) I've argued that occasionally with younger poets. One of them told me once when I said, "You aren't interested in history": "That's what you think." He didn't feel that way.

WP: I'm a great admirer of Walker Percy, but in some ways he seems to me a narrower kind of writer than the great writers of the past.

LS: He is very narrow. He gets some very intense effects from being narrow. You get that same kind of narrowness increasingly in modern writing. I think Hemingway had more of a sense of a context of history, say, than Walker Percy does. Percy is shrewd and knows a lot, but he doesn't have any great social dimension to his writing. He is primarily a satirist. He is primarily interested in being, in the dilemma of being, in very personal terms. He approaches this theme most closely in essays written for mostly Catholic publications.

WP: If I could shift the conversation around to another Catholic writer, how do you feel about the canonization of Flannery O'Connor, which seems to have taken place with great rapidity? As you know, since you were on the editorial board of the Library of America, she was the first recent writer to be included in that series, which is, or at least pretends to be, canonical.

LS: I was on the board for about ten years, and I'm trying to remember exactly what happened. One problem that they had was that it took a lot of money, and they began to realize that, if they didn't get some recent writers—which was pretty hard to do because of the difficulty of getting copyrights—it was going to be pretty hard to maintain the series. They found out that they could get Flannery O'Connor. That's one explanation, but on the other hand there's no question that she's phenomenally popular. She is read for literary reasons and also, I think, for religious reasons.

WP: Allen Tate was not willing to include her among the great Southern writers.

LS: Tate's own brand of Catholicism was different from that of O'Connor. Tate was deeply influenced by Eliot. Everything that he wrote when he was younger indicated that sooner or later he was going to end up as a Roman Catholic. Actually, however, he was never a very good Catholic in practice. I don't remember specifically what he said about O'Connor, but I do know that she took her writing extremely seriously. She was a student of Andrew Lytle, who always insisted that his students have a maximum artistic integrity. Of course, Lytle is nearly ninety years old now, and his teaching was a long time ago. He also taught Madison Jones and James Dickey, but I think he believes Dickey took a wrong turn and is no longer a serious writer. Andrew was disappointed in *Deliverance*.

WP: He thought it was too commercial?

LS: Yes, but of course, there may be more personal things. Writers are always quarreling about something.

WP: I know that Walker Percy has a great admiration for O'Connor, but I think they're very different writers.

LS: From what I gather, Flannery O'Connor has something of, or perhaps more of, what Walker Percy has, that is, an appeal to persons looking for salvation. I've heard Walker talk about getting calls in the middle of the night from people wanting help.

WP: I don't know that I believe that, as Auden says, literature makes nothing happen. But I'm not sure either that it can save your soul.

LS: Yeah, I know that Warren, in his lectures called "Democracy and Poetry," was just appalled by what Auden said. Warren had the feeling for the religious background of Southerners—and I think he searched deeply for meaning in his own life—but he didn't bring his search into his work the way O'Connor and Percy do.

WP: I know that you're a great admirer of Robert Penn Warren. *Understanding Poetry*, which was of course done in collaboration with Cleanth Brooks, was dedicated to the proposition that poetry could not only be understood: it could be understood by undergraduates.

LS: The kind of poetry that Brooks and Warren praise in that book is not necessarily the kind of poetry Warren wrote. The book came fairly early in Warren's career, but it was after the period of his early poetry. Some of the early poems are rather extravagant. He published one poem about "the purple hills of

Hell" that was a notoriously bad poem and which he did everything that he could to suppress. He completely wiped it out as far as he could. There was a time after *Understanding Poetry* when Warren didn't write any poetry at all. But then he married again, and in spite of the fact that Eleanor Clark was, and so far as I know still is, an ardent Trotskyite, the marriage worked, and he began to write poetry again. He really dated the time of his poetic renaissance from the birth of his first child.

WP: I've often wondered if Warren's renewed interest in poetry grew out of his declining novelistic powers. I feel strongly that there was a very rapid decline after *World Enough and Time* in 1950.

LS: There was, but it's hard to tell which was the cart and which was the horse. He became so absorbed in poetry. He always considered himself to be primarily a poet. There was a time, I think, when he wrote novels because he wanted to make some money.

WP: And he did, with *All the King's Men* and *Band of Angels*, both of which were sold to the movies.

LS: All of his novels after *All the King's Men* sold. Some of them tend to be potboilers. Warren himself told me once that he put great store in a novel called *Flood*, but from the time when he began to write poems in the fifties, he was more and more obsessed with poetry. He told me not long before his death that the worst thing about getting old was that the poems don't come any more. He wrote poems almost on a daily basis. And when you read them and read what he wrote about them, you realize that he got caught up almost obsessively in the theme of self. In *Brother to Dragons*, he tried his hand at a larger kind of historical poem, and he kept coming back to that poem and rewriting it. His cruder manner in the second version of *Brother to Dragons*—his departure from iambic pentameter for one thing—was part of what he thought of as finding his own voice. On the other hand, he insisted that poetry is a discipline, and he did not like free verse.

WP: Warren, of course, is an accepted poet, but there is today a constant revision of the canon, an unceasing search for new figures.

LS: A lot of the minor figures are interesting and ought to be revived. Many of them are very interesting even if they're not intrinsically very important, but that's only historically speaking. The effort to elevate some of these people to the same stature as Melville or Hawthorne is foolish. And that's what they do. Some of them will, for example, say almost anything in order to prove a point about the victimization of women. Or about the victimization of Blacks.

WP: In my interview with him, Ernest Gaines made what I thought was an interesting point. He said that the Black audience wasn't large enough to support a novelist and that most of his readers were white.

LS: That's true. I admire Gaines, and Ellison is a writer I admire very much. I think that in the sixties he was sort of overtaken by events, and that many of the younger Blacks began to consider him almost an Uncle Tom figure. He came down very hard on the younger Black writers who said, we've got to recover our African roots. He said, you're in America now. And they rejected him. And he never finished his second novel. Or at least never published it.

WP: *Invisible Man* is right smack dab in the American tradition.

LS: And it's written in the American language, not in some African language. It seems to me that Ernest Gaines has struck a balance. He's a great admirer of Turgenev and Faulkner and other writers. He's not making any bones about not writing in an African tradition.

WP: Like most people my age who are interested in criticism, I'm pretty much a product of the new criticism, and although I realize that some of them, like R. P. Blackmur, for example, could be obscure, they were committed to the idea that the language of criticism should be pretty much the language of the general educated public, that if you were reasonably intelligent, you ought to be able to read criticism and enjoy it. I don't think that's true of a lot of recent criticism.

LS: The New Criticism did develop its own jargon, but it was never so ponderous as what you get in deconstruction. The American devotion to deconstruction has caused Europeans to laugh at Americans. Derrida, for example, is pretty well passe in Paris. People come and go on the Parisian literary scene, but it's a mystery why Derrida is still such an obsession in America. Why have American academics become so obsessed with deconstructionism in general? For one thing, I think they have associated it with feminism and Marxism. But the idea that language is always part of a conspiracy makes the whole process of criticism seem not to be worthwhile. Just as a theory, deconstructionism is one thing, but as an applied theory, it's another. You get involved with all kinds of things that don't grow out of literary criticism per se. You get involved with an effort not to understand literature but to destroy it.

Readers who are interested in the ideas discussed in this interview are referred to the following books:

Simpson, Lewis P., ed. *The Federalist Literary Mind: Selections from the "Monthly Anthology and Boston Review," 1803-1811, Including Documents Relating to the Boston Athenaeum.* Baton Rouge: LSU Press, 1962.

Simpson, Lewis P. *The Man of Letters in New England and the South.* Baton Rouge: LSU Press, 1973.

Simpson, Lewis P. *The Dispossessed Garden: Pastoral and History in Southern Literature.* Athens: University of Georgia Press, 1975.

Simpson, Lewis P., ed. *The Possibilities of Order: Cleanth Brooks and His Work.* Baton Rouge: LSU Press, 1976.

Simpson, Lewis P. *The Brazen Face of History: Studies in the Literary Consciousness.* Baton Rouge: LSU Press, 1980.

Kennedy, J. Gerald and Daniel Mark Fogel, eds. *American Letters and the Historical Consciousness: Essays in Honor of Lewis P Simpson*. Baton Rouge: LSU Press, 1987. Contains a bibliography of all of Simpson's longer works complete to date of publication.

Simpson, Lewis P., James Olney, and Jo Gulledge, eds. *"The Southern Review" and Modern Literature: 1935-1985*. Baton Rouge: LSU Press, 1988.

Simpson, Lewis P. *Mind and the American Civil War: A Meditation on Lost Causes*. Baton Rouge: LSU Press, 1989.

Chapter 2
Scholarship in the South: A Conversation with Lewis P. Simpson, Part Two

WP: Since I talked to you last time, you've published an autobiographical essay, "Living with Indians," in *The Southern Review*. Do you plan to write more reminiscences of that kind?

LS: Well, I've been asked that by a number of people, and I don't know. I might. It's not easy to do, but I might do something. I'd like, for example, to do more about my father. Some things I can't quite bring myself to write about. People are still living who might be offended, you know how it is. And if you try to evade the truth, you are likely to start inventing or fictionalizing, and you start getting into pretty sticky ground, that marginal boundary ground between the memoir or the autobiography and the novel.

WP: And the novels lie about what happened anyway.

LS: Well, sure. Of course. I think I try to make this point in the last part of my memoir. We all live by illusions. Memoirs, autobiographies, are just about as much based on lies, if you want to call them that, as out-and-out fiction is. I remember a book about how to write a successful novel in which the big thing is the necessity of creating a believable illusion of reality. But in doing a memoir— do you do the same thing? History is a trick the living play on the dead, Voltaire said. But a couple of centuries later when history is written and rewritten every hour or so, we know it is also a trick played on the living. But if you don't seek deliberately to mislead, if you recognize that the memory is always a liar, maybe with luck you can give a reasonably honest account or report of what you remember as an individual.

WP: The recent event which caused the most discussion at Southeastern where I teach was the Civil War series by Ken Burns. Did you watch that?

LS: I watched all of it. Ken Burns was here when we had that conference in 1985 marking the fiftieth year since the start of the first series of The Southern Review. It was advertised as an international conference; and we did have a few people from abroad. At that point in time, Burns had just finished his Huey Long movie, and we got in touch with him. He was going to show his film here anyway, and he agreed to come out and show it for us. Some of us had lunch with him. He was already talking about the Civil War being his next project. I thought the Huey Long film was remarkable. I don't know if you saw it or not.

WP: Yeah, sure.

LS: I've seen other things that he did, and I think Burns has a real genius for this sort of film. I was sort of amused when he said that he was trying to get enough money to produce an original film, a fictional film, a play of some sort, and to get away from documentaries. I think he has a genius for documentaries and I was amused at that. Talking to Ken I remembered a Civil War documentary on television a few years ago which used still photographs. I found out Ken had the idea of making that pretty pervasive in his film and he did. I think that was the great feature of that mini-series, the use of still photographs, employing camera techniques which have been developed in more recent years to display them. The history of photography is not very long, and the Civil War was the first war photographed. Much of the war was recorded by artists who sketched on the field as they always had, but the camera proved to be a revolutionary way of seeing war. I don't know much about the history of photography, except through my friend, Charles East, who is an expert on it. The coincidence of the Civil War in America and the development of photography made it possible for the first time to make a record of that war such as had never been made before.

Shelby Foote, incidentally, became a star, a prime-time star, as a result of the Burns film. (Laughs.) He was very effective. Most of those shots of Shelby were filmed up at his home in Memphis, and he was just sitting there talking. He did the whole thing in a very short period of time. Knowing everything about the war, having this wonderful Southern voice, and having almost total recall, he could just sit there and talk out of his abundant knowledge of the war and his abundant knowledge of the people of the South, and so on. In a way he seemed to me to hold the whole thing together.

WP: I assume that you approved of the so-called experts. My feeling was that I would have been happier if they had all been left out.

LS: I have heard that objection before about other documentaries and I have agreed, but this time I wasn't so disturbed about it. The film would bore without Shelby, also without Barbara Fields. I thought the documentary about Melville done some three or four years back had entirely too much of that talking by professors.

WP: What they do, of course, is to have different people present different points of view with the theory that the viewer can make up his own mind.

LS: I thought that Burns had worked out a pretty good balance between representing the progress of the war through still photographs, letters and diaries, and the commentary. I think that Shelby provided necessary perspective, but that if they had cut out some of the other speaking parts, it wouldn't have made much difference. I thought that during the last two or three episodes somehow the film didn't seem to hold together too well, but all in all it was a remarkable performance.

WP: Were you surprised at the amount of passion and controversy that series generated?

LS: Not particularly, because the Civil War is still a subject that stirs very deep emotions in people. I wasn't surprised about the South, but I was a little surprised that there was so much reaction from other parts of the country, not just from the South. I don't know how many letters and phone calls there were about the series, but it drew a tremendous audience, I think the largest audience that public television has ever had. There is something about the Civil War that is deeply rooted in the American consciousness. This would seem to be so even though the population is so different from what it was a hundred years ago. I don't know how to explain it except that the Civil War has to do with the very fiber of the nation. After the Civil War, the nation was really another nation, a different republic, a Second American Republic. It was a deeply bitter war, the most catastrophic war in comparative terms of casualties that I believe had ever been fought up to that time.

WP: Have you worked on any non-fiction films?

LS: I have worked a little on documentaries here and there as an advisor, enough to know they're very hard to do. I guess the biggest one I ever worked on was the one on Faulkner, called "A Life on Paper." It ran, I think, ninety minutes. I also worked on another documentary called "Climate for Genius," which was in six parts. It was filmed on location in Oxford, Greenville, and Natchez and was about the works of several Mississippi writers but especially Faulkner and Eudora Welty. In each part a panel sat around on location discussing works relevant to the place at hand, etc. Louis Rubin, Dan Young, and I were in all six parts, I believe; Shelby Foote was with us at Faulkner's home and in Greenville, I recall, Elizabeth Spencer in Natchez. I also worked on a documentary about Alabama culture called "Alabama Heritage." These films were far less structured than "A Life on Paper."

WP: Where is "A Life on Paper" available?

LS: It was filmed under an NEH grant by the Mississippi Educational Television Authority in Jackson and shown on PBS. I imagine it can be acquired even yet through one of the companies that distributes educational films. The script writer for the film was Faulkner's Hollywood friend, an old Hollywood scripter, Buzz Bezzerides.

WP: He wrote the screenplay for the Nick Ray movie, "On Dangerous Ground." He is a very slick kind of writer, isn't he?

LS: I don't think "slick" is quite the right word. But he had spent his life in film. He worked with Faulkner when Faulkner was making a living doing Hollywood jobs. Took care of him when he was drunk too. He had a kind of absolute regard for Faulkner's genius as a writer. But he was committed to Freudianism. I remember the original script gave an interpretation of Faulkner in almost totally Freudian terms. It had to be modified considerably. In fact, many changes had to be made in the original conception of "A Life on Paper" in the process of putting that film together. It did come out pretty effectively, finally. There's no way in a documentary to avoid using a certain amount of commentary, certainly not if the film is designed for a broad spectrum of people. Some in the audience will know nothing about the subject of the documentary, and some will be experts, as in the case of "The Civil War."

WP: Well, everything is commentary. The selection of photographs is commentary.

LS: There are people that argue that when you broadcast a baseball game or a football game, there should be an absolute minimum of commentary. They tried that with football I remember, and somehow the people didn't want it. They would rather listen to that endless palaver which almost drives me crazy sometimes. They want every second filled up. No people in history have been so addicted to endless and meaningless noise as we are.

WP: If we could turn now to a subject we touched on in the first interview, what relationship do you see between the legacy of the Civil War and the Agrarian movement and the essays in *I'll Take My Stand*.

LS: When you talk about the essays in *I'll Take My Stand*, I think you have to take into account the separate individuals who wrote them.

WP: You don't see the Agrarians as a unified literary or political movement?

LS: Not in the way they've often been presented. They were all highly individualistic people. I suppose the only one of the Agrarians you could call an unreconstructed rebel—a pre-Civil War "fire-eater" in a way, a pre-Southern War for Independence rebel you might say—was Donald Davidson. If you read some of his poems about the Civil War you can see how absolutely determined he was to preserve the cause of the South, or at any rate to celebrate the cause and hardly to admit it was lost. When Tate sent Davidson the manuscript of the most famous poem about the Civil War, "Ode to the Confederate Dead," Davidson saw that it was a metaphorical comment on the state of the modern world and was upset with his friend. Where are your dead, the real Confederate dead? he asked Tate. Other Agrarians—I think of Warren—saw the Civil War as a great, ironic tragedy. Warren's meditation on the war published during the Centennial observance is one of the finest things ever written about it. Andrew Lytle took a considerable interest in the war, championed Bedford Forrest in a way. But Lytle actually had a far more complex view of American history than the Forrest book indicates. Allen Tate may have been the greatest writer about the Civil War among the Agrarians. He wrote not only the "Ode" but the greatest novel about the war, *The Fathers*. The most overt interpretation of the cause of the Civil War in *I'll Take MY Stand* is Owsley's essay. And I guess all the participants in the manifesto more or less shared this mythic view that the war was fought to preserve the Agrarian principle on which the nation was founded in opposition to the innovative and corrupting industrial principle. So the subtitle: Agrarianism Versus Industrialism. This is the theme of the "Statement of Principles" Ransom wrote as preface to the manifesto. Ransom really got excited for a time about the Agrarian movement. He worked out a kind of rationale for the movement in the prefatory statement—kind of tied together, or tried to, the diverse directions of the individual essays. His idea was not to promote a revolution in any positive sense but to encourage the recognition that civilization in the United States was going the wrong way. If nothing else the South, maybe by joining with the West, could try to hold the line against further industrialization. You have to admit the Agrarians had a point; you can't look at the utter pollution of the world in the last fifty years and not admit it.

WP: But by that time, the late twenties, weren't they beating a dead horse?

LS: Yes, in any practical sense the book was anachronistic, completely anachronistic so far as the facts of history were concerned. Of course, as they moved through the changes of the thirties, most of the Agrarians realized this. The only one that remained true to the faith was Donald Davidson. Later Ransom made a kind of formal renunciation of his former views about science and education and industrialism. He admitted that he had been beating a dead horse, that he should have been more realistic about the benefits of science and so on. Davidson took terrible exception to that; he got really upset.

WP: Of course, Davidson and Tate were arguing about poetry and politics while the book was being written.

LS: At one point, Tate had worked up a detailed program for a "Southern reactionary movement." He sent the thing to Davidson and Warren. It included a practical program. One part of it was publication. Tate envisioned not only a magazine but a newspaper. (Laughs.) It was all preposterous. Tate was dreaming about a political and economic program which could not be actualized.

WP: I was reading someone recently who said that Tate's conception of himself was removed from reality, that he was in fact a kind of modern type, the scholar gypsy, who stayed at one college a while and then moved on.

LS: Tate was pretty rootless. Even his childhood was rootless. He once conceived a work to be called "Ancestors of Exile," in which he would present the American condition as essentially one of exile—the exile of the Europeans who came to another world and could never go back home—the "ancestors" of his own exile. I think Tate wanted to put down roots in the South, to have a home and so on, but it never really worked out for him. He became a rover and a wanderer, a sort of elegant Bohemian, always in need of cash but dedicated to literature.

WP: I believe Warren also moved around during the early part of his career.

LS: Warren had rather the same problem. I've written some about this. After Warren got his undergraduate degree at Vanderbilt, he went off to Berkeley and then he became a Rhodes scholar and went to England. When he came back to Tennessee, he said, with a certain exaggeration, that he had spent four or five or six years of wandering and now wanted to come home. He got a job at Southwestern in Memphis, but they only gave him a one year contract and didn't renew it, so he appealed to Vanderbilt, his old school. They gave him a three year contract, and he really expected that to be renewed. He lived in a house some miles from Nashville because he wanted to live out in the country. He liked the house and the job; the only trouble was that they didn't renew his contract. That was a blow to him. At about that point LSU was adding faculty, even though the country was in the depths of the Great Depression. There was, in fact, a rather remarkable faculty in English created during that little period—a tribute to the good sense of Dr. William A. Read who was chairman of the department-so Warren ended up coming down to LSU about the same time that Cleanth Brooks was invited to come. And when Warren came down here, he thought that here would be the place where he would at last put down his roots in the South. He rented a cottage on what is now called Hyacinth Avenue in South Baton Rouge.

WP: What year would that have been?

LS: Nineteen-thirty-three or thirty-four, I believe. The place on Hyacinth is still there. At that time, it was in what was still a semi-rural area. It had originally been built in the 1870s as the home of a dairyman. Then Warren managed to get a little money and bought some land out on the Old Hammond Highway, a beautiful piece of land with red oak and water oak trees on it. He built himself a cabin with a metal roof. It's still there and it's still preserved. He built this himself with the aid of, as he put it, one out-of-work carpenter. It's an interesting place and very, very tiny. Warren lived there with his first wife until 1941, and you would have thought that what he wanted to do was to build that little cabin-like place and live there until he got the money to build a big house. But that was not his idea. He wanted a house that already had some years on it, a place situated in one of these magnificent live oak groves. He didn't have live oaks out there on Hammond Highway. He found a place down in Gonzales in Ascension Parish. Is that Ascension Parish?

WP: I think so.

LS: That place is still there. I've visited all of the places Warren lived in the Baton Rouge area. This was not as old a house as he probably would have preferred, but it was situated on twelve acres of land, and it had—still has—a beautiful stand of moss-covered live oaks. It's on a bayou. The house is still the same, except that it's been added on to at the back. The original structure has not been disturbed, and you can still tell what it was once like-a big old bungalow with a great big gallery running all around it, certainly a very Southern kind of setting. Warren fell in love with that place; it was going to be the place where he was going to live for keeps he said. He moved there in the fall of 1941, but by spring he had become completely disaffected from LSU. He never had felt that he had been getting a fair shake at LSU for one reason or another. As I recall, the story is that Minnesota offered him a professorship with a $400 raise. He was so reluctant to leave LSU and move north that, as I recall, he was willing to stay here for $200 more. He was refused the two hundred bucks by the upper administration. By this time the Second World War had started, and everything at LSU was centered on the war and nothing but the war. It was a big military school anyway—long and affectionately known as "the old war skule." In 1942 the president, a retired army general, and others were interested in nothing at that time except the war, and both *The Southern Review* and Warren went by the board. So Warren took the offer and left, but he left with great reluctance.

WP: You think he never really wanted to leave the South?

LS: There are statements by Warren which indicate that he felt like an exile. I remember once that I had made some incidental comment about literary exiles in a letter, and he wrote back: if you really want to know something about exile, I can tell you; in effect, I've been an exile all my life. I remember I wrote back a short note asking him to write an article or an essay on that topic for *The Southern Review*. He never did. What I say about Warren and exile is in the *Sewanee Review* this summer, by the way.

WP: Of course, Warren wrote about himself off and on, but he never really wrote an autobiography. Somebody must be writing a biography.

LS: Yeah, Joseph Blotner, the biographer of Faulkner.

WP: I'm sure it'll be a thousand pages long.

LS: Joe told me he wasn't going to make it that long, but he does tend to work at great length. I'm sure there must be other people, but he's the only one I know of right now who's trying to turn out a real biography. I try to make the point in my study of Warren that he was always engaged in writing what he himself called a "shadowy autobiography."

WP: But haven't most of the Southern writers in the twentieth century been exiles? Madison Jones even wrote a novel called *An Exile*.

LS: Yeah, they have. It's a phenomenon. You look at Tate, for example. I don't know that he would have been the same person at all if he had stayed in the South. Or that Warren would have been the same person if he had stayed in the South. Andrew Lytle pretty much stayed in the South although he did spend some time in the East.

WP: I think the ones that left may be more numerous and generally of higher literary quality.

LS: I guess. Maybe that's so. I think the writers living in the South today are in a little different situation as a whole. There are a lot of them in North Carolina.

WP: Ernest Gaines told me that although he lives here now and intends to continue living here, the most important thing that ever happened to him was moving to the West Coast when he was fifteen or sixteen.

LS: I don't doubt that. Of course, Ernest Gaines was very different from the earlier generation of black writers who left the South very deliberately, fled like Richard Wright. The whole question of black writers' relationship to the South is very interesting. In recent years some black writers have come back to the South.

WP: You would see them as being different from the white writers.

LS: Yes I would. All modern writers have had the problem of alienation from society and thus the problem of self-definition, of defining for themselves what society does not hand to them, that is, a sense of vocation. But for the black writers of the American South this problem has been, and still is, more intricate and inhibiting than it is for white writers. The black writers feel the need to define their literary heritage. So do white writers. It's a lot harder for black writers. The white writers know that ultimately they come out of the European culture. If they reject this heritage, they know what they are rejecting, and I guess they know what they want to put in its place. This is where the black writers come from too if they accept the white civilization. But typically the black writer wants to come from somewhere else. In recent history black writers in the South, it seems to me, have been trying to find out what that place is. Today a multicultural label is being pinned on all writers in America. Are there "African-Southern American" writers as well as "African American writers"? If there are, I suspect that African-Southern writers are contributing to what may become, after the present militant multiculturalism cools off, a new American cosmopolitanism. They were already doing so in a way back in the time of the Agrarians. One thing you can say about the whole Agrarian group is that they were very cosmopolitan people—in the old sense, that is. They really weren't farmers, except for Lytle who knew a good deal about farming. Warren didn't. Tate had a place in Kentucky for a while that his brother had bought for him, but he wasn't a farmer. They wanted to be in Europe and elsewhere. First and last Warren spent a lot of time in Italy. Tate spent a lot of time in France. Ransom loved England. He was a real anglophile and stayed in England all he could. Even Donald Davidson spent nearly all his summers in New England at the Breadloaf School. Southerner that he was, he still liked to go to New England, which is where Warren and Cleanth ended up permanently. I don't think Davidson ever traveled much though otherwise, except to fight in France in 1917-18.

WP: I think that as Tate grew older he felt increasingly mistreated by the literary establishment.

LS: He felt that the man of letters was not well treated by the modern world. He was an almost perfect expression of that kind of alienation. In all of these writers, there was a kind of sense of belonging to a spiritual community, a literary priesthood.

WP: Do you still have that now? I don't think so.

LS: No, no we've pretty well lost that feeling, not only in the South but generally. You have an almost perfect characterization of the faith in the literary priesthood in Malcolm Cowley's pieces on Hemingway and Proust, or take Tate's essay on Hart Crane. It's part of romanticism in a way, I guess, the feeling that you get certainly in Shelley speaking of the poet as the unacknowledged legislator of

mankind, in contrast, say, to Doctor Johnson's feeling for writing as a public vocation whether you made any money out of it or starved to death. You can't imagine
Johnson's being alienated.

WP: Johnson was a creature of the city.

LS: In the eighteenth-century sense, yes. Art in other words becomes more
and more a kind of religion, even a substitute for religion sometimes. But the feeling is not really articulated fully until you get down to Baudelaire, who said that
the man of letters is the world's enemy. You define the bourgeois as the great
enemy. This gives you the intensity that Baudelaire saw in Edgar Allan Poe. The
artist has a kind of feeling that he belongs to a priesthood of art. I certainly think
that you do see this in Tate's dedication to his craft. You see it most strongly in
James Joyce.

WP: You also see it in Wallace Stevens.

LS: It is very strong in Stevens, even though he was a businessman. It's that
split between the world of art and everything else. The idea of the artist has
become more diffused in some ways and more marginal.

WP: I don't think artists of today take art as seriously generally.

LS: That's true. It's not taken as seriously. I'm writing a piece on Walker
Percy. The idea of the novelist as an artist is pretty strong in Percy. But he was
born in time to experience such a sensibility.

WP: I've been thinking about Percy, and it seems to me that there's a discrepancy between what some critics call his Christian existentialism and the very
traditional form of the novel that he used. I have a feeling that he was never quite
radical enough in his alteration of the novelistic form to find a form that really was
successful in projecting a lot of what he wanted to say.

LS: Percy was kind of a self-trained novelist. I don't think he was very traditional. He picked his techniques primarily from Camus and other twentieth-century French writers. He said that Sartre gave him a clue of what he wanted to do if
he wrote fiction. He decided that, if he couldn't get readers for what he wanted to
say by means of philosophical articles, he might as well try fiction. He tried his
hand at it and wrote maybe two or three novels that he threw away before he finally came out with *The Moviegoer*. He had learned from the French writers how to
write *The Moviegoer*, how to write a kind of philosophical novel. Percy was a
medical man who had left the profession, and he always thought of writing in
medical terms, as for example in his essay, "The Novelist as Diagnostician."
Walker had a burning desire to try to say effectively what he felt about the dimin-
ishing of the spiritual in the modern world.

WP: I think of him very much in the line of traditional Catholic satirists like
Evelyn Waugh and Gabriel Fielding.

LS: He developed a profound doubt about language, about what the fate of
literature is for that matter. Will he have a permanent place among the American
writers? I doubt that it will be as strong as that of, say, Flannery O'Connor, but at

least for a number of years he will remain of great interest. As you know, at least until the last part of his career he wasn't really selling very well, although he'd gotten to be very well known among intellectuals, and he will remain an intellectual's writer I suspect.

WP: But who isn't? I mean is there anyone who is not in that group now who is any good?

LS: Well, I guess not. If you look at the Southern writers today, will you find anyone like Percy? I don't know enough about what is going on among the so-called Catholic writers to make a judgment there. They are kind of an anomaly in American literature. We don't have a Roman Catholic tradition in American literature the way they do in France or even in England. In the South you have Walker Percy and Flannery O'Connor, Bill Corrington, Allen Tate, Caroline Gordon—all dead now. At present there is Walter Sullivan. At the moment, those are the most prominent Southern writers I can think of we may associate with Roman Catholicism.

WP: I know that Billy Mills is trying to get together a book of essays on Corrington. I did an interview with Corrington, and he came across like a rednecked good ole boy, but he was way beyond that intellectually.

LS: He was a great admirer of Eric Voegelin, who wrote *Order in History*. Now, that is not easy going, and it's about as far away as you can get from a honky tonk atmosphere. But Bill had a way of dealing with honky tonk kind of people from the country music world. He had a pretty wide range.

WP: I think his short novels are his best work.

LS: There's no question about that. He had a gift for the short form.

WP: He had a high opinion of *Shad Sentell*, but I think he was mistaken about that.

LS: I knew Bill for a long time, and he used to send me copies of everything he wrote, and I thought that *Shad Sentell* was pretty weak. The publisher finally ended up publishing just a minimum of the manuscript that he had written.

WP: I thought it was too long even the way it was published.

LS: Anyway, I never tried to evaluate it. I thought it was more in the league with some of his detective stories which he and his wife Joyce were writing during his last years.

WP: I've read all of those except the last one, which just came out, and I think they had a vigor that *Shad Sentell* lacked.

LS: I think you're right there. I don't think there was much vigor in *Shad*. Perhaps I shouldn't say that since I didn't read it carefully. It was published by some rather obscure publisher.

WP: Who promptly went bankrupt. Bill had just published *Shad* in '85 when I interviewed him, and his health seemed okay then.

LS: As a matter of fact, I saw him at a national conference on Eric Voegelin's work in New Orleans in 1987. I spent two or three days with him there and that was the last time I saw him. By then, he had already had a heart attack.

WP: Had he reformed his life style?

LS: No, he hadn't. That was one of the problems. He was still smoking cigars and he was still living just about the way he always had. He seemed to take a very fatalistic attitude. He apparently had had a pretty bad spell, but he was not about to give up his life style.

WP: I interviewed him at his house in New Orleans, which has since been sold, in a big room filled with expensively bound sets of the classics which he told me he had bought from Blackwell's or from some other English book shop with the first money he got from the movies. He apparently just told them to ship him standard sets of all the important writers. That seemed to me a very Southern thing to do. I can imagine an old Southern planter doing that. He was a great admirer of William Gaddis's *The Recognitions* and of Cormac McCarthy.

LS: McCarthy is a very strange writer. I've read his novels with fascination. There's no better stylist writing. He has a great gift of words.

WP: When I reviewed one of his earlier novels, I think it was *Child of God*, I wrote that it reminded me of Faulkner with all the history left out, but I'm not sure you can say that about *Blood Meridian*.

LS: I think you can say something about him in terms of the old Southwestern humorists like George Washington Harris. It's pretty dark stuff. McCarthy doesn't go to college campuses or to literary conferences. He lives a very secluded life. He moves around a lot, seems to want to be completely isolated. In terms of style, he's a far stronger writer than any other Southern writer I know of right now. He started writing in the early sixties, I believe.

WP: *The Orchard Keeper* was his first one.

LS: I think it won the Faulkner prize. His novels have a very melancholy vision of human nature.

WP: I think *Child of God* and *Blood Meridian* are at the far end of hell some place.

LS: I think they are. Dante knew that a person may be so far lost that the only chance he has for salvation is to be taken down to see hell. McCarthy seems to envision that we are so far lost that the only chance for our redemption is to visit hell. There's no way to save us otherwise. This might be the simplest interpretation of McCarthy: here, I will show you what humanity is really like, and then there might be some chance for redemption.

WP: You know something about the history of Texas. Was there any appreciable research or historical background in *Blood Meridian*? I know Madison Jones wrote about similar terrible events in Tennessee in *The Innocent* and I know that he did use historical events.

LS: I think there is a historical background, but *Blood Meridian* is not a historical novel. Of course everybody knows life in the West encouraged lawless people. There wasn't much law in Texas for a period of time, but it wasn't very long historically speaking. Anyway, history is not the point in McCarthy's novel. It's the utter depravity of the human race that he is after. The band of cutthroats in *Blood Meridian* are evil incarnate. I liked Walter Sullivan on McCarthy in his piece at the 1985 Southern Writers Conference—"Southern Writers in Spiritual Exile." He talked about the judge in the novel as a "parody of God" and pointed out that the intensity of McCarthy's sense of evil comes from his implied recognition of the opposite of evil, which is good. There may not be much hope in McCarthy, but he does believe in the necessity of evil and thus has the basis for a possible belief in the necessity of good. You can compare him to Warren in this regard. Walter's essay came out in the collection of conference things, etc. the LSU Press published. It's in his new collection of essays too, *In Praise of Blood Sports*.

WP: I'd like to turn now to the history of *The Southern Review*. It seems to me that when it was revived, the magazine was in a much more difficult position intellectually. The first *Southern Review* knew what the intellectual agenda was, so to speak.

LS: It's illuminating to study the first *Southern Review*. One thing we need to remember about the first *Southern Review* is that the editor was neither Brooks nor Warren. The editor was Charles W. Pipkin, the Dean of the Graduate School, and Brooks and Warren were managing editors. Pipkin, a political scientist who like Brooks and Warren had been a Rhodes scholar, became Dean of the Graduate School at the age of twenty-nine. He was a real genius, but he burned out early and died in his very early forties, as I recall, about a year before *The Southern Review* ceased publication. The agenda of the original magazine is not a very easy subject to deal with because there's no explicit indication of how much Pipkin influenced it. There's no question that, as far as the general management of the magazine was concerned, the major influence was Brooks and Warren. It was not an issue-oriented magazine. You see the 1935-42 magazine referred to occasionally as a journal founded to advance the Agrarian principles, which is not true; or that it was founded to advance the New Criticism, which is maybe a little bit truer, and so on, but you realize how problematic it is to say that it had a specific agenda. I did look through it and see what a variety of things it did publish. And I never got the sense from talking to Warren or Brooks that they, or that Pipkin, felt that they were trying to advance anything like a formulated program.

WP: They certainly must have had strong feelings about some writers like Eliot, and Stevens, and Pound, and some others.

LS: Yeah, though they weren't able to get much by Eliot. He contributed an essay to the special issue on Yeats they did. They had nothing from Pound, and only one piece about him. But they had several poems by Stevens. They were both deeply interested in poetry and began to develop *Understanding Poetry* while they were here at LSU.

WP: How many of the New Critics were published in the first series? Did they publish Blackmur?

LS: They published a good deal by Blackmur. They published Ransom, Tate, and they published themselves too, though nothing by way of criticism by Warren except one book review. They published people like Leonard Unger, Austin Warren, Arthur Mizener, and Morton Dauwen Zabel too, and they published a good bit by Kenneth Burke. Blackmur's "Humanism and the Symbolic Imagination" first came out in *The Southern Review*. Brooks on Eliot's *Waste Land* also. And Ransom on Shakespeare's sonnets. Tate published "Literature as Knowledge" in *The Southern Review*. Burke published his rhetorical analysis of Hitler's *Mein Kampf*. There was a lot of important critical comment. Allen Tate felt, one or two of his letters certainly show this, that *The Southern Review* was going to be an organ for a group of people who would express his idea of a Southern reactionary movement, but I think he soon realized that that wasn't exactly the way it was going to work.

WP: What was the attitude of the magazine—if there is such a thing and, of course there isn't—toward Faulkner?

LS: It didn't have any really. There were seven volumes published from 1935 to 1942, but there's not a word in the whole thing about Faulkner except one negative review of *The Hamlet*, which formed a small part of a much longer multiple review, and which referred to it, I believe, as "another explosion in a cesspool."

WP: And that was all there was about Faulkner?

LS: As far as I can remember, that really was all I could find anywhere in the magazine about Faulkner. The funny thing is that Warren had got on to Faulkner and had become deeply interested in Faulkner, I believe, even by 1935. He was not a well-known writer at that time. He had acquired a certain notoriety because of *Sanctuary* and because his other books were considered dirty, but he wasn't a bestselling writer. The first American to write a really substantial essay on Faulkner—not that it's necessarily still valid—was George Marion O'Donnell. He did an essay on "Faulkner's Mythology," which came out in the first issue of *The Kenyon Review* after Ransom started that. George said that Faulkner's works were based upon "the Southern socio-economic ethical tradition."

WP: What year would that have been?

LS: Nineteen-thirty-nine, I believe. That really was the first go at Faulkner from the point of view of trying to explain Faulkner's work as a whole and something of the epic scope of it. O'Donnell was a kind of disciple of the Agrarians, more of a disciple than anything else, you might say. He was something of a theoretical Agrarian. He had written about Faulkner even as a high school kid. He was a very precocious child who had grown up on a plantation named "Blue Ruin" in Mississippi. Charles East knew him, and I have heard Charles talk about him. Other people, I'm sure, were interested in Faulkner, but they just didn't publish anything.

WP: Why didn't the Agrarians pay more attention to Faulkner? Was it because he was drunk when they saw him? Or was it simply that he was outside the academic community?

LS: I think it was partly that he was an outsider. Faulkner was foreign to the Vanderbilt Agrarians. He was not comfortable around academics. He didn't finish high school. There certainly was no warm relation. When *The Southern Review* was started, there was a conference in Baton Rouge. The records of that conference—or at least the records of the proceedings—were published in 1985 in *The Southern Review*. A large number of writers were there, mostly from the South. But Ford Maddox Ford was the most distinguished of the non-Southerners who came. Warren was the chairman, and he made some reference to the fact that Faulkner had been invited but had been undecided and hadn't shown up. It would have been surprising if he had come. I think he had gone to a literary conference at Virginia in the early thirties, but generally he avoided all that sort of thing.

WP: Did he feel that real writers didn't go to conferences?

LS: I think he did. This was in the time before writing had been so assimilated to the campus. Allen Tate for example did not want to associate himself with the campus. He did it only out of financial need finally. He wanted to be an independent writer and that was the ideal.

WP: But in those days creative writers weren't generally treated very well by the academics.

LS: No, they weren't able to get in, at that point didn't want to get in, a lot of them. You still had that old kind of bohemian attitude. That was a part of Faulkner's makeup certainly, and Tate shared in that attitude.

WP: But my impression is that Tate became pretty bitter at the end because the academy had slighted him.

LS: Well, I don't know. Tate avoided the campus as long as he could. He was testy toward it. Warren obviously never was. He was pretty much an academician. He seemed to feel that the teaching and the writing were all compatible. Tate didn't want to give up the life of the free-lance writer.

WP: Of course, Warren was a great teacher. James Wilcox studied under him in the late sixties.

LS: I remember he did. Wilcox was over at Thibodaux a few years back when Warren was there. I saw him there.

WP: He wrote a novel for him, and Warren criticized it and commented on it page by page.

LS: Was that at Yale?

WP: Yes.

LS: He would do that. He liked to teach. He didn't like to teach every semester. He said he felt a certain need for a captive audience some part of each year, so he generally had a class each spring at Yale.

WP: By 1965, when *The Southern Review* resurfaced, Faulkner's reputation was well established.

LS: That's true. During the earlier period, Faulkner was not well known at all, but by the time of his death in 1962, he had been established as a monumental writer.

WP: You said that *The Southern Review* in 1935 didn't have a program, and I know that a magazine has to take what it gets, but to what extent do you think a magazine can guide and shape critical perception?

LS: All I meant was that I thought that Brooks and Warren had a sense of direction about the relationship between poetry and criticism and so on, but you can obviously start a magazine with a very rigorous program in mind, as F. R. Leavis did with *Scrutiny*.

WP: There's no doubt about that.

LS: The whole question of what you do with a magazine depends upon what you want to do with it. If you have one editor, a very strong editor, he can dominate the magazine and it becomes his magazine and his point of view, and it can do very well.

WP: That's exactly what Leavis did, and you can argue in a very real sense that *Scrutiny* is Leavis's best work.

LS: But we have to remember that Brooks and Warren were full-time teachers.

WP: How did the new series of *The Southern Review* get started?

LS: The first series had never had a big circulation, but there weren't very many magazines published then. In 1935 there wasn't much competition. There was *The Virginia Quarterly Review* and *The Sewanee Review*, the oldest academic quarterly, around since 1890.

WP: Was *Partisan* around at that time?

LS: *Partisan* which was founded in 1935 as a Marxist, an anti-Stalinist, publication was not academic. It claimed to have a circulation of about 15,000 at one time.

WP: That would have been huge.

LS: But *Partisan* has had a checkered history in recent years and is now published at Boston University.

WP: What was the circulation of the first series of *The Southern Review*?

LS: Never more than 1,500. It had some circulation abroad, and I think they said they sold more copies in Japan than they did in Baton Rouge. Of course, readership of literary quarterlies has always been much heavier in libraries than among individual subscribers. If you don't have a big library subscription, you won't have enough circulation to justify the magazine. In any event the first series of the magazine had made such a strong impression that there were all of these people in the university, particularly in the English department, who were strongly in favor of bringing it back. But we couldn't get the money. Then through a combination of circumstances money was finally made available in 1963. Don Stanford and I were appointed coeditors. It took us about a year and a half to put things together. The first issue came out in January of 1965. Of course, it's now been going much longer than the original series.

WP: Were the first editors in 1935 paid or did they get release time or what?

LS: As far as I know, they got no release time. They were young men. They worked very hard, and they both had a tremendous capacity for work-they were never to lose that. They didn't get any special concessions. They just went at it and did it. And they not only edited the magazine, they taught and wrote critical articles and books and novels and what not, and began that famous series of textbooks. It was a different situation by the sixties. I think they gave us one class off. Considering the amount we had to do, that wasn't very much.

WP: How many hours were you teaching at that time?

LS: I think they had just got it down to nine for full professors.

WP: So you were teaching six hours and editing the magazine.

LS: Yeah, but with teaching and graduate work, dissertations, and a lot of committee work, and everything else, carrying on editorial work was not easy.

WP: Looking at the twenty plus years of the new series, do you think that you were successful in what you set out to do?

LS: In some ways I think the magazine was more successful than we hoped. Very early in the game, you could see what was happening. Even after twenty years plus, there was no problem at all about establishing the image of the magazine. It was still there; people all over the country remembered it. This didn't mean that you were going to get everybody in the world to subscribe to the new series by any means, but they knew about it and they read it. It wasn't any problem to reestablish it and pretty soon we started to get good manuscripts.

WP: How successful do you think the magazine has been in attracting the best younger writers?

LS: I would say reasonably successful. I don't think we had the pick of the lot, but how are you to judge? The literary situation has become so ambiguous. The old-line publishers have all been bought by big corporations that are diversifying, as they say. The big national magazines are gone. There is nothing much left of the old literary world in America, where you had *Harper's, Atlantic Monthly*, and *Scribner's* at a kind of upper level, and *Saturday Evening Post, Collier's, Woman's Home Companion, Ladies Home Journal*, and *Cosmopolitan* at a more popular level, but all in the market for good fiction and articles and paying well too. There weren't many literary quarterlies; they were small, elite publications. Now there are a lot of them, nearly all associated with campuses. They don't pay very well, or not at all. One market is *The New Yorker*—it pays well to writers who get in the stable and are willing to give it the first refusal on stories. There isn't any central kind of magazine world any more I mean. Trying to believe in some kind of center, the quarterlies belong to an organization called The Coordinating Council of Literary Magazines.

WP: What was the division of responsibility while you were coeditor of *The Southern Review*? What was your chief responsibility? How did you decide whether you were going to publish a piece?

LS: For some time we actually had three editors, two from the Baton Rouge campus and one from what was then the Louisiana State University at New Orleans campus. The New Orleans editor, who had the rank of Associate Editor, was Rima Drell Reck, a distinguished student of modern French letters. We would meet once a month, mostly in Baton Rouge but sometimes in New Orleans, and decide about submissions. As time went on the situation changed, and it seemed more feasible to put first one coeditor and then the other in charge of the individual issues. LSUNO began to seek more autonomy and became the University of New Orleans and the magazine's editorial relationship with the New Orleans campus ceased. So we followed a division of responsibility that seemed to work to the advantage of the magazine. It is a division still adhered to. Contributions to a given number are determined by one of the two editors. He decides. There is no editorial board. It sounds awkward but in practice it has worked in a situation in which the editors are part-time editors, part-time teachers, and part-time Lord knows what, whatever called on to do by way of work on departmental and university committees, professional organizations, etc. An absolutely key person in the operation of *The Southern Review* is the only full-time person, the Business Manager. For the past several years Evelyn Heck has served admirably in this capacity. There is a part-time copy editor; and a student helper or two. I ought to add that during my time on the *Review* my part of the editing was always in part directed toward what we called "the Southern dimension of *The Southern Review*." The coeditors had a kind of logical division of interests with my interest in American writing and American history, particularly Southern history and writing, and Don Stanford with his interest in modern poetry, in British writing generally, etc. He retired before I did, and James Olney came to the staff—a man also interested in poetry, he has a fine book on Yeats, but also is one of the leading students of autobiography as a literary mode, and not least, of writing by black authors, American and African. James has given the magazine what it really lacked, close awareness of black writers. After I retired Fred Hobson came aboard for a couple of years. A noted student of the South, he was a great acquisition, but he left to go back to his native state, North Carolina. Never have seen anybody with as much tar on his heels as Fred. Now Dave Smith, the well-known Southern poet, a Virginian, is on the staff with James as coeditor. Don Stanford and I are consulting editors and do some writing for the magazine.

WP: How many of the pieces were commissioned?

LS: No fiction, no poems. Almost without exception, however, the book reviews or review essays. Some of the regular essays. I am not sure of the percentage; never tried to figure it. A "special issue"-one devoted chiefly to a single figure, say-might be planned carefully enough to mean several commissions. But I started a biannual series of specials called "Writing in the South," and these issues were mostly, I think, taken from what came in. Of course you could suggest contributions, or solicit them, without direct commissioning. The number of manuscripts coming in meant there was always a stack on hand. We figured the submission rate at about 15,000 a year if you count individual poems. Poets usually send more than one poem at a time, you know. One thing about getting submissions is you get more and on the whole better ones if you pay for each piece published in a professional way. For a long time we paid, I think, twelve dollars a page for prose and twenty dollars a page for poems, but there was a way to do better in the case of an unusually distinguished person. The pay is a little better now but not much. The chief thing is to pay something, maybe small but respectable. This doesn't mean you won't get less than respectable submissions. Many people are very naive about publishing. You get a good bit of "greeting card" verse, or of a quality like that. You get people too who will send something and say, "Send my check as soon as possible." You get a few who don't take rejection slips very gracefully and will write something like, "You can rot in hell before I'll ever send you anything else." There is a lot of pathos actually in this business.

WP: What was the circulation and was the magazine self-supporting?

LS: The questions are in the past tense, and I don't think of my association with the *Review* in the past. It goes on. The circulation remains, I believe, at between 3,000 and 4,000 per issue. We have had printings of 4,500. Some issues will have more over the counter sales than others-at the outlets in bookstores and newsstands handled by the distribution agency that represents the magazine. It is very hard to get and maintain individual subscriptions. I remember a statistical analysis of the readership of selected American quarterlies in libraries a few years ago; it showed *The Southern Review* with something like 12,000 readers each quarter. Right up towards the top. But the idea that you can go out and get 12,000 subscribers is a pipe dream. All the quarterlies are heavily subsidized, most by universities and colleges. The dream of an independent quarterly is still around. Some time ago the *Kenyon* at Kenyon College was revived with a big fund from, I believe, alumni of Kenyon. A major advertising campaign was put on, with the idea that something like 25,000 subscriptions would come in and the *Kenyon* would soon be self-supporting. It didn't work. At best subscription payments, plus advertising money, in any one year are not likely to total more than the cost of printing one issue and paying the contributors to any of the quarterlies I know about. I mean the ones that sort of belong to the major league. No literary quarterly of any size and distinction can exist at all without being heavily subsidized. Not in America at any rate.

WP: What were some of the pieces which you published that you were proudest of?

LS: I guess you mean the pieces that I worked with in particular-things in the issues I edited. A perilous question that I can't answer categorically. Among things early in the game I think especially of Arlin Turner on Mark Twain and the South, and an interview with Walker Percy by Carlton Cremeens. Later on there was an important piece by Walker Percy on Walter Miller's *A Canticle for Leibowitz*, Ransom's modification of his attitude toward Eliot, William C. Havard on the "new mind" of the South and on *The Children of Pride*, Louis D. Rubin, Jr. on "Southerners and Jews," and Walter Sullivan on "Southern Writers in the Modern World: Death by Melancholy." Still later there was James M. Cox on Jefferson's *Autobiography*, a major essay on American autobiographical writing; also Cox on Shelby Foote's narrative history of the Civil War. There was Warren on Mark Twain and also on Theodore Dreiser; Brooks on Walker Percy. I can't begin to list all the nonfiction things I have liked. I wouldn't fail to mention, though, Charles East on the death of Huey Long, and Robert B. Heilman on Long and the Harry Williams biography of Long. The late John Finlay on "The Dark Rooms of the Enlightenment" represents a very unusual moral essayist. If you go to poets, any number of poems; but I always think of Joyce Carol Oates and of getting on to her poetry when nobody much had. Also of an appealing poet I published when he was a very old man and whatever star he had had was set, John Hall Wheelock. Wendell Berry, John Finlay, Henry Taylor, Dabney Stuart, Turner Cassity, Brooks Haxton, Pinky Lane-any number of poets and poems. Fiction? Fiction flowed from Joyce Oates's electric typewriter into all the quarterlies of course, still does. John Hazard Wildman, John William Corrington, Elaine Gottlieb, Charles East, Martha Lacy Hall, David Madden, Louis D. Rubin, Jr., Elizabeth Spencer, Peter Makuck, Robb Forman Dew—many names come to mind. Among the stories in the *Review* by the older writers, I remember Elizabeth Spencer's "The Cousins" vividly.

WP: Who were the most important young writers you published?

LS: "Young" isn't always a definitive term. I suppose Martha Hall did not think of herself as being in the youthful category when she published her first story in the *Review*, but it was a first story and opened up a career in fiction that is still developing. But in terms of being young in years when they first came out in *The Southern Review* we could claim Joyce Oates, Peter Makuck, Robb Dew, Brooks Haxton, John Bennett, Jefferson Humphries, and others. Andrew Hudgins is another young writer to be mentioned. I don't think that young writers today, no matter how good they are, have the kind of emergence that we associate with Eudora Welty. Writing schools graduate an awesome number of writers who are competent. I think the processing of writers through writing programs, however, may modify real talent, turn genius into mere competency, so to speak, at least make it more difficult for the truly gifted person to recognize his or her own gift.

WP: Are you satisfied with the turn the magazine has taken in recent years?

LS: Yes. I think the new editorial perspectives that have been opened up by James Olney in the five years he has been with the *Review* and the new contributors have given it a new dimension of possibilities. I have mentioned his knowledge of black writers. I don't think I said that he has behind him the experience of a white Midwesterner who went to graduate school at Columbia, then taught in Liberia for some time. Also that he taught for some time in a black college in the South. At the same time he has cultivated a deep knowledge of Yeats and Eliot and the moderns, including the French. He speaks fluent French, by the way. He continues a cosmopolitan character that the *Review* derived from the original editors. This had been perpetuated by Don Stanford and Rima Reck. My own orientation wasn't parochial I hope, nor was that of Fred Hobson. Nor is Dave Smith's. The South has been far more related to Europe than most of us realize. Allen Tate once said that he and his Agrarian companions would have to be the last Europeans, there being no Europeans left in Europe. I hope the magazine will go on being a cosmopolitan publication in the best sense of the term, though I know that in some ways American culture, like culture everywhere, is becoming compulsively attracted to narrow particularisms—ethnic, political, sexual, religious, and so on. We live in a time of ideological madness.

WP: Do you think it will ever be possible for another magazine to have the impact that the original *Southern Review* had. If so, what conditions might make that favorable?

LS: Frankly, no I don't think it possible; and I can't imagine any future time when the possibility might exist. The historical circumstances cannot possibly rise again in the so-called post-modern age. That is a silly term. Modern means here and now, and you can't be post-now. But you can be anything if you assume that words don't mean anything, have nothing but ideological referents, and that has been the tendency in the past twenty years or so, certainly in the hothouse of American academe, and unfortunately literature and language have come to have almost the whole of their self-conscious existence in this rather fetid hothouse. Only in the most marginal sense is there a literary life left—the life that Hemingway or Faulkner knew, a life that came down from the Hebrews and the Greeks and the Romans but also once lived in the printing houses and streets of Paris and London and Rome and the old Berlin, and in New York, and after a fashion even in little cities like Nashville, Tennessee, and even in country towns like Oxford, Mississippi. This was the life I have attempted to describe as existing in the Republic of Letters. This was the secular yet spiritual community of minds that followed the downfall of the medieval mind. Out of it I have argued came the Declaration of Independence, the U.S. Constitution—also the Confederate Constitution. Out of the Republic of Letters came the American Republic, which was an idea, not an ideology. But the difference between idea and ideology is hard to define, and idea is easily transformed into ideology.

WP: Finally, what sort of writing do you have planned for now or in the future?

LS: I suspect I've shot the small wad I had, probably shot it pretty decisively ten years ago in *The Brazen Face of History*, and further back in *The*

Dispossessed Garden. But I liked doing *Mind and the American Civil War.* It won the only book award I've ever had. I am by choice basically an essayist, like my friend Jim Cox, like Allen Tate, too, who always said he wasn't a long distance runner. I think there are too many long distance runners. Many books would be better if written as essays. At least critical studies would be, and a lot of historical studies, too. I imagine some good essayists have been ruined by the necessity of writing bloated books in order to get tenure or be promoted. We always say, "But where is his or her book?" when inspecting a dossier. Writing is a habit like breathing, and it is a kind of premature death to quit it. I have a book in the wings called *The Fable of the Southern Writer* that I want maybe to take from a little and add to a little, too before it is published. I've recently done another essay on Faulkner—something on the Civil War and Faulkner; well, it is on Mark Twain as well. I've done another essay this spring on Walker Percy and read it as a lecture. I would like maybe to do more on Walker, that is, if I dare to. He is a formidable subject, maybe a last expression of the Southerner as European. Speaking of things just published, I have a long piece on Eric Voegelin in a new collection edited by Ellis Sandoz. This piece is called "Eric Voegelin and the Story of the Clerks." It is about Voegelin's relation to the concept of the "clerk"—the European intellectual—as defined by Julien Benda in a once famous 1920s book called *The Treason of the Clerks.* Walker was interested enough in this to read it, even if he didn't go for Voegelin's awkward vocabulary, when he was running a persistent fever, a symptom of the illness that would kill him. In a letter to him I said that he, like Allen Tate, was a clerk—meaning in context that he was a "good clerk" who would not betray the vocation to letters by what Voegelin called "ideological deformation." Walker liked that, liked he said to be called a clerk like Tate. I have written a good deal about the vocation to letters. Maybe I will try to say something more in this respect. (1991; slightly revised, 1992)

Chapter 3
Telling it Again: A Conversation
with David Madden

"Did I ever tell you about the time I tried to get my little brother off the chain gang?...Oh, I did?...Okay, I *will* tell it again.
——-*Pleasure-Dome*

Sharpshooter, David Madden's eagerly awaited novel of the Civil War, is in a final revision. Madden, a tireless reviser of his own work, even in some instances after it has been published, works on a manual typewriter in a large room dominated by a huge railroad desk. On this desk are usually five manuscripts in progress. The room has bookcases on all sides, and the novelist writes with his back to a high stained glass window. The book cases are filled with fiction and with reference works used as historical background for *Sharpshooter*. A number of Civil War photographs are tacked to the wall. There is also a reproduction of Winslow Homer's wood engraving from *Harper's Weekly* of a sharpshooter's lanky frame perched in the top of a tree.

Madden, a prolific writer, has been for twenty-three years writer in residence at Louisiana State University. He has published nine volumes of fiction and has written or edited twice that many volumes of criticism. Madden's first novel, *The Beautiful Greed*, appeared in 1961, his most recent, *On the Big Wind,* in 1980. His two best-known novels are probably *Bijou* and *The Suicide's Wife*. *Bijou* was a Book-of-the-Month Club selection when it appeared in 1974, and *The Suicide's Wife* (1978) was made into a television movie starring Angie Dickinson. Madden's short stories, collected in *The Shadow Knows* (1970) and *The New Orleans of Possibilities* (1982), are intimately related to his novels and often deal with the same subjects and characters.

Madden responds to my questions slowly and carefully, stroking a cat which he is holding in his lap and sipping on a cup of coffee. His answers tend to gain force as they go along. On subjects that he feels deeply about—such as the charge that he reuses old material from his books—he alternates between a forceful defence of his own position and a bemusement at the injustice of the criticism.

WP: David, in what sense, if any, do you consider yourself a regional writer?

DM: I wouldn't use the term "regional," but I would probably use the term "Southern." Now of course, you could say that "Southern" is regional, but that leaves us only with the North and the South, so it's not much of a region concept. In the sense of East Tennessee, that would be a region. I would say that I'm definitely a Southern writer. In that sense I'm regional. "Regional" has such a bad connotation; it's almost as bad as "lo cal color" as a term. As a matter of fact, John Gassner once told me—I was his student at Yale Drama School—when he saw *Cassandra Singing* in play-script—he says, I want to warn you to stay away from regional identification because it can kill you the way it did E. P. Conkle (laughs), who seemed terribly ancient to me even then. So I take his advice to that extent, but not to the extent of denying, as Walker Percy says of himself, that I'm a Southern writer. I'm very much a Southern writer even though I wouldn't hesitate to write about any locality or any other kind of people than the Southern. In other words, I don't feel confined to the South, but I do definitely identify myself with the South.

WP: People my age had a close identification with Thomas Wolfe. I remember when I was seventeen or eighteen, we used to read *Look Homeward, Angel* out loud outside of the student union where I went to school. I judge from *Bijou* that, between say thirteen and eighten, you must have had a close identification with Wolfe also.

DM: Yes, very much, very strongly. As you know, the last long chapter of *Bijou* deals directly with Wolfe, and Lucius's admiration for Wolfe is a motif running through most of the novel. In fact, he steals a copy of the *Portable Thomas Wolfe*, which in my own life was not the "Portable," but the Penguin "Short Stories," to give it added value. In other words, he's making a connection between an action and a literary value, and they seem to be inseparable for him. So then, Wolfe had a great influence on me, but pretty early I decided I'd better cut myself away from him as a literary influence.

WP: I remember when I was in college, teachers told me I wouldn't like Wolfe as well when I got older as I did then.

DM: That's true of me because I was asked about three or four months ago to give a reading-sort-of-lecture at a meeting of the Thomas Wolfe Society in Raleigh, North Carolina, demonstrating Wolfe's influence on me when I was a kid. And I reread some things and he had pretty much the same impact, but I continue to be horrified by some of his stylistic excesses which undercut the kind of effect he clearly and obviously was striving for. I use him often as an example of the writer who consumes the experience as he describes it by over-writing so that the reader doesn't really experience the experience but rather experiences his writing about the experience, which is a totally different thing. I as a writer believe in doing anything I can to set up a context which will stimulate the experience in the reader in a controlled fashion rather than describing an experience directly in the style itself. Do you see what I mean? And I think that there's a combustion which takes place there which ruins his intentions, so you say, "Oh, what beautiful writing!" rather than, "that was a fine experience he just put me through." I think most readers confuse the two. I think most readers think that the effect of beautiful writing is the same as experiencing what the writer is expressing.

WP: You grew up in Knoxville. Were you aware of James Agee at that time?

DM: No, not until about the third year I was writing *Cassandra Singing*, which took about fifteen years to write. When I was about twenty-two, I became aware of him. Well, I was aware of him earlier, but I really became aware of him when I realized that *A Death in the Family*, which came out about 1957 when I was writing *Cassandra Singing*, was set about two blocks from where I was living and that he was being hailed as a really fine writer about Knoxville. And I wanted to be the writer to write about Knoxville. So I began to kind of compare my writing with his and to feel in some sort of competition with him.

WP: I judge that your story, essay, or whatever it is, "James Agee Never Lived in This House," pretty much represents your ambiguous and changing attitude toward Agee.

DM: Yes, as do all my critical writings about him, and over the years, the ambiguity hasn't much altered. But that's not why I wrote the story—it *is* a short story, but with deliberate mixing of the informal, memoir esay and a sudden turn into pure fiction in the middle, a combination I was glad appealed to James Olney when he accepted it. I've had a lingering compulsion to write a story about the lady (as I imagined her) who lives in the house in Frenchtown, New Jersey where Agee wrote much of *Let Us Now Praise Famous Men*. My original intention was to tell it straight up to where she refuses to let me see the house and then to tell the reader, directly, the many imagined perspectives I had on that situation—Agee admirers bothering a lady living in that house. So when I was in Knoxville a few years ago to give a talk on *Famous Men* and Robert Coles, the main speaker, had an accident, and they asked me to fill in, I wrote they story in one sitting and read it the next day, and decided it needed little revision. In the midst of writing it though, the old lady wouldn't stop talking, so I let her talk. I've read it all over the country now and folks seem to love hearing it. I certainly love *doing* hwe voice.

WP: Were you aware of Agee's film criticism in *Life* and *Time*?

DM: No, not until—I probably read it but I wasn't aware who he was or that *he* was doing it. My editor for *Cassandra Singing* and *Bijou* was his close friend and editor, David McDowell, so I really didn't become aware of the film criticism until it came out in those volumes David McDowell published at McDowell-Obolensky.

WP: I had a letter or two from McDowell about some reviews that I had written, and I think that he is unquestionably one of the great editors of the twentieth century.

DM: He is one of the few editors I've encountered who is truly in the Maxwell Perkins tradition. He is the kind of person I thought all editors were supposed to be, or were trying to be.   In other words, every editor wanted to be as good as Maxwell Perkins, and what you would do is to compare every editor with Perkins, and find them either as good as or wanting, and I thought that David McDowell was pretty close to Perkins.

WP: I think of you as an intensely dramatic writer because in a sense your characters seem to talk themselves into life. Is that the dramatic influence, do you think?

DM: I don't think it's the theater. It's the story-telling tradition, the dramatic immediacy, the Southern mountain story- telling tradition as exemplified in my grandmother, who was very dramatic in the way in which she would tell a story. She used her whole body, and she made up voices, and she would even make sound effects with her voice, and so on. And so story-telling was extremely immediate to me the way that radio drama was with out the image, and movies were in a very obvious imagistic way. I got interested in the theater because seeing a play was like just another more vivid version of what my grandmother was doing. It was a live actor on a stage being spotlighted the way my grandmother was a live actor sitting in a chair, which was her stage, and her spotlight with the lamp beside her. I was wonder ing today why, given my sense of the dramatic, which comes from storytelling and from actually seeing a lot of plays and from wanting to be a playwright, I haven't been successful as a play wright, why I haven't been able to write a play that would work on Broadway. Now, I've written a lot of plays, and almost all of those plays have been performed, but none in a really big Broad way sense, or Off-Broadway.

WP: Without digging into your personal life, could you say something about the way personal experience went into *Cassandra Singing*?

DM: The only thing personal went into the early versions and not into the published version. The personal element was simply the locale of Knoxville, Tennessee. I shifted the locale to Eastern Kentucky because just the locale alone of Knoxville, Tennessee, was having the incredibly inflating effect that writing about onesself usually has, as with Wolfe and some of Fitzgerald. When you write about yourself, you go on and on and on. Well, I was only writing about the locale, and I was commit ting the same autobiographical fallacy, so I changed the setting. Now, my father was a kind of a alcoholic, a drunkard, the way Coot, the father in *Cassandra Singing* is, and I sort of had him in mind, but the biographical details are not there at all. So that's one of the two or three works of mine that are the most imaginative, the most totally imaginative.

WP: I suppose that in terms of number of copies sold *Bijou* has been by far your most popular novel.

DM: Well, not by far; *The Suicide's Wife* sold pretty well.

WP: I assume that at some point *Cassandra Singing* was optioned for film because it says on the back of my venerable paper back copy, "Soon to be a Major Motion Picture."

DM: I was commissioned by Tony Bill, the producer of *The Sting*, to go to Warner Brothers and write the script for *Cassandra Singing*. I was in residence there for about two or three weeks in 1969, soon after the novel came out, and I was among the last resident writers. John Milius, who is still writing and producing (*Red Dawn, Flight of the Intruder*) shared an office, or shared a secretary—he had a room and I had a room and she was in the middle—and we were the last, I think, along with Evan Con nell (*Son of the Morning Star, Mr. Bridge, Mrs. Bridge*)—writers to be right there on the property. I finally came on home to write. I did the Faulkner thing with the full knowledge of the producers because they're no longer that excited about having the writers around and economically it wasn't working out. It was one of these independent deals and the reason it didn't get done was not that they weren't satisfied with it, but because a group of sort of hippie types took over the Hollywood scene.

WP: Yes, in 1969 and seventy-two.

DM: The guys who did *Woodstock* pretty much took over at about that time, and they didn't want to inherit projects that were underway. So it was a typical Hollywood story. *Bijou* got more interest from the movies than any book Crown had published, and yet it didn't come as close as *On the Big Wind* to being done because no one could figure out a way to translate that story into a film, which is incredible to me because most readers see it very easily as a movie, you know. The way I see is is to confine the entire movie to the movie theater, making the movies on the screen an actor in the movie, not just a background and not even just an ambience, but a real presence in the movie, so that when you're looking at Lucius talking to an usher or a customer, those people have as much power in the screen as Alan Ladd does on the screen in the theater in the background. So that you always feel that all of the actors or the characters on the screen are always competing with the characters in the movie. And I could never get them to see that. In fact, one producer who considered it said that for aesthetic reasons, we don't think it works, which is ridiculous, since it was the aesthetics that I was really emphasizing. I was making an aesthetic judgment and what she meant was that, (laughs), you know, it wouldn't sell, that it wasn't a typical kind of Hollywood movie.

WP: I assume that there would have been a kind of contrast between the world outside, which represented the world of more or less mundane reality, and the world inside the movie house, which was larger than life.

DM: Well, but what I wanted to get was not so much that—you could just imply that; everybody has that in their own background —I could bring that into the theater. I could bring every-day drama, every-day situations into the lobby of the theater, because in those days a theater was like almost a town meeting hall.

There was a very rich kind of life of characters coming and going who were clearly identified, and there were events taking place in the lobby and backstage and in the restrooms, and it was a very living sort of organism. And the stuff on the screen was just part of a larger picture, as I tried to suggest in the scenes in the Bijou. For instance, when the father comes in and says, hide me, so-and-so broke out of prison and he's tryingto kill me, and Lucius takes his father back stage down stairs and in to a cave. That event competes with any event on the screen. The interesting thing is that Lucius never sees that what he's caught up in is just as interesting as the movies he's seeing. He thinks the movies is where real life is.

WP: I think in a way you may have been too successful in that novel in that, after you get away from the novel for a while, that theater reverberates in the mind and expands so that it becomes something as big as the theater in *The Phantom of the Opera*—

DM: Yeah, right.

WP: —-and I think that may have been the quality—

DM: That's what I want. That's what I want to get in the movie. In fact I have revised the novel, cut it from seven-hundred pages to a hundred-fifty on the principle of: we'll leave nothing in the novel that does not take place in the Bijou. There are a few scenes outside the Bijou that I would rewrite to take place in the Bijou because it's their value that I want to capture, it's the character relationship that I want to capture, not the event for its own sake. So a parallel kind of—a similar kind of event—could be transposed to the Bijou.

WP. I hope you can get a publisher to publish it. But the only two novels I can think of that were published in revised versions were that one by John Fowles (*The Magus*) and a novel by Ira Wolfert (*An Act of Love*).

DM: Well, two of Faulkner's works were published in different versions, *Sanctuary* and *Sartoris*, or *Flags in the Dust*.

WP: Yeah, but they weren't published until after the writer was dead. [Amazingly enough, neither novelist nor interviewer thought of Henry James.] One of the things that strikes me about your work is that, in a sense, you seem to move in to history, That is, you have moved from *Cassandra Singing* in to what seems to be a central kind of experience, that is, from things which are located outside of history to *The Suicide's Wife*, which are located very specific ally in history.

DM: Well, now the reason I did that—somebody writing for an encyclopedia got that all wrong—she said that that meant that this was a feminist novel because it took place among all those public events of '68, but the reason I chose '68 was not because Martin Luther King and Robert Kennedy were killed and all those other horrible events were happening, but because I wanted a year in which a great many things were happening to contrast with what some people might see as nothing happening in her life, what she perceived as nothing happening in her life, but what I hoped that the reader would perceive toward the end as being something very important happening in her life. As she became more and more interested in the kind of external events that had been fascinating other people, I wanted the irony of the reader becoming far more interested in her, who had no life, than they were in those public events that they had experienced and that she was relatively missing. Do you know what I mean?

WP: I understand.

DM: And so it had nothing to do with my commenting on historical events. I was simply using them to bring something out in her, to contrast with her. Actually it was something that she was experiencing in a way that most other people wouldn't experience. Her experience was simply, "Oh, you mean that there are really other things happening out there, you can really get interested in these things?" That's different from using my them to get you, the reader, interested in those events. Now, you come to the Civil War novel I'm working on now, *Sharpshooter*, then that's where what you're saying really applies. That is really true. There for the first time I really am interested in historical events.

WP: *The Suicide's Wife* strikes me as very much an American novel in the sense that—well, this is not specificaly an American technique—but it's the Hawthorne way of telling the story, with Hawthorne beginning *The Scarlet Letter* with the events which most writers would write about having already taken place. It begins in effect a new story there. *The Suicide's Wife* begins with the death of the husband, and the story is about what happens to the wife.

DM: That's why it's really strange that people say they wish they knew more about the husband and why he killed himself. That's not what the novel is about. The novel is about the woman wondering why he killed himself. She has so little to go on that what we're supposed to be interested in is the process she goes through, not whether she finds out, not what she finds out. None of that. We're just meant to be caught up in the proces and to respond with her to it. We're not meant to say to ourselves, oh, yeah, that's fascinating, that's more and more fascinating, and now he's coming alive, he's getting richer, yeah, I can see him more clearly now. That's not it at all. You're supposed to be experiencing it from her point of view. Whereas in the movie, they tried to fill in all that stuff.

WP: Considering the structure of the novel, you could never find out anyway. It has to remain a mystery.

DM: They tried to do it in the movie. They showed him having trouble with the school...

WP: That's a mistake.

DM: ...which was really phony. I've forgotten, but there were some more phony details that aren't even true of teachers. They just didn't trust the story as it was. Why they were attracted to the story is a mystery—if they didn't trust it.

WP: I have at home a paperback edition of *Brothers in Confidence* but I couldn't find it. I assume that wasn't published in hardcover.

DM: No, not that way, It comes out in *Pleasure-Dome* as you know. The paperback is kind of a collector's item. It's really rare. I think they're charging $30.00 for that.

WP: I'll keep my copy.

DM: A lot of people kind of like the purity of *Brothers in Confidence*, you know, just being by itself. Some people even go further back and say they prefer the very first novella version. I fleshed out the novella for *Brothers in Confidence*. The way that happened was Peter Mayer at Avon wanted to do the novella the way it appeared in *The Southern Review*, which would give us a paperback of seventy pages, just blow it up and space it out, and maybe we can get seventy pages. He says, no, that's the way I want it, just the way it is, until he realized that it was only going to be this thin seventy page book. Then he said, "Well, I don't know if I can get away with this. Do you happen to have more material? Is there a longer version?" It so happens I was doing *Bijou*, I was caught up in the richness of the relationship between the brothers when they were younger, so it was very natural to draw on all that. In fact, I think there were some scenes that I had cut out of *The Southern Review* version that I reinstated, and so that was how we got it to be just long enough—barely—to be in paperback. So it wasn't an artificial filling is what I'm saying. It was a very natural amplification.

WP: I think that the paperback publication of American fiction now is something of a public disgrace, but I do think that Avon over the years has published more good fiction than any other paperback publisher.

DM: *Miss Lonelyhearts*, *Call It Sleep*, and that's all Peter Mayer. He's a very good editor. He's another good editor.

WP: Were you satisfied with *Pleasure-Dome* as a sequel to *Bijou*?

DM: It's a sequel only slightly in my mind and maybe in yours. People who really know a lot of my work may see it as a sequel. I kind of thought of it as a true sequel, but it got out of hand and got too long. I didn't want another long novel. Originally, it was supposed to be in five parts rather than two, so that we were supposed to go with Lucius into the merchant marines. That was going to be a total revision of my first novel, *The Beautiful Greed*. You see, I wanted this sequence: he leaves home, goes into the merchant marines, then we were going to have him in the Army, which is a novel I'm going to write—I haven't written yet, but am going to write—but I have written one section which is in *The New Orleans of Possibilities*, "The Cartridge Belt." "The Cartridge Belt" is really the centerpiece of a short novel about the army. Okay, so we're going to have the merchant marines, then the army, then he was going to get out of the army and go into these other two experiences. Then, there was going to be a fifth dimension, which was where he would be teaching. So the con-man concept, the artist as con-man, the con-man as artist, would have another dimension: the teacher as con-man. It would be a lot richer. So that was to be a five part thing with two new elements, the army and the teaching. I had three elements already written, and they got too long, so therefore as a sequel *Pleasure-Dome* kind of doesn't flow. It relates to

Bijou but doesnt't flow the way it was originally conceived. In the editing process, things got eliminated, things got changed, and we ended up with something which is not a true sequel.

WP: I found to my amazement when I was looking through my books today that I was quoted on the dustjacket of *Pleasure-Dome.*

DM: Yeah, that was a very good review that you did.

WP: I think I must have reviewed *Bijou.*

DM: You reviewed more than one or two.

WP: I remember in my review of *Pleasure-Dome*, which I looked at, I expressed some hesitation about whether or not the two main stories in that novel went together. Do you feel that they do?

DM: Yeah, well, that's another problem too. Some people think that they do and some people think that they don't. But then again you have to remember that it is two parts of what was once five facets. At some time, I think I had a sub-title, "The Romantic Adventures of...," or something like that. Each of the five would be another way of looking at the temperament of a young romantic in his encounter with reality, with the everyday world. Even so, when it came down to just being the two, I had fewer opportunities to play one thing off another, but if you really look at that, the way the thing goes together is not so much in terms of the character situations—and of course they don't go together that way—but the mentality and sensibility of the main character who is telling the story. So what you're getting is the same sensibility looking at a similar kind of experience in two totally different contexts, because he goes on to con Zara Jane in the Jesse James story just at he did these other people in the story of the brothers, but for a different reason, a personal reason. It's his way of looking at the world; it's his vision of the world and how he imaginatively recreates the world. First, we see how his two brothers do that. They take reality and change it right there on the spot; then we see how Lucius working with this old lady take a myth and transforms it and works on it and has that effect upon a witness, which is the kid on a motorcycle. So that's a similar thing; the kid on the motorcycle is a lot like Bucky, the little brother.

WP: Was there any pressure put on you by the publisher or by the editors or by anyone else to write a longer more expansive followup to *Bijou* since that was an extremely successful book?

DM: No, as a matter of fact—maybe....*The Suicide's Wife* cameout before *Pleasure-Dome,* didn't it?

WP: Yes.

DM: Those were bought at the same instant, and I think *The Suicide's Wife* was finished. It was written right after *Bijou,* and it comes, in the sequence of publication, right after *Bijou.* The nice feeling by a lot of reviewers was that—oh, he's gone from this very long thing to this very short thing, and they're totally different for other reasons—and there's generally a good response to that. We like this. A lot of reviewers seemed to enjoy saying, I don't see how the same guy who wrote *Bijou* could write *The Suicide's Wife*. I as a writer liked that; it was a very good feeling to be able to do it and to have people see that and to consider it a value. Then with *Pleasure-Dome*, as I say, it was going to be as long as *Bijou*, but I really didn't want it to be that long. The editor seemed to feel that those five different stories were really a little too different. Now, when we get to *On the Big Wind*, we have about twelve stories, and they're all very different from each other.

WP: What happened to the stories that were cut from *Pleasure-Dome*?

DM: One of them was published in *The New Orleans Review*, and that was a totally rewritten version in the first person of *The Beautiful Greed*, my first novel. The novel was originally in the third person, and it was also short. So it is published. The army novel is in a first draft, and the teacher novel I'll probably never write. That's too much out of the sixties and the guru scene of teaching— you know, the old guru approach to teaching.

WP: I know you do a great deal of criticism, and I know that you're interested in James M. Cain and the so-called tough guy writers, but I don't really see any of that, or at least not much of that, in your own fiction. Is there some reason for that?

DM: Well, I think the interest in Cain was very close to my interest in movies because the way I got interested in Cain was through the movies of Cain's books, *Mildred Pierce* and *Double Indemnity*. And I think I like the best of the tough writers because they are very crisp and imagistic in the way the good crime movies were. So that's an element which doesn't really get into my fiction, an interest out there separate from my fiction. The only thing is I wrote a detective novel called *Hair of the Dog*—you probably haven't seen it—and which I really like and which several people like Richard Poirier and I think Robert Coles the psychologist really like...

WP: Where was it published?

DM: And I can't get the damned thing published. Well, I published it in *Adam* magazine as a serial, but I can't get anybody to publish it as a book, and it's really kind of a charming sort of lyrical Southern semi-satirical detective story. It's not a tough guy story. It's very fast-paced and very succinct. I wrote it in eleven days the way Simenon writes his novels. In fact, I read Simenon's statement that he wrote all of his novels in eleven days, and I decided to write one in eleven days. It's eleven chapters long, I wrote it in eleven days, and that's it.

WP: One of the other characteristics you have in common with him, you go about it slightly differently, is that when he started writing a novel and he didn't like it, he would just write it and publish it and then give the characters different names and do another version of it, and sometimes end up with three or four different novels until he got what he wanted.

DM: Could you give me an example of that later? I'd like to see that. I can do that by the way—if you want to comment on the way I write—I can decide, I can will this, I can say—I spent fifteen years on *Cassandra Singing*—starting tomorrow I will write a story a day for five days, and I'll go to my file of stories and I'll look through it. And the five stories will leap to my attention, which excites me—and one or two of them may be stories which haven't particularly excited me lately, but for some reasons they will under those conditions. I can take that schedule and actually write a story a day, and spend maybe two or three weeks rewriting each later on. Out of one of those experiences—I've done it three or four times—came "Traven," which is *Brothers in Confidence*, written in a day. "The Day the Flowers Came" and two or three others that I can't remember right now, but there was one stretch—no, "The Singer"—three of my best stories were written within a five-day period and rewritten with not a hell of a lot more work. On the other hand, I can spend fifteen years writing *Cassandra Singing*, and six years writing *Bijou*, and six years writing this *Sharpshooter*; and so what I'm saying is that there is this ability to write very intensely and to get totally absorbed in the first draft and to be able to get it down the way Simenon did.

WP: I notice that you're interested in art. You have a print of Rockwell Kent over there and—is that Hopper over there?

DM: Yeah.

WP: I collect Winslow Homer wood engravings from *Harper's Weekly*. And I see you have a copy of "The Sharpshooter, which is probably his most famous one.

DM: I write about that. Just today and yesterday I was writing about that, and I'll show you what I was doing with it. Drawings are very important in Sharpshooter, and photographs of the Civil War. Willis Carr meditates on them very deeply. In fact, he is a sketch artist, the sharpshooter, and the Homer sharpshooter is the one I have in mind for him, except that he is a Rebel and not a Yankee the way the one in Homer is. Homer did a sketch, or a woodcut, and then he did a painting a few years later. I think his first mature painting was the one of the sharpshooter.

WP: How long is this book going to be?

DM: First, it was seven hundred pages, and I cut it down to about four hundred, and then I reinflated it to about six, but I want to cut it back down to under four hundred manuscript pages.

WP: I sort of hesitate to bring this up and to express this point of view, but I'm of the opinion that you should go full-bore with the fiction and sort of let the criticism take care of itself. There are a lot of good critics around, and I realize that there are a lot of Southern writers like Warren and others who combine fiction and criticism and sometimes poetry, but I feel that, if you hadn't written so much criticism, you might have written more novels.

DM: You could say this. It definitely is true that all that critical work has detracted from the fiction, but the way I was able to do that has absolutely nothing to do with the profession of teaching, absolutely nothing to do with academia. I've been here [at LSU] a long time and whatever situation I have here is almost totally based on fiction and very little attention is given to the criticism. Noboby ever says a word to me in the department about my criticism. Well, maybe a word.

WP: That's ironic. It's a reversal of the usual situation where they're telling some poor devil he has to publish on John Donne when he wants to write the great American novel.

DM: I have the same attitude toward fiction that I have to all the other genres. To me, any form is exciting if I decide to work in it. To me, there's just one creative flow. I have the same attitude toward everything I do. There is one university. There's not a thousand universities. There's only one. I don't have any allegience to LSU, just to the idea of a university, you see. So if I'm visiting a university, it not as if I'm going from where I belong, LSU, to Cornell, where I don't belong, doing a lecture. The creative flow is all one, and whatever you do in it is just as important as anything else. But still it is true that it would be better to have written thirty novels than to have written twenty books of criticism and ten books of fiction. By the way, every one of those books of non-fiction is pretty distinctive. Nobody ever did a book like *Tough Guy Writers of the Thirties*, and somebody imitated *Rediscoveries* recently.

WP: Some novelists seem to think that writing too much criticism is bad for a novelist because it makes him overly analytical.

DM: The easiest way to test the premise behind that question is consider mine as a good example: since I have written and published criticism during the same period over which I've written and published fiction, one could look at the fiction, characterize it, then look at the criticism and characterize it, and then ask: do both fiction and criticism share a similar analytical quality? I expect the answer would be that the fiction, when it isn't clearly in the oral story-telling tradition, is never overtly intellectual or analytical and that the ciriticm, while certainly analytical, is full of imaginative conceptions and developments. As I've said, to me both fiction, general nonfiction, and criticism, even textbooks, come out of an undifferentiated flow of creative energy, directed at an imagined, receptive audience. Another way to test this often heard theory is to look at more and more cases, such as Robert Penn Warren, people who have consistently published both criticism and fiction. My tone of voice suggests I have my own answer, and it is emphatically no, because, for one thing, in the crucial stage of revision, all fiction writers become, essentially, literary critics.

WP: I love both of the *Rediscovery* books. Was the second one as well received as the first?

DM: No, it was hardly noticed. Why is one of the mysteries of book reviewing that I hope someone solves quick because Peggy Bach and I are about to send in a third volume called *Rediscoveries: Non-Fiction*. I think somehow or other the books just never got to the reviewers because it's clearly the kind of book they would almost all snatch up.

DM: Do you know the imitation *Rediscoveries*?

WP: No.

DM: Well, the imitation just kept referring and referring to *Rediscoveries*.

WP: The only criticism I had of the Redicsoveries books was that one or two of the rediscovered books were so well-known that they shouldn't have qualified.

DM: Well, that happens when you get contributors who insist on writing about a certain book.

WP: What part do you think a novelist should play in the community life of his time?

DM: As a novelist, no part at all. I think that the novelist more than justifies his existence and his role as a human being in society simply by writing good novels, but I think that every citizen should do certain things. And those are the things I do. I have a tremendous reverence for the democratic process and for democracy as a concept. I think it's the most humanizing political structure ever devised. I have a real, vital desire to see it work and to participate in it, and when I see it being violated, it's extremely upsetting to me, so I get drawn into—or leap into—various kinds of controversies. When I write some thing to the paper, or when I go on television to express an opinion, it's not out of an obligation as a novelist to participate at all, and it's not as a novelist that I'm speaking, not even in the censorship cases. Of course, when it happens to be my own novel, then it's very hard to separate the two. Of course, I do separate them, but it's very hard for anyone to understand what I mean when I say I separate them. What I do is simply my own concept of an active citizen. And I guess that it's simply my own attitude as a teacher that teaching's part of my creative flow and that probably gets into my attitude toward the democratic process. I guess I love processes in which things get worked out, the teacher process, the student process, the writing process, the acting process, the democratic process.

WP: The writers that you admire most—Henry James, James Joyce, Fitzgerald, Faulkner, Wright Morris—are not people who, at least in their work, seem to express any kind of social commitment except in the most general way.

DM: That's good. I'm glad you mentioned that because that's what I mean when I say that I don't think a novelist has any particular responsibility to take part in political experiences or issues, because I'm personally more interested in the art of fiction than I am in the subject matter of fiction or the themes of fiction. I'm interested in creating an aesthetic experience for a reader rather than in reporting on the way people happen to be living in a certain decade. In other words, I would hate to have people say in classrooms of me what is too often said of other writers: he drew a very convincing portrait of Victorian society at the turn of the eighties or something. To me that is absolutely no accomplishment whatsoever. I want a sense of accomplishment about what I write, and I don't want anybody to say that, in *The Suicide's Wife*, he really captures what it was like to be alive in

1968. (With animation.) You go to hell man, I wasn't even thinking about that, you know?

WP: I would like to ask your opinion about some other serious writers of your generation. What do you think about George Garrett?

DM: George Garrett stands out, stands way out, from all other fiction wlriters or poets that I know as a man who has a generous attitute toward the writers around him. He helps more writers than any other writer that I could mention, and I think he's a good writer and one of the most valuable men on the literary scene today. Peggy Bach and I dedicated *Rediscoveries II* to him.

WP: Reynolds Price?

DM: I feel some communion with him. We were published in the same year, and Granville Hicks reviewed both of us in the *Saturday Review* within months of each other, and he was on the cover, and I was not. So ever since then, I've had this feeling that Reynolds Price and I were competing with each other. Now, this kind of thing is not very important to me. This kind of thing is not very meaningful to me, but it's just a kind of little sidelight that I've been following for the past twenty-five years. How's Reynolds doing? How am I doing? The real fact is that I read only one novel of his, the first one and I saw these incredible similarities between—what is it, A *Long and Happy Life?*—

WP: *A Long and Happy Life* was the first one.

DM: —-and *Cassandra Singing* because it starts off with a guy on a motorcycle with his girl hugging up to him. I felt then and I still feel that the writing was precious. Now, some people feel that about Cassandra Singing too, but I tried my dammnedest not to write with a Faulknerian lushness.

WP: Cormac McCarthy?

DM: Well, Cormac McCarthy is the worst offender as far as imitating Faulkner goes. I think Reynolds Price is a much better writer than Cormac McCarthy.

WP: I want to put in a good word for McCarthy. I like him a lot.

DM: I like *The Orchard Keeper*, but I liked it only because I could say to myself, well, it's a first novel after all, eventhough it's slavishly imitative of Faulkner, but then all the others have been slavishly imitative of Faulkner—even what is it?—Suttree, the last one.

WP: Well, *Blood Meridian* is the most recent one, but *Suttree* is the one he spent years and years on. He worked at it off and on for twenty years.

DM: I wish him well. We're both from Knoxville, you know. I tried to get friendly with him, but he was very standoffish.

WP: John William Corrington?

DM: I haven't read much of him, but I can say I'm not attracted to him. I'm not drawn to his work.

WP: Are you familiar with Ron Hansen, who wrote *Desperadoes* and *The Assassination of Jesse James by the Coward Robert Ford*? I thought of him in connection with the Jesse James story in *Pleasure-Dome*.

DM: He and I are in correspondence about that. He loves *Pleasure-Dome* for the Jesse James stuff. He was about to write that when he read *Pleasure-Dome*. We were at Bread Loaf together. I liked it pretty well.

WP: Are you talking about *Desperadoes*?

DM: I don't think I read either one of them all the way through. I sort of dipped in to them, then wasn't drawn to them, but I think he's probably very effective.

WP: Which of the older generation, the revered elders, do you feel most drawn to? What about Warren?

DM: Well, Faulkner mainly, Conrad. Camus. Wright Morris. Robert Penn Warren's *All the King's Men* mainly. I've got a kind of collection, a pantheon of my favorite writers that I'll show you. Dickens has joined the pantheon. Joyce.

WP: What about the Wright Morris books of prose and photographs, especially *The Home Place*?

DM: You know I did a book on Morris, and you saw my essay on the influence of photographs on Southern writers. I'm going to do a book out of that essay and include Morris for contrast.

WP: Is there anyone else that you particularly admire that we haven't mentioned?

DM: Jules Romains's *The Death of a Nobody* affected my writing deeply. Michel Tournier. I think *The Ogre* is one of the finest books to come out in a long time. And *The Garden*, by Yves Berger.

WP: I reviewed that.

DM: That's a wonderful book.

WP: Weird.

DM: It's imitative of Faulkner, but in a way that transcends imitation. It's not imitative, rather it's influenced by Faulkner.

WP: I think the Latin American writers have used Faulkner in a much more creative way than the Americans have. They can't misuse him. They're far enough away from him that he's not overpowering in the way that he is for the Americans.

DM: In the same way that the Italians have used Hemingway. I've been reading Vittorini and those guys, and I think that Vittorini is better than Hemingway in some of the things that he does stylistically.

WP: Shelby Foote was so much under the influence of Faulkner that he disappeared, and he never really reappeared until he turned to non-fiction and did that three volume narrative history of the Civil War.

DM: I've been reading a lot of Civil War history for *Sharpshooter*, and I think that, leaving out Grant, his Civil War writing is among the very best, but it's also full of infuriating mannerisms that I find detestable and that I picked up in so many books about the war. People write about the Civil War because they're really full of a sense of the importance of the Civil War, and the incredible horror and magnificence of it, but as soon as they start writing about it, they somehow seem to have to show us that they're above it, and they get condescending in their word choices, and they trivialize things in an incredible way. They take great generals and say, well, now I'm not going to fall for this great general thing, so they start describing these generals in a way that really trivializes them. And then when it suits their purposes, they'll soup up the language to make them sound really magnificent. Foote is one of the worst at that.

WP: What did you think about the Ken Burns's film on the Civil War which got so much attention recently.

DM: The occasion of this kind of massive assault on the public was terrific, wonderful. It was a fine happening. But the film itself was rather static and predictable in its technique and seriously irresponsible in its misuse of photographs, the single most unique archive of the war, misused from the beginning, of course, when Brady took or was given credit for more photographs thn he deserved, and when others did as he did, and when books on the war decades later cropped and knowingly mislabeled them for the same reason Burns did: to illustrate, above all, whether appropriate or not. He used one photograph in two or three totally different contexts, while using most of them authentically, and so the misuse of some distorts the effect of all. The camera playing over photographs was certainly allowable, but it got monotonous, and so did the music. Most of the voices, however, were very effective. My various criticisms aside, I watched every frame eagerly and the whole series, I am happy to observe, woke a lot of people up, North and South, to the fact that this was the central event in our history, with the most reverberations, and most serious, throughout our history to the present day, with Desert Storm, coming in conveniently for timely comparison.

WP: The series seems to have made a media star out of Shelby Foote. According to a friend of mind, his accent seemed to get thicker with each battle.

DM: The anecdotal sensibility thrives on accent, as Andrew Lytle's, for instance, does, and Faulkner's did. You know, I often wonder why it is that Southerners, when they deal with serious human dramas, feel compelled to structure the telling as a kind of folkloric joke, with a humorous punch line at the end which brings to the pursed lip of the teller the trace of a smug smile. I have thoughts on that, but they are long, long thoughts.

WP: Your story, "The Demon in My View" connects the Lucius Hutchfield material with the death of General Sanders and the *Sharpshooter* material.

DM: Yes, because "A Demon in My View" is a short novel follow-up to *Bijou*—Lucius much older returning to live inside the abandoned theater—and it was while reading some knoxville history for *Bijou* that I read about General Sanders being taken wounded to the Lamar Hotel (the Bijou theater was built inside the hotel, so to speak, the hotel remaining on the side and above the front part of the building) after a sharpshooter in Bleak House tower, so the legend goes, shot him out on Kingston Pike. I knew the story of the shooting all my life, but not that he died in the bridal suite of the hotel. So I like the feeling of that story merged with Lucius's story.

WP: Your have the tendency of a certain type of novelist to connect materials from different novels and stories. Do you ever feel that, like Wolfe, you're really writing just one big story? When did you start that? Is that desirable?

DM: There is nothing inherently closed, or complete, about a story of the lives of characters, although any given story or novel in which they figure should, to my mind, be a complete work of art. I want first of all to create works of art, so places and characters interest me on many other lievels; they are inexhaustible. The new place (London Bridge for a novel in the works) and new characters have no special value in themselves. Wolfe was, I feel, writing about places and people, his own places, himself, his own people and friends, so that being his primary focus, plus grand language in which to talk about them, and not art, it enhances our life-long enjoyment of Wolfe to think of all he wrote as one vast story.

WP: Who are some other writers you like?

DM: Another writer I really admire is Davis Grubb. I'm fascinated by him generally, but I haven't read anything besides *The Night of the Hunter*, And William Styron's *Lie Down in Darkness* is one of my favorite books. Another favorite writer of mine is Virginia Woolf. Graham Greene. Henry James. Fitzgerald is another major writer for me, but only in The Great Gatsby. Only *The Great Gatsby* for me is a great work of art. But you're right when you say that I go for writers who don't have a social concern at their center. These are works that you can read over and over and over again. What is magical and fantastic about them is rechargeable by virtue of their artistic qualities, whereas I could not possibly read *Man's Fate*, which is about the Chinese revolution, a second time. There's no way. You would have to hold a gun to my head to make me read it a second time. It's okay the first time because I'm interested to see how he's hand ling this social event since the artistry is not very commanding.

WP: I think Dickens is the only exception I can think of to that statement.

DM: Yeah, but you know the issues aren't alive for me. All the issues are dead. I say, yeah, that's sort of interesting, he handles that well. *Hard Times*, I guess, is the best example people would point to of his social consciousness, but the social problems were not what interested me in that book. What is good about a book transcends those transitory interests. The proletarian writers are the best examples of all. There's only one or two you can force yourself to read. *The Disinherited*, by Jack Conroy, but that's only because it's a picaresque story of a guy who goes from one job to another. It's kind of nicely written, but most of them are really, really bad books. But the tough guy novels, written in exactly the same decade, which have no social purpose whatever, I can reread and reread. I can reread *The Maltese Falcon* over and over.

WP: I think anybody could. But what about *They Shoot Horses, Don't*

They? which I was looking at last night.

DM: I could reread that several times, about four times. (Laughs.)

WP: You don't see that as being social.

DM: No, that's existential. I think the metaphor of the marathon is a better existential image than you find in Camus.

WP: You wrote an essay about Jessie Hill Ford (*The Liberation of Lord Byron Jones*), the Tennessee novelist whose career as a novelist was interrupted by a personal tragedy. What interested you about that incident?

DM: The essay grew out of one of Willie Morris's last assignments at Harper's. He asked me to cover the killing and the trial and a 300 page book exploded out of my visits to Tennessee. He and I had been talking about the irony in the many parallels between the facts on which Ford based *The Liberation of Lord Byron Jones* and the events of the killing and after. Also, the elements Ford's imagination added also had parallels in the events of the killing. And further, how all Ford's earlier writings seem to prefigure both the real and imagined events of the novel and of the killing. Many writers saw all these things, but somehow they struck me so deeply, I wanted to capture them in a long essay or a bok, and over a decade later, I derived from the massive writings and long-thinking over the years, the memoir "On the Loose." As with the Agee short story, James Olney felt a somewhat new approach was being taken, and I felt it, too. And I see some relation between my memoir of writing about Ford and my story about Agee. I'm working on several long pieces about my feelings about certain writers—Wolfe, Faulkner, Nathanael West, O. Henry.

WP: Apparently, Ford never recovered, at least artistically. So far as I know, he hasn't published a book in almost twenty years.

DM: No, he's been working mostly on movie and television scripts. I wish he would write about that experience, but I sense that he never will.

If you don't mind, I haven't really said too much about this, but I want to say something about how I was using earlier mater ial in my books. Several people have commented on my reuse of earlier material. Some see it in its proper light and others distort it as if I have to do it, as if I'm really desperately reaching for material to do new work. But if you just look at the very works they're also discussing—these are people who are talking about all my work, well, sometimes they are people who just know about the work and are talking about new work—but if you knew all my work, you would know that I'm prolific and that I have a rich body of raw material and that I don't need to reuse old material. To me, writing is not material anyway.

WP: I also know that that's what Faulkner and all the other Southern writers have done.

DM; The point is that the reason I'm doing it is for the very same reason Faulkner did, which is that no story is complete and total and finished and consumed. Every story has so many rich possibilities and dimensions in relation to so many other stories, and as time goes on, you begin to see these connections and you want to bring them to a fuller realization than you did before. I want to do a short version of *Bijou*, not because I want another book, but because I think it will be better than the earlier version, you see, more intense, more concentrated. That's just my feeling about it, whether anybody agrees with it or not, that's my feeling about it. And it's incredible that anyone would consider that a negative factor in the development of a writer. I showed you my drawer full of story ideas, you know, versions and things that I've started and not finished. I've no paucity of material. My material comes as much from my imagination as it does from my life, so that it's incredible to me that anybody would construe that reuse as a negative. It's like telling the same story again, but in a different way. The reader is supposed to enjoy that along with the writer. If the writer truly enjoys it—truly enjoys it, and if it's good in the first place—redoing it could not...I don't see how that could be a negative factor. The reader has to be able to enjoy that just as much as the writer does, if you liked it in the first place. Wright Morris does this all the time, in a very sort of subtle different way: similar situations, even the exact same lines, totally different context. And to me that's wonderful, that's rich and exciting.

WP: I judge from what you said in one of your essays that you've had some difficulty in getting *Sharpshooter* published.

DM: Yes, it fulfills nobody's expectations for a commercial or serious Civil War novel. No romance, for instance. But the revised version is more accessible, I think while still having the effect I wanted—of a sharpshooter, who was almost a child, having been in most of the battles with Longstreet and having, probably, been the person who shot General Sanders, but who somehow feels he missed the war. I imply that he has lived it much more vividly in his retrospective mulling over of facts and in his imaginings than if he had come out of it feeling, as most men did, that he had fully experienced it. And in the end—a major part of my revision—he almost starts all over again when he recalls with surprising vividness, his relationship with a black Union prisoner, who had been a slave of the Cherokee nation, under his guard tower at Andersonville—who taught him how to read and write—Cherokee language—and who he shot when he steeped over the deadline. And interested publisher awaits my revisions.

WP: It seems that writers today, no matter how well they are regarded, constantly have to start over. Does that discourage you?

DM: No, nothing discourages me because I live in my imagination. Oh, on the third level it very much does, because, yes, writers today with ten works of fiction out there, must start all over in a sense. Why a publisher thinks a new serious writer is a good investment, I don't know, when they ought to know what I would think is very well known, and that it that the majority of writers don't really keep on writing new, good fiction. I don't really mind having my new works considered in isolation if editors would only do that. But, they insist on getting the whole picture, past, present and future, before venturing with the new book. I have just finished reading six-hundred pages in manuscript of the letters of William Goyen, one of the finest writers of the past half century, and, like most other writers I know, he had a hell of a time publishing his later works and was, even though he had been an editor himself for seven years for a major publisher, constantly surprised and hurt by lack of faith in the books that got published and lack of recognition for a body of work everyone agreed was superb. But he lived in his imagination, where there is no time, no fixed place, no transience, but purely, what I call the world's one breathing. (1984, extensively revised, 1991)

Chapter 4
The Long Haul: A Conversation
with Shirley Ann Grau

Shirley Ann Grau's first book, *The Black Prince and Other Stories* (1955), published when she was twenty-five, was enthusiastically greeted by reviewers as marking the debut of an important Southern writer. Grau's first novel, *The Hard Blue Sky*, which followed three years later, dealt with the lives of the inhabitants of an island off the Gulf Coast. *The House on Coliseum Street* (1961) chronicled a young woman's troubled search for fulfillment. *The Keepers of the House* (1964) won the Pulitzer Prize for fiction and was greeted with wide acclaim. Grau's most recent novels, *The Condor Passes* (1971) and *Evidence of Love* (1977) show, in my opinion, an increasing restiveness with what she regards as the restrictive label implied by the phrase, "Southern novelist." A second collection of stories, *The Wind Shifting West* (1973) was notable for an extended range of subject matter and variety of technique.

"Hello," she says. Remembering a remark in one of her stories, I do not offer to shake hands. The interview is conducted in an office in downtown New Orleans which the author shares with her husband. She shows a justifiable pride in her literary achievement and a willingness to extend the interview beyond any boundary which I had hoped. During the course of the interview, her other lives intrude. There is a telephone message about her recently married daughter. A philosophy convention is in town, and someone calls wanting her husband's phone number.

WP: People are always interested in the minutiae of writing. Could you tell us something about your writing habits? Do you begin with a draft in longhand?

SAG: Oh no, I haven't written in longhand since I was ten or something like that. Typewriter. I'm going to shift very soon to an electronic, but that's as far as I go with the new technology. I did go down and take a course in IBM computering, the PC, but it's not for me. There is one kind of writer I think it's suited for, the one with a great output. I have a dear friend who produces probably 60,000 words a month. His output is just phenomenal. He has one of those huge Laniers.

He's got it so programmed that he feeds it the characters' descriptions, their names, their relationships, and it will correct any slips he makes as he roars through. And in his case speed is absolutely essential.

WP: Do you do several drafts?

SAG: I think everybody except perhaps these terribly prolific guys does rewrite. I type, do some corrections by hand. Mrs. Wessing, whom you met, cleans it up, and I mess it up again at least three times, but not usually more than three. Actually, she's the one who needs the word processor to save her all that typing.

WP: Do you have a set time that you write?

SAG: I prefer afternoons, but then, as today, things cutacross it, and I can't do it. Of course, I never have liked rigid schedules.

WP: Why has it been so long since your last book?

SAG: I decided that I'd worked really hard since I was about six and that I was going to have some fun. My grandfather quit work when he was forty. He figured he had enough to live on, so he said that was it. He was going to sit down and read and travel and enjoy himself. I made it a little past forty, but then I decided that I was going to enjoy myself. Of course, after a while, that gets a little boring. After I married off Number One Daughter I went back to work. By that time I was tired of having fun. I'm not one of those dedicated people who move everything out of the way for a career. It's part and parcel of a complete life. I know just how my grandfather felt. You know, time to move on. That's also the good thing about writing. You carry it with you. If an engineer drops out for a few years, he might as well never go back—he will be totally out of touch with the technical movement of things—but it doesn't matter with a writer.

WP: I'd like to turn to a question which I know you're sick of hearing: In what sense if any do you consider yourself a Southern writer?

SAG: It seems sort of silly to ask what you mean, but the term "Southern writer" is usually most uncomplimentary in the literary world. It's, oh, "another" Southern writer. So nobody's going to go for something that is, to start with, a criticism. I suppose the Southern regional writer has pretty well vanished. He's a bit like a dinosaur now.

WP: There's still some of them around, I think.

SAG: There are a lot of new Southern writers. I've been awfully impressed by the current crop of first novels within the past six months or so, but they are not regional writers in the sense of local color. They have more in common with John Updike than they do with George Washington Cable. It's interesting.

WP: Did you read Sheila Bosworth's *Almost Innocent*?

SAG: No, a friend of mine whose opinion I value very highly said, It's a spinoff from *A Confederacy of Dunces*, and so I didn't pick it up.

WP: During the period when you started writing, it was almost impossible for a man at any rate to avoid the influence of Faulkner, who was kind of overpowering at that time.

SAG: Faulkner was big in the fifties. Indeed, he was.

WP: I can think of one or two places in your works that remind me of Faulkner, but in general you seem to have almost totally escaped that.

SAG: I have a very low opinion of Faulkner. Of course when I was in my teens I read absolutely everything and was really sort of overwhelmed. In high school I began climbing my way out of it. Now it seems to me that he's—this is an awful pun—all sound and fury with very little behind it. Stunting, all sorts of technical stunting, but very little substance. Also I was offended, badly offended, by the treatment, by the attitude toward blacks. I think his time came, his time went. He's left a mark, but he looks as old-fashioned as Hemingway now. It's a strange sort of thing. Novels are much more flexible now, much smoother; the craft is better.

WP: Your first two books, the collection of short stories *The Black Prince* and the novel *The Hard Blue Sky*, give an impression of great originality. Whatever influences there were seem to have been very much disguised. But what would you say the influences were? Eudora Welty?

SAG: To start with, I only barely remember the books I read. I admire Eudora Welty tremendously. She is so darned deliberately small that, while I admire her, I get perfectly furious. I keep saying, open up, it's all there, it's beautiful, please expand it. I admire Carson McCullers tremendously. I don't think the biography they did of her a few years ago was any good at all.

WP: Katherine Anne Porter?

SAG: She's very good, yes, indeed, though *Ship of Fools* left me confused. Still she's very good.

WP: You started out writing when there were a lot more markets for short stories than there are now.

SAG: Oh, yes, my timing was perfect. For a young kid coming up, there were endless ways to make a living. You started writing travel pieces for *Holiday*. Any number of writers broke in that way. It also kept a regular paycheck coming in. Then you could move through the magazines into longer fiction, but now—well, I don't know. There are more hardcover publishers now, though there are fewer magazines. (Pause.) Still young people do get published; this is what amazes me.

WP: Do you still write short stories?

SAG: Yes, I've got a collection coming out. I signed the contract last week, so it'll be out around the first of the year, more or less.

WP: You're unusual among writers of today because all of your books have been published by the same publisher.

SAG: I like continuity, yes. The short stories will go to Knopf again, yes. I've worn out one generation of editors and one generation of agents, and I'm now down to the second. I'm still with the same agent. Well, she, poor gal, is dead, but her son is there. And Alfred Knopf was my first publisher. He died a few months ago at ninety something, an extraordinary man. When he retired, I stayed with the firm. We muddle along together. I complain to them and they fuss at me. They're one of the few publishers I can think of right now who values continuity.

WP: *The Hard Blue Sky* is unusual among first novels because it does not draw upon personal experience in the obvious ways in which first novels usually do.

SAG: That's a matter of principle with me. Way back, when I was first starting, in college, I took a good hard look at what happened to novelists, particularly American novelists—they write one autobiographical book and then, out. The best example I can think of is Harper Lee's *To Kill a Mockingbird*, which is a lovely, charming book, now twenty-odd-years-old perhaps, and no successor. So, I thought, dear Gussie, this is not going to be me. Therefore, I've never written about personal experience. Places, sure. *The Hard Blue Sky* is pretty clearly Grand Isle, or Last Island, back when I was a child, but it contains nothing personal. There's nothing personal in any of them.

WP: Did you ever consider actually showing the effects of the storm, of putting that in the novel, or did you plan to leave that out from the very beginning?

SAG: We're talking about a novel I really don't remember very well, but it seemed to me that the storm wasn't really the important point in the book, that anything the storm did would be anticlimactic—I wasnt't writing a weather report—that whatever happened, it really didn't matter, it was beyond the range of the novel. You could run a novel forever, you know. People get born, marry, and die, and you can go on and on, but there are logical forms, and it seemed to me that the story was ended long before the storm got there.

WP: Do you think those people are still down there?

SAG: You mean, are they still rattling around inside in my head? Sure. Is Grand Isle like that now? No, no. It's a landing strip for helicopters for servicing the offshore oil rigs, or it was the last time I was down there. I wouldn't want to go back, no.

WP: I think *The House on Coliseum Street* is my favorite among your books.

SAG: It's mine, too. Everybody said, "Antihero, antihero," about the girl in that book. I got really quite tired of that word. (Pause.) That book would be so easy to do a spin-off from. I apologize for using televisionese, but you could take the characters from that and use them, the three younger sisters and Mama, but you know you always have more ideas than you have time and energy to write about.

WP: One of the things that interests me about your writing is what you leave out. I remember when I was reading *The House on Coliseum Street*, I thought, well, here is that girl who has four sisters. We have this short novel, how is she going to tell us about all of them? And, of course, you don't. You tell us basically about two of them.

SAG: Yes, two. It seems to me, when you construct a novel, the most important thing—I'll put it that way—is what you take out. I'm quoting some sculptor, somebody like Matisse probably, who said that sculpting stone is only a matter of cutting away the parts you don't want. And in a sense, that's what a novel is. a story with the parts you don't want removed.

WP: Another example of that was in *Evidence of Love*, where the painter was introduced who may or may not have been the mother. Did you want to leave that up to the reader to decide?

SAG: It seems to me that so much of life is equivocal. We really don't find answers to ninety percent of the things we look for. Again, that's about ten years ago, so I may remember it a bit wrong. It seemed to me that it really didn't matter whether she was or was not his mother; she functioned as one. It was his need for a mother that was the point, not whether this was the right Mama. It could have been. The time was right; everything was more or less right.

WP: Did you think of *The House on Coliseum Street* as as case study or as naturalistic or as anything of the sort?

SAG: No. I never think in classifications like that. I just don't. That's not the way my mind works. (Pause.) All of the novels have some basis in fact. They have quite a lot of basis in fact. None of them are the stories of any one person, if that's clear. It's a great many people stirred up together into one character.

WP: By fact, you mean personal experience, people you knew?

SAG: They're all amalgams of real people. The incidents are mostly all true, but they did not happen to those people. You take a bit here and a bit there. Like a jigsaw puzzle. You take an odd shaped piece from here and an odd shaped piece from there and put them together where they fit. (Pause.) I suppose most of my ideas come from newspapers. I read quantities of newspapers, a lot of obituaries. That's life in a couple of inches.

WP: I realize that your career is in progress, so to speak, but looking over the books that you have published up to this point, it seems that *The Keepers of the House* is the center, the kind of linchpin, of your work. I get the impression that the critics, at any rate, sort of had you kind of pigeonholed up to, and perhaps through, that book, and they felt that after that point you didn't quite develop the way they wanted or expected you to.

SAG: You know, I don't think you can pay too much attention to reviewers because reviewers are swayed by fashion. They adore very young beginning writers. They adore very old writers. In between is a long, dry stretch. But that's what you have readers for.

WP: Perhaps the most impressive aspect of your novels is your mastery of male characters. I read *Almost Innocent* and the Mary Gordon novels, and I don't believe in those men for a minute. The knock against American male novelists has always been that they didn't understand women. But certainly the reverse is generally true.

SAG: I've always had many men friends, even in high school and in college. I mean just friends. I was always encouraged—probably because my father wanted a boy and got me instead—I was always encouraged to do things the boys did. As a matter of fact, my younger sister was a perfect little Marilyn Monroe, you know, blue eyes and lovely blond hair, and I remember my grandmother taking a look at me one day and saying, well, she'll have no trouble, but you're going to have to take up hunting to find a husband. (Laughs.) So I did. It seemed to make perfectly good sense. I was always a pretty good shot, and I didn't mind taking fish off hooks. So I tended to be where the boys were, so to speak. And because I'd known them for so many years I think they just never gave a thought to me. I was a very good friend. A hunting companion. So I just got to see boys as boys. And then you just extrapolate from there as the boys grow up. I never thought of these reasons before, but any number of people have told me my men seem real.

WP: *The Keepers of the House, The Condor Passes*, and *Evidence of Love* are all large novels in the sense that they cover long periods of time and have large numbers of characters, but they're not large novels in the thirteen-hundred page Tolstoyan sense. Did you have a model for that kind of writing? How did you arrive at the long novel in short form, so to speak?

SAG: It seems to me that every novel has a different frame. Those have the generation frame. The skeleton that holds them together is the transition between generations. Why did I do three in a row like that? I don't know.

WP: I tend to think of those novels as the *Doctor Zhivago* form, the epic novel which depends not upon its form, but upon poetic insight.

SAG: No, I like novels to be essentially dramatic constructions. Again, the exception might be a very short novel which could probably be held together simply by the beauty of the prose the way a long poem is held together. I think novels are dramas, storytelling of various degrees of value.

WP: Which of the classic novels do you read? You said you read newspapers. What else?

SAG: I read newspapers very simply because that's grist for the mill. I must take four or five a day. My mail man hates me. Never the first page, the back pages. (Pause.) I read poetry. I reread *Tristram Shandy* last week, which has nothing to do with anything, except I like it. I suppose I don't think of novels as being classic novels. I did read the Russians very enthusiastically once. I gave up because I really never figured out what they were doing. They were so ill-made and so bad, but still had a quality that very few other books have. I got very frustrated trying to find out what it was and how they did it. Finally I just couldn't read any more. I put them under the bed in the guest room in sheer disgust.

WP: When I was reading *The House on Coliseum Street*, I kept thinking of Edith Wharton's "Summer," which is about the same length and is on a related theme.

SAG: The last Wharton novel I read was *The Age of Innocence*. I read it again while I was waiting for my last child to go through her music competition. She's very good, and I think she's curiously undervalued. It's good. In many novels from that period, you look at what, at the moral structure, and you say, how could people think that? It seems like the back of the beyond.

WP: I think Willa Cather is a great writer, but again she's not much read now.

SAG: It's because she's so gentle, I think. (Pause.) Also I read the complete *Red Badge of Courage*. It didn't solve any problems in interpretation, but it was most, most interesting. *Maggie* is an intriguing book—it's a very bad one—but it is intriguing.

WP: In comparison with a lot of novelists, you have not published or shown a great deal of interest in criticism. Is there some reason for that? Did you just want to devote your main attention to fiction?

SAG: I write a few newspaper reviews a year simply because there are some books I want to call attention to, and the quickest way to get people's attention is in a newspaper. The last one was the most recent biography of Fitzgerald. It was a great disappointment. *Invented Lives,* I think it was called. I only do about two reviews a year, usually for the *Chicago Tribune*. And last year, I did a travel piece for the Chicago paper. Travel—well, hardly. It was about New Orleans and I was here. I think I was able to point people to things in New Orleans that they wouldn't normally see, not the French Quarter, for heavens's sake. In general, I think that fiction writers do well to stay out of criticism. Do you remember John Gardner? A marvellous fiction writer, but he wrote something called *On Moral Fiction*. It was extremely peculiar. I think fiction and criticism are two separate functions, and that each is better left to itself.

WP: I was struck by what you said in the Lafayette lecture about novelists not necessarily being intelligent.

SAG: Was that ever published?

WP: I got a Xerox copy. The story that I heard was that it's in the process of being published.

SAG: Great. I haven't seen it. I'm not sure I have a copy.

WP: I think of all those people who are trying to write novels who seem to think that because they can do an essay on Yeats or Hopkins that they can write a novel by a kind of act of the will.

SAG: It almost never works that way. It's just as separate—well, let me put it this way: no one really expects to be able to write music. They wouldn't dream of sitting down to toss off a sonata or a symphony. But because everybody speaks, they think they can write. It doesn't follow. It doesn't follow at all.

WP: I think the character of Margaret in *The Keepers of the House* is an absolutely striking creation.

SAG: I knew a gal who was very much like Margaret. I'm talking about taking a character and putting it in a situation it didn't actually ever face.

Occasionally, among black women, you get this extraordinary figure. (Pause.) They're hard to believe; they're so much larger than life.

WP: I was fascinated by the obliqueness of the relationship between William and Margaret. That struck me as Faulknerian in the way that you showed him meeting her and then you sort of drew back. You didn't really tell a lot about the way she felt about it or he felt about it. Or did you have that feeling?

SAG: Again, that's part of the cutting away of things in a novel. It wasn't of primary importance, I don't think. That novel was actually rather objective, I think, perhaps more so than the others who followed it. It was more to do with actions than with feelings.

WP: He goes into the swamp looking for a still, and I kept thinking about what was going to happen, and what happened was not what I expected to happen at all.

SAG: That's right. He went on a bet, didn't he? [It was, however, a bet that he himself had inaugurated.]

WP: I thought that what would happen was that they would see him, or he would get shot, or that something of that sort would happen. But nothing happens except that he goes on this voyage or journey and that meeting her is the end result of it. Is that what the whole thing is working towards, but he doesn't realize it?

SAG: I suppose, but again, I don't look at it abstractly. It just seemed to be where the story line needed to go.

WP: I was also fascinated by what I might call the predictive power of the novel, the way in which the politician and the circumstances described there seem to prefigure what was in fact to happen somewhat later in the South in history in general.

SAG: Well, it seems to me that if a writer is in tune with the times, he's going to point the direction in which things must go. Things have a logic, and any writer who can gauge it accurately is going to point to the short term future.

WP: How did you feel about the critics who saw or claimed to see some sort of a relationship between *The Godfather* and *The Condor Passes?*

SAG: Actually, *The Condor* was earlier. It was published in the *Atlantic* earlier.

WP: Do you feel that the movies or the mass media generally have been an influence upon your novels?

SAG: I think they probably influence everybody. They're there, they're all present, they have to have an effect—on everybody, not just me. Everything does. I can hardly wait to see what the word processor is going to do to writing style.

WP: God help us, it's going to be bad.

SAG: It is, I think, going to influence the speech patterns, the word patterns. Lots of people think they can tell when Bible reading slipped out of the common background. They swear they can see a change in the style, so the effect that this mechanical marvel is going to have on us could be equally obvious.

WP: When reading good writing, when reading you, I am often amazed by reading bits of information about flora and fauna and miscellaneous bits of information. I think, where did she learn that?

SAG: I told you, my grandmother advised me to go where the boys were. (Laughs.) It's there. The country and its flora and fauna were just there, too.

WP: Do you think of any of your stories in visual terms. I'm thinking of one of the stories, "The Way of a Man," which begins with an extremely visual description of a house.

SAG: That was a long time ago. (Pause.) That's thirty years ago. It's just totally gone. Sometimes you write a story and then you use it in slightly different form in something else. And that complicates the process of remembering a little more.

WP: How many of your novels began as short stories?

SAG: I don't know. Probably, *Condor* was the last of them. [Apparently, this statement is not true; the story, "The Patriarch," included in *The Wind Shifting West*, was the origin of *Evidence of Love.*] I really don't remember. I don't even keep records of what was published where.

WP: From what I've read, the reviews of *The Black Prince* were superb, but the reviews of *The Wind Shifting West* were not as favorable. Were you as satisfied with that collection as with the first one?

SAG: I don't think you're ever satisfied with any of them. Also, as I said before, there's a critical tendency to overpraise young and overpraise old. I can hardly wait for the novel I'll write when I'm seventy-five.

WP: I really like the title story of *The Wind Shifting West*. I think the ambiguous sexual encounter in that story is just about the best of that type of thing I've ever read.

SAG: It seems to me that fiction is almost like the Rorschach test. Everybody sees it differently. That's why you can reread it, of course. Any decent piece of fiction you can reread and see quite differently.

WP: You don't think of it as a Rorschach test for the writer too?

SAG: Probably. But for example when I read one of Breece Pancake's stories and then read it again a month later, it seems quite different. [Pancake was a young West Virginia writer of great promise whose collected short stories were published after his suicide in 1979.] The emphasis is different, the whole import seems different. Now the words are the same; it's what I'm bringing to it that's different. It seems to me that one great part in the acceptance of fiction is the reader. Yet everybody seems so totally interested in what the writer puts that I think they rather overlook what the readers contribute. It's the other side of the thing, you know. What good fiction always has is a certain ambiguity, and the reader fills it in. It's an interaction, it's not just words carved on granite, like a tombstone. It's a very active give and take.

WP: I feel that most of the reviewers who looked at *The Black Prince* felt that they could fit those stories within a recognizable framework of Southern writing, but by the time they got to *The Wind Shifting West*, they had a lot of trouble with a story like "The Last Gas Station."

SAG: Oh, yes. I like that one. Actually, my publisher did tell me once a few years ago it was very difficult because I kept changing with every book.

WP: You mean difficult for him as a publisher?

SAG: No, difficult for readers because there was no one set thing that was predictable. But as I said, we often yell at each other. (Pause.) I don't want to do what some very good writers do—look at Hemingway—a good writer, but he kept imitating himself. And you end up right in the bottom of the pond that way. Every book, it seems to me, must be different.

WP: That story would fit very well in a collection of genre fiction. I can imagine that in an anthology edited by Stephen King.

SAG: Oh, yes. Realism gets to be a little tiring at times, and your urge is to expand it, do a ghost story, push it back, do something like "The Black Prince," the title story, do a myth-make, a legend-make, forget the ordinary and do something outside the ordinary logical progression. So, do a ghost story. I'm trying to think if I have one in my new collection. There was one in *The Wind Shifting West*. The Vitnam story, "We Three," I think it was called. One day, I really am going to do a ghost story, and one day I'm also going to do a simple short love story. I haven't done that yet either.

WP: "We Three" reminds me of Henry James because you don't tell us whether she's mentally ill or truly haunted.

SAG: That isn't really the choice. She is truly haunted. He's simply there, forever and ever. It's always seemed to me that people carry everything around with them as they go along, just like a hermit crab growing crustaceans on his back.

WP: Another of my favorite stories is "The Long Afternoon," about the bratty little girl who has to stay home.

SAG: (Laughs). Oh, I did that a very long time ago. Indeed, I lived next door to her.

WP: Could you tell us something about your work in progress?

SAG: I just did a collection of short stories. These will all be about women. There are nine of them, or is it ten?

WP: Are you working on a novel?

SAG: Indeed. When I finished the stories about two months ago, I began a novel.

WP: Were any of these stories published in magazines?

SAG: I didn't have time. I decided I'd move them out.

WP: I'm really fascinated by what your next novel is going to be. You have that series of three novels with strong patriarchal figures, and by the time you get to *Evidence of Love*, your control of theme and material seems totally masterful to me. It's the kind of control I associate with the great European novelists.

SAG: I've flipped again. I've changed again. I feel that every novel must be different. I picked up the people from one of the stories. You see, I often use short stories the way a painter uses a sketch pad. You outline the characters, and then you come back and put them in a novel. This one shouldn't be frightfully long, so far as I can tell. A novel is a year's work, and so it'll be next Spring before it's ready to go.

WP: Your books have a great deal of contrast. Some of them are about very rich people, and some of them are about very poor people. Many writers can do one without being able to do the other. But I think that the old man, Edward Milton Henley in *Evidence of Love*, is totally convincing and totally fascinating.

SAG: He's really more or less real. The man that I modeled him on is a kind of a relative by marriage. He had that same Old Testament quality.

WP: I think most readers coming across that book would see it as a rather bleak picture of the human condition.

SAG: Uh-huh. (Hesitates.) Well, I always thought it was sort of funny. Only one reviewer noticed that. But it's heavily ironic, yes. One day I'd love to go back and do a little bit more with my Unitarian minister, Stephen. The exaggeration of a scholar is a fascinating idea and one that's not often done. A man for whom ideas are more real than things. But the story has not come to me yet that I can put him in. I wait with all these pieces and eventualy they coalesce. It's like a very slow and imperfect computer, but that's what it is. You file it all away and wait to pick up the rest of it.

WP: In certain respects, I don't think you carry as much of a didactic burden as a number of the current generation of Southern writers, or even those of the past, in the areas of ideology or religion or whatever.

SAG: I don't know. For example—in Flannery O'Connor, you can see the Catholicism very cearly, but with Welty, what? I can never figure out what Southern writers have in common, for example, in ideology.

WP: It always seems to me that the two poles of the Southern novel are gossip and melodrama, and the Southern writer has to contend with them on each side.

SAG: Oh, I see what you mean.

WP: But I was really thinking more of the religious business, with fundamentalism on the one side and Roman Catholicism on the other.

SAG: I guess I've never, never, looked at it that way. My family was really quite fundamentalist. But it simply didn't take with me. It all washed over my head. Certainly the young novelists right now are secular, that is, the ones I know.

WP: Walker Percy said in a lecture I was reading that was given in the same series a year or two before you gave yours that the modern South is Christ haunted.

SAG: "Christ haunted" sounds like Poe, doesn't it?

WP: I think he'd probably go along with that.

SAG: When I was young religion had a rather important part in Southern life, but I'm not sure that it had that place because it was religion or because it was the structure of society. A church is a social club. I very cheerfully went to Baptist hayrides and picnics. On the surface today, it might seem that the South is very religious because there are an enormous number of churches, and people go to them. I don't think that means too much. And it is also possible to mistake the South's conservatism for religion. They're not the same.

WP: Do you have a commentary upon the difficulty of raising a family and being a writer at the same time?

SAG: Not really. My children have all been very healthy. That helps. It's simply part of everything else. As the children would say, "No big deal."

WP: Have you ever considered writing screenplays?

SAG: Yeah, I get offers. They all have involved West Coast or New York, and I don't particularly want to go live in either place, even for a short period of time.

WP: Do you write poetry?

SAG: No, there's no audience for it. I write what there's a possible, a probable, audience for. It's always been important to me to earn a living by what I do. I guess you could lay that off to the fundamentalist background: you make your own way as soon as possible.

WP: How did you come to do the Lafayette lecture?

SAG: The first time I was to do the lecture I was caught in a flood. It was Spring. It had been raining, but you know it always rains. The day of the lecture I woke up bright and early at seven to get an early start, and found four feet of water in my street. And a friendly little policeman was paddling around—he had gotten a pirogue from somewhere. I couldn't find the man who runs the lecture, so I called a friend of mine in the Lafayette psychology department and told him, for goodness sake, put up some notices so people wouldn't come out in the rain. We rescheduled it for, I think, September. A lecture like that encourages reading and the world of books. I like that. I always wanted to do two things, I guess: one was to have a bookshop and the other was to work for a newspaper. I'm not likely to get either one, which is why I still like to do those little newspaper reviews.

WP: A lot of women writers like Elizabeth Spencer have worked on newspapers.

SAG: When I started out, you had a choice: you could go to work for a newspaper or go immediately into freelance. I elected to go immediately into freelance, and thanks to *Holiday* magazine, I came through. Of course, I was very lucky to have a fine agent.

WP: I understand you grew up in Montgomery, Alabama?

SAG: I came back here to college. I went to a little school in Montgomery called Booth, which was totally unaccredited, so suddenly my family looked at me and decided they'd better do something if I was going to get into an accredited college. By the time I got shipped down to New Orleans, I was a classics scholar. The little school in Montgomery taught Latin and Greek, and I insisted on finding a school in New Orleans that taught Latin and Greek. The Ursuline Convent did—isn't that amazing, but they did—and so I went there. Obviously there's no market for a classical scholar, so I shifted to English at Newcomb.

WP: What can a creative writer, a novelist or a short story writer, learn from philosophy, if anything?

SAG: I don't know. I wouldn't even know how to approach that.

WP: I meant to bring, but forgot to, my paperback edition of *The Keepers of the House*. There were at least two versions of that published, the one before the Pulitzer and the one after, which had a large yellow circle on the cover.

SAG: They stamped it, yes. I don't have any control over that. By the way, *The House of Coliseum Street* is coming out in a reissue this fall [1985].

WP: By and large, publishers are just not keeping quality fiction in print. The only way a writer can be remembered by people that read—graduate students and people like that—is by having his books in paperback, because they don't buy hardcover books, particularly hardcover books.

SAG: Assuming that you can even find a bookshop to cooperate with you, hardcover out of print books are devilishly expensive. That's another thing I always wanted: a small publishing house to do nothing but reprints. There are so many marvelous books that are out of print.

WP: I think you could make a list of the fifty best novels published since the second world war and half or two-thirds of them would be out of print.

SAG: And a lot of them have fallen into public domain. People forget to renew copyrights very, very often. Now, publishers will, but many publishers have gone out of business. For example, Duell, Sloan had some marvelous titles back in the forties. Duell, Sloan is out of business. Now those will come due. Unless an author or his heirs are awfully good at bookkeeping, they're going to miss that twenty-eight year renewal date.

WP: Do you go to the movies very much?

SAG: Not vey much. *Amadeus* was here and I missed it.

WP: Have you done much teaching?

SAG: I did one term at UNO. It's entirely too time-consuming. There's no way to teach writing by lecture. The only way you can do it is to sit down page by page and try to shake the little heads loose from their preconceptions. I've got a couple of kids I'm more or less running through the mill now. I think they will make it. They send me manuscripts and I write insulting comments in the margins.

WP: One criticism that bothered David Madden was that he felt that some people had unfairly accused him of rewriting old stories or reusing old materials in new novels. I wondered if you had any feeling about that.

SAG: You mean periodicals as against hardcover publications?

WP: No, I was thinking of material that you had worked into a novel.

SAG: It's extremely conventional. I've never heard anybody criticize it.

WP: I think for him it was partly a matter of rewriting whole novels in a different way.

SAG: I always thought it was moderately unfair to take a magazine publication and hardcover publish it. And yet I've done it all my life.

WP: You published stories in *New World Writing*, didn't you?

SAG: That publication was a good idea. I don't know why it died.

WP: There is a myth out there that there are all those great unpublished manuscripts.

SAG: I'm sure that there are not. Again, everything you say you have to make a hasty exception to. There probably are one or two.

WP: You do hear stories about books like *Zen and the Art of Motorcycle Maintenance* being turned down by fifteen or twenty publishers. But it was eventually published.

SAG: It had a lot of rejections, but all within a relatively short period, a couple of years. Sure, that can happen. Lots of novels bat around from publisher to publisher. But they get published, assuming the writer doesn't have what my daughter calls a hissy fit and yank them off the market. But most seriously I think there are very few unpublished books worthy of publication. If you have this neurotic rejection reaction, you've taken yourself out of it. You wouldn't believe the bad novels there are. (Sighs.)

WP: From your students, from publishers, or what?

SAG: From students, from friends of friends. I collect people. This is my hobby. Some people collect paintings. I collect people, so I'm forever being asked to look at manuscripts. In all these years I don't think I've come across more than two that were worth publishing. (1985)

Chapter 5
In the Quarters: An Interview
with Ernest Gaines

My interview with Ernest Gaines takes place on the sun porch of the house furnished for him by the University of Southwestern Louisiana where he is writer in residence. Gaines is a big man with a commanding presence, a deep voice, and hair graying at the temples. He nearly always wears a beret. He seldom hesitates for a word and he speaks rapidly and forcefully.

With but a few excursions outside Louisiana, *Catherine Carmier* (1964), *Of Love and Dust* (1967), and *A Gathering of Old Men* (1983) are set in the "quarters" of a large plantation near Bayonne, the imaginary town which is Gaines's equivalent of Faulkner's Jefferson, and recount the changing lives of the people who lived there from Civil War times until recently, when their jobs disappeared and their houses were razed in the name of agricultural efficiency. Even those novels which are not set primarily in the quarters, *The Autobiography of Miss Jane Pittman* (1971) and *In My Father's House* (1978), are dominated, even obsessed, by its presence and its memory.

After the short walk from the English department to his house, Gaines gives us a tour of the house and of the converted garage back of the house which serves as a study and where he does his writing. The shelves are filled with books, mostly on literature and history, which seem to have been read and casually replaced. Only the section on black literature and history is neatly arranged.

The house, which is spacious and uncluttered, is filled with framed photographs of the tin-roofed house where the novelist was born; of people from his past, including one of his remarkable, crippled aunt who served as a model for Jane Pittman; and of the author himself, aged around twenty and remarkably handsome. The face in the photograph is inscrutable, but the author himself, some thirty odd years later, is remarkably open and candid, and displays none of the hesitation before difficult questions which I have sometimes sensed in other interviews.

WP: How did you first become interested in writing?
EJG: I probably started writing when I was only seven or eight or nine

because I lived on a plantation at False River. Very few of the older people who lived on the plantation could read or write. Both their reading and writing was very limited, so I would always write their letters for them and then read the letters that they would get in the mail. I also read the Bible and things like that for them. I became interested in writing when I went to California at the age of fifteen. I went into the public library at the age of about sixteen. I got in the library because my stepfather told me I had to get off the block. After school, I would hang around with the kids, and he said, okay, off the block or you're going to get yourself into a lot of trouble. So I ended up in the library, and that was the first time I'd ever been in the library. I'd go about an hour. Of course the public libraries you had in Louisiana in the False River area where I came from were all segregated. So I went into the library and I saw all these books and I started reading, and I read, and read, and read. I did not particularly care for the way blacks were depicted by many of the writers, especially the Southern writers, the Southern white writers, but I would read them anyhow. I would read any writer who wrote about the land. I went through Steinbeck, Willa Cather, the European writers, the nineteenth-century Russian writers. Out of all this reading, I never did find my own people in those books. It was then about the age of sixteen that I began to write about the people I had left in Louisiana, about the place and the people of Louisiana. That's what I started on.

WP: I read that you wrote the first version of *Catherine Carmier* when you were sixteen.

EJC: At sixteen. That was my first project. My mother had a baby about that time, when I was sixteen, and I had to babysit for her. His name was Michael. I had that entire summer, and I had my mother rent me a typewriter. I didn't know a thing about typing. I had never taken a typing class, but she rented it for me. I kept Michael asleep. I made him sleep, and by the use of one finger at a time I pecked away at it until I got a novel. I wrote about a hundred and fifty or seventy-five or eighty or ninety pages, whatever. I sent it to New York, and of course it was not a book by a long shot. They sent it back to me, and I took it out into the yard and put it in the incinerator. About nine years later, when I was at Stanford, that would be in fifty-eight, I started on it again, and four years after that, I finished it.

WP: As far as you can remember, how much of the original novel that you did when you were sixteen was retained in the final version?

EJG: Very little, because in the beginning there was only the love story between Catherine and Jackson. I don't even know whether her name was Catherine then. I didn't know what the characters were all about then. I know it was a love story, and that was about all. But it did not have him going to the South for a little while and then going back to California. It did not have Lillian's leaving and going back, you know, passing for white. I don't think it had the murder of the small child. I don't think he was in there. It was just about a guy who comes back and sees a girl, the girl he was in love with when he was a little kid. I hope I can say that. I mean I was only sixteen when I tried to write it. I don't know what it was all about. I know it was about a darker-skinned family on one side and a mulatto family on the other side. That was the original idea, the conflict between them.

WP: After reading your other novels, the thing that amazed me about *Catherine Carmier* was how complete a representation it was of your themes and point of view.

EJG: I think one of the things I discovered when I was quite young was that I knew what I wanted to write about. Of course, many things have changed since then. The civil rights movement came along since that book was written. I've done much more traveling and much more reading. But I feel that I knew from the beginning what I wanted to write about. What I've learned from the writers I've studied is how to write, but I knew all the time what I wanted to write about. I didn't need any one to tell me what to write about. I didn't need the kind of topical subjects to write about that were popular during the sixties. I didn't need any of that.

WP: I remember when I was growing up I was much impressed by *Native Son* and by a novel which is almost forgotten now but which got an enormous press at the time, *Knock on Any Door*.

EJG: WIllard Motley's novel, yeah.

WP: I always thought that Motley was an extremely interesting writer who could have been a great writer but who somehow never managed to fulfill his potential.

EJG: Motley took on a subject that I think most of the important black writers of that time would not have attempted. He was writing more about white characters than about black characters. I think that if you were an important black naturalistic writer of that time that you had to write about the thing that was closest to you. I don't think he was doing that. I don't think that was his aim. He could tell his story in other ways. What he wanted to say, he could tell through white characters as well as through black ones.

WP: When did you become aware of those important black writers?

EJG: That is a good question because I did not become aware of the important black writers until after I left college. I grew up in California. I grew up around San Francisco. When I first went to California, I went to Vallejo, California. Then, after I had been in Vallejo for five years, I went into the service just after the Korean War, and then when I came out, I went to San Francisco State to study English lit and creative writing. Later I went to Stanford for an advanced degree in creative writing. During that time, black writers' works were only mentioned. We did not study Ralph Ellison, we did not study Langston Hughes, we did not study Willard Motley, we did not study any black writers. *Native Son* was mentioned; the other books were not even mentioned. I was in Alabama this last weekend, and they asked me the same sort of question about black characters and black writers, and I said, the only black character I ever studied in all my college years in San Francisco was Othello. I did not study any black novelists at that time.

And I was so far behind in most of my work that I had to spend most of my time catching up. In high school, junior high school and college, I had to spend most of my time catching up with the average student there. When I went to California, I think I was in the ninth grade or the tenth grade, and many of the students had read books that I should have read when I was much younger, so I had to read all those books and catch up. And then later when I went to college, I had to read all those books that I should have read when I was in high school and had not read. So the writers I was reading were white writers. Instead of reading black writers, I was reading Faulkner, I was reading Mark Twain, I was reading Hemingway. We were reading English writers, we were reading French writers, these were the people we had to read. So I did not have time to go out and to read black writers. I had to read all the books that were assigned. Then of course I was trying to write at the same time. Between the reading and the writing, all my time was occupied. It was after I had gotten out of college, after I had left the university, that I began to catch up on the black writers.

WP: I think Catherine is one of your most appealing characters. Reading that book, I thought that she really came alive. She's just as real as somebody who lives next door.

EJG: I really had a lot of problems with that book. At that age, it's really difficult for a young male writer to write about a young female. It was much easier to write about Miss Jane because I did a lot of research, and I did a lot of reading so I could get the voice of an older person and the things she would be interested in. But writing about this young gal who was in love and unable to fulfill that love was pretty difficult for me. I suppose *Catherine Carmier* must have taken me twice as long to write as *Miss Jane* took.

WP: While your books show the destructive effects of racism, you allow even the unsympathetic characters a certain amount of room to move around. That is, they don't know that they're always bad guys. My feeling about James Baldwin, for example, is that he never did manage to get it right.

EJG: Yeah, well, different people say different things about me. A person at a university back East I won't mention the name of because I'll be going back there—a friend of mine just left there—and this guy who's chair of the English department said that Gaines's whites in *A Gathering of Old Men* are stereotypes, so my friend said, well, what about the black ones, and he said, well, I don't think they're stereotypes. A lot of whites have accused me, but not all of them because most of my readers are white and my books are taught all over this country and published all over the world. A lot of whites have accused me of making my whites devils and my blacks angels. I just don't agree with that at all. At the same time, a lot of the more militant blacks have said I have not been hard enough on my white characters. It's awfully hard to please everybody, so when anyone asks me who I write for, I just say that I write no one especially. I just try to write well. If I wrote for this group, then that group over there is going to say, you're not doing it right. If I wrote for that group, the other side is going to say the same thing, so all I try to do is write well. I just hope that I'm still fair with my characters.

I honestly think that I'm as fair with my white characters as most of, as probably all, of our white writers are with their black characters. I'm not trying to measure myself against them, not at all, but there are certain reasons why you may not be fair.

You mentioned Baldwin a moment ago. I think that with a person like Baldwin who grew up in a Harlem, in a certain area where you don't have this exposure to all people, your vision can be narrowed. So much happened to so many Southern white writers. Their visions are here; they see blacks but they don't know how to reach them. They think they know the blacks. The writer says, I know him, I know him, but he really does not know him because he really does not communicate with him, or with people on his level. He knows those who work in his yard or those who work in his kitchen, or the ones who clean up the place, but he does not know those people who are not doing that, so his views are as narrow minded as someone who lives entirely in a single area.

The best thing that ever happened to me was that I went to California at the age of fifteen. I had lived here long enough to know a little, but I hadn't lived here long enough to become too bitter about things. I had lived here long enough to have my mind really open to learn. If I had lived here another seven or eight years, my mind might really have closed down on things, but when I went to California, I went to an integrated area in Valle jo, California, about thirty-three miles northeast of San Francisco. This was just after the war, in forty-eight. I lived in an area in army housing along with poor whites. All these people had gone to the West coast to get jobs in army supplies and navy yards and air force bases and all this sort of thing. So we were all housed in the same general area, and I was there with poor whites, Japanese, Philipinos, Latinos, and all of these people at that age. So I began to realize even at that young age that people were different, that this person believed this and this person believed that, and that people had different languages and different philosophies, that this person loved his home and that his home had an influence on how he thought. So I began to see that at a very early age, at fifteen, sixteen, seventeen. I knew these people. I went to school with them every day at an integrated school. If I had moved into a completely black area, say like Watts in Los Angeles where there is a completely black area, or say the south side of Chicago, or Harlem—any place like that where you had no other exposure—I maybe would have had that kind of narrow view, or a more narrow view. I would maybe be willing to see things but maybe unable to see things because no light had come in, because there was not enough sun light to let me see all sides of things.

WP: What did you think about *Invisible Man*?

EJG: It's a difficult book for me to read even now. It's a difficult book for me to understand even now. I always preferred his book of essays, *Shadow and Act*. But this is sacriligious to say things like that about *Invisible Man*. I'd like to say it's a great book and I love it very much and it has everything in the world for me, but I can't honestly say it. It's a very difficult book for me to understand, although I read a lot about what others say about it. I read what Ellison says about it, what black critics say about it, what white critics say about it, but when I get down to reading the book myself, it just doesn't give me that understanding of what's in it.

WP: I see that Ellison has a new book coming out called *Going to the Territory*. I assume it's a book of essays and not his novel.

EJG: I think it is. I spoke to Robert Penn Warren and to his wife at the Southern Review literary conference a few months ago, and they did mention that a collection of essays was coming out.

WP: I was interested in *Of Love and Dust* that after Marcus had killed a young man in a fight he was sent to work on the plantation until his trial came up. I assume they used to do that sort of thing.

EJG: Yes, they did. I've known situations where that has happened. The plantation owner could bind you out, and you could work on the plantation until your trial came up, and then if you were not sent to prison you could work for him because he had gone bond for you. I've known other situations where the white bosses have gone to the prisons to get the guy out and he refused to come out. I've known cases like that. I've known one of each.

I had a good friend—he's dead now, he was killed in San Francisco—who was sort of like the boy in "Three Men," who refused to go out with this guy who wanted to bind him out. Later he went to Angola to serve his time and when he came out of Angola, he was told to get out of Baton Rouge. Later he went to Houston and he was run out of Houston by the cops and he went to San Francisco. He was a pretty rough guy, and he was killed by a woman. She shot him point blank with a .38.

WP: I think you show the racist, paternalistic system very well in "Three Men" where the young man gives himself up to the authorities because he hopes that the man will take care of him. (Pause.) I know this seems like it happened a thousand yearsago, but what was your reaction to the enormous controversy about William Styron's *The Confessions of Nat Turner*?

EJG: Well, I could see why the critics criticized the book exactly as they did. My criticism of the book was with its form rather than with the philosophy or context he was speaking of. I just did not think that a person of Nat Turner's background would have spoken in Styron's language. I can see why the book was criticized by those black critics who have all the right to feel and to believe that Nat

Turner was a genuine hero and not this demented person that Styron depicts.

WP: Frederick Karl in his book on the American Novel, *American Fictions, 1940-1980*, says that in his opinion the controversy was extremely unfortunate because he thought that it injured black writers, that it kept them from dealing with large and controversial subjects.

EJG: I think he's nuts. I don't agree with him at all. I wrote *Miss Jane Pittman* after this. That's a large subject; it deals with life in the South for a hundred years. I think Alice Walker's book *The Color Purple* is a large subject. I think that if he means the naturalistic approach to the novel, then I don't know who else is doing this. But I don't think that has anything to do with taking on large subjects.

WP: As a response to the human experience naturalism seems to have died around 1950.

EJG: Yes, it did.

WP: *Bloodline*, of course, is a collection of stories which contains "The Sky is Gray," which I have read is one of the most anthologized of all modern short stories. It's certainly one of the most loved stories and since the television version of it done for the American Short Story series, it's been read even more.

EJG: That story is so well known by people, black and white, Southerners and Northerners. I really don't know why. I think it's a good story, as I think all of them are good stories. I don't think it is so much better than all the other stories, but that's the only one that people really talk about, and they talk about it so much.

WP: I would try to answer that question. I think it gives pretty nearly the whole range of human experiences. It's got an openness and a fullness and a great-hearted quality that we associate with a certain kind of great art, with Dickens and writers like that. It's a wonderful story. (Pause.) Did you have anything to do with the movie version?

EJG: No, nothing at all, just as I had nothing to do with *Miss Jane Pittman* when they made that film. They made it out there near Stockton, California., at a place where a lot of westerns were made and a lot of movies which deal with farm people, but I was not involved. I was invited to be on the set during the time of shooting. They shot about three weeks and I was there about two of the weeks, but I had nothing to do with it at all.

WP: I wonder why they didn't ask you to write the screenplay.

EJG: They never do. They might ask you to look over the script after it's been written, but they never ask you to write anything. They never did ask me to write *Miss Jane Pittman* or "The Sky is Gray." They have others to do it.

WP: All the people I've interviewed so far, with the exception of Shirley Ann Grau, have written screenplays. Have you written any?

EJG: I've been invited to write them, but I got out of it. I told them I didn't think I could do that. I'm not going to do what they tell me to do, so I got away from it. I don't think I would ever write a screenplay which didn't have something to do with my own work. I would like to work on my own novel or short story, but I'm not interested in going to Hollywood and in doing what they want me to do. And I know how much they change things, and I don't want to do that.

WP: Do you know Charles Fuller, who wrote the screenplay?

EJG: I met him, but I don't know him personally. He's the same guy who wrote *A Soldier's Story*.

WP: Also, all the people I've interviewed have had a background of growing up with the movies, which I basically don't see in your novels.

EJG: I grew up with the movies, but I also grew up with the radio, I think. We didn't have television, but we used to listen to these great radio programs during that time. I think I learn ed a lot about dialogue from listening to radio programs, especially the plays. I think they had this show on Sunday evening, which had all of these great plays, and I could imagine what the entire thing looked like just from hearing people talk about it. I think that in much of my dialogue, the short sentences or whatever—maybe a writer shouldn't explain what he does or how he does it, and I really can't explain it. Critics are constantly asking me what writers influenced me, and writers have influenced me, but I think that listening to radio shows have influenced me. I used to listen to the old *Gunsmoke*, with William Conrad playing Matt Dillon—I think he's about five-seven or five-eight and he's about that wide (gestures), so he couldn't make it in television—and I really thought it was some of the best dialogue I had ever heard. So radio as well as the movies have had some influence on my work. I don't write for the movies, I write to be read aloud.

WP: David Madden likes to associate his storytelling with the oral tradition of the mountains where he grew up.

EJG: I would rather tell a story than have someone read it. I do a lot of reading. I was at Auburn in Montgomery this past weekend, and people there had read the stories—they had read *A Gathering of Old Men*, and yet they said, when you read it, I get something else out of it. I write to be read out loud, especially when I'm dealing with the first person point of view.

WP: When I read "A Long Day in November," the story about the man who burns up the automobile, I was remind of Ellison's story, "Cadillac Flambeaux."

EJG: I don't know that story.

WP: It's about a man who burns up his Cadillac, and it's one of the stories he published, I think around seventy-two or three, and which was supposed to be part of this epic novel which never appeared, and I wondered if he could have seen your story.

EJG: Oh, he saw it. The *Bloodline* stories were published in sixty-eight, and he chose that book as one of his favorites for that year. He knew all about that story, but whether or not that had any influence on his story, I have no idea.

WP: Well, there aren't that many stories about people burning cars. (Both laugh.) Which brings us to *Miss Jane Pittman*, a story so real that a lot of people think that she actually existed...

EJG: I've heard that too.

WP: ... and which was enormously popular. I assume that that book has sold as many, or almost as many, as all your other books put together.

EJG: Oh, yes, many times more than all the rest put together. That book has sold I would say somewhere in the neighborhood of fifty thousand in hardback and continues to sell in hardback after fifteen years. And we've sold a million plus in the paper back. It was the film that really sold that book. Before the film, it had about three hardback printings and about three paperback printings. Now, we have about fourteen, fifteen, hard back printings and about twenty-three, twenty-four, paperback printings.

WP: What did you think of the film?

EJG: I like the film for the amount of time they had to work, two hours. That book covers over a hundred years in time, so they're giving us roughly a minute to a year. A lot of people don't like it, but I do. It brought some things out. It changed too much, of course, but it brought some things out. If we had had four to six to eight hours, I think we would have had a major film, because it would have taken the time to rewrite the script well, it would have taken time to get better actors—there were three or four actors in there, Cicely of course was great, but we would have had better actors, better writing, more time, better camera work and everything else if we had had the time, but since it was made for television and since the producers didn't know how the American public, which means of course the American white public, would accept the film, they made a fast quick film which didn't cost very much money at that time.

WP: There is certainly an amount of oversimplification of the novel, but I think that, for a television movie, for any kind of a movie, it's certainly very good. You've been very fortunate I think in the two adaptations of your work.

EJG: Yes, I agree with you because I know others who have not been so fortunate. Faulkner was never so fortunate.

WP: How many real people are there in your novels? Do you take characteristics of somebody you know and involve them in different actions or what?

EJG: Well, let's take *Miss Jane Pittman*, for example. I didn't have anyone in mind for Miss Jane physically. I didn't know what anyone a hundred years old would be like. But I used some of the characteristics of my aunt too here. My aunt never walked in her life. She crawled all over the floor, but she cooked our food, washed our clothes, did everything. I gave Miss Jane her moral strength, her courage, but Miss Jane was not based on anybody. Catherine was slightly based on a girl I knew. Lillian was not based on anybody I knew at that time. I think I've known more Lillians since I wrote that book than I did before. In *Of Love and Dust*, Marcus had some of the characteristics of Muhammad Ali. He loved to talk. He said, I'm good and I can prove I'm good, like Muhammad Ali, Cassius Clay at that time. Marcus was slightly based on a guy that I knew, the same one who was killed in California. As a matter of fact, the boy in "Three Men" that kills and the boy in *Of Love and Dust* are the same. It's the same sort of story, it is the same story, except that in *Of Love and Dust*, he comes out of prison—he says, I'll take my chances outside—and in "Three Men" he remains in the prison. But my characters are not usually based on any particular person.

In "The Sky is Gray" now, much of what little James goes through—and my middle name is James, you know—I went through. But it's not me. I did have the toothache as a child, we had to ride in the back of the bus in the mid-forties, we could not eat up-town, we could not walk in a place and get warm or anything like that, and his mother was somewhat like my mother. I had to kill birds in order to eat, and I am the oldest of my family, so I had to look after my younger brothers and sisters. I went through all of that in a period of say ten years, but I crowded all of that into his life in a period of a daytime.

WP: How did *Catherine Carmier* happen to be reprinted by North Point Press?

EJG: It had gone out of print, and they asked to reprint it. They were picking up earlier works that had gone out of print, and I knew Jack Shoemaker, the editor.

WP: I love their books. They're well designed and beautifully printed.

EJG: Yes, with that extra jacket and all.

WP: I thought one of the most moving parts of *Miss Jane* was the story of the two brothers, Timmy and Tee Bob, and of course that wasn't in the movie.

EJG: They wanted to put it in the movie. If that movie had been longer, four hours, it would have been in there. But God, I'm glad what they tried to put in the movie, they left out. They had Timmy up there eating with them in the house. They had Robert Samson coming down into the quarters and admitting that Timmy was his son to different people. They had all kinds of crazy things like that. A white probably would have said that to Miss Jane, but he never would have gone around boasting about it. And he surely would not have had Timmy sitting around on the patio eating with him with Tee Bob and Tee Bob's mother.

WP: I assumed that they just left that out because that was just too delicate a subject for them to handle.

EJG: Well, they could not bring in all the subplots. They only had two hours, less than two hours with commercials, so they had to stick with Cicely, they had to have the camera on her all the time. Miss Jane is in all the scenes in the first book of the novel. In the second book she's in most of the scenes, but then the other characters begin to take over. In the third book, "The Plantation," that's the love story between Tee Bob and Mary Agnes LeFabre. In the last book you have the Jimmy story. So as she gets older, as you move through the books, Miss Jane is less and less involved in the direct action, but because the film is so short, they had to have Cicely's face on the screen all the time.

WP: What is your feeling about the enormous success of that book? I know that a writer is always happy to have a book that's so successful, but some writers feel that such a success detracts interest from their other works or makes it almost impossible for them to live up to what the public expects.

EJG: I don't think about trying to live up to anything. I just try to write as well, to write better, the next day. People are always asking me, what is your favorite book, and they expect me to say *Miss Jane Pittman*. Certainly it's my most popular book, but I don't have a favorite book, and if the world and the reading public feel that *Miss Jane* is the one they want to read, it's okay with me. I'm always more interested in the book I'm working on now, or the book I will work on ten years from now, or twenty years from now. I'm not interested in *Miss Jane* any more, other than in the royalties which will come in from it. It has no effect on my trying to measure up, simply because I think I have done that. I've written as well in the *Bloodline* stories, in *Of Love and Dust* for a straight dramatic novel, in *Catherine Carmier* for a delicate love story. I don't have a favorite book. There are certain qualities in each that you find more admirable than you find others.

EJG: My favorite of all your books is the one that you didn't mention, *In My Father's House.*

EJG: Thank you for saying that. I was talking to a guy in Alabama the other day who said that was the least of the books he liked.

WP: It's got the stark inevitability of Greek tragedy.

EJG: That was my aim. That was my aim.

WP: There's nothing wasted in that book. It's totally honest and almost foreordained from the beginning, from the first page.

EJG: A great man falls, and what he's going to do when he gets up. He feels that even God had failed him. He could not even please God any more.

WP: But I can see how someone who reads *Miss Jane* and "The Sky is Gray" and then comes to *In My Father's House* would be put off by it because this is much more grim.

EJG: Oh, yeah, I've met a few people who liked the book, who said, this is one of the better ones, but most people, the doctors here at USL, feel that no, this is not your best. They give different reasons; for one thing, there's a lack of humor anywhere in the book—there's no humor anywhere—and it is so grim, and we don't particularly feel with the subject. I think it's the least taught of all my books. When you said that it was in the style of Greek tragedy, that was my aim, but I don't know if you can do that. I think if I were a playwright—but no one has shown any interest in it, no one has ever put out any kind of money—I think I would really like to work with them and then I would try to bring out that idea of Greek tragedy in that story.

It's very difficult for me to read [to an audience]. I can't read that book. It took me longer to write that book than any other. When I read from my books,I never read from it unless someone requests it. I will read from *Miss Jane*, I will read from *A Gathering of Old Men*, which I was writing on afterwards. I think in order to read *In My Father's House*, you would need to read it in one sitting to get everything out of it. It's not a book you can read a part of and put down. You can section *Miss Jane* to read, you can section *A Gathering of Old Men*, but with this book I don't know that you can pick out sections to read and leave a satisfied feeling with your audience.

WP: I think *In My Father's House* is one of the most important Southern novels of the past thirty years, and I think that, if people don't like it, that's their problem. But I don't think it's totally without humor. What about Chippo?

EJG: Chippo, yeah, yeah, but I think people get so involved with that father-son relationship that they overlook people like Chippo and all the others. It's a book that I don't read.

WP: More than any other writer I've interviewed, and more than any other Southern writer I can think of, you deal with the church and its influence on the lives of the people you write about. I think I'd be honest in saying that most white writers who wrote about that kind of fundamentalist white church could not deal with it without a touch of irony. But you seem to me to be looking at it straight-on and saying, well, this institution may have faults, but it's doing a lot to keep this society together.

EJG: A certain part of society, yes, I agree with you there. I think that my younger people may not see it as the older ones did. You know Marcus's idea was that he wanted to go to church because there were a lot of women around the place. You have the young man in "The Sky is Gray" who disagrees. Then you have Jackson who comes back in *Catherine Carmier* and who says it's all bourgeouise stuff and that he doesn't go along with that. He's not a nihilist, but he has sort of nihilistic leanings. You do have that; however, I do have the church as the institution which has kept the older ones going. And of course that's what Jimmy says in the last book of *Miss Jane Pittman*: this is all we have. I have no flag, I have no guns, I have nothing else, and I need this strength—the church—in order to be able to continue.

WP: You know that Baldwin was a teen-age preacher in Harlem before he moved away from the church. Do you think the church in the city still has the same kind of viability you depict in your novels?

EJG: I know that in San Francisco there's a church on every corner. There's a bar on this corner and a church on that corner, and it still seems to have its strength with the poeple. At least I see them out there all the time. I don't go, but people pass right by me, and I drive right by them, so I think the church still plays its role in the cities. Take for example Dr. King's church in Montgomery—I went by it just the other day— the Dexter Avenue Baptist Church just off the capitol, just a short walk from the capitol, from Jefferson Davis's statue. I think the churches are just as strong as ever with some of the people.

WP: The novelists that I've talked to seem to agree that religion is not much of a preoccupation with the people they know or are interested in.

EJG: Religion is not a main theme that I'm interested in. It's always there, just like the color of the skin. You can tell that this person is black, you can tell the kind of house he lives in, you can tell the kind of food he eats, you can tell how he lives. And so the church is there at all times. Usually my male character has reached a point where he has to make a decision: my decision is whether I follow the man or I don't, and I don't know that he, except for Phillip Martin, relies on the church to give him strength at that particular time or on some thing else deep inside himself. The boy in "Three Men," Procter, tell the young guy whom he saves at the end, whom he will stay in prison to save, okay, you pray, I can't, but pray as a man would pray, maybe that will help me take the beatings I'll have to take. I'll try to be a man, but I cannot get down on my knees. And it's the same in my other novels and stories. For example, in a comic novel like "A Long Day in November," he goes to the church and the church fails him, so he has to go to the voodoo woman. They go back to the more basic things, further and fur ther back, but the church is always there somewhere in the back of all the stories and all the novels. I lived on this plantation, and of course the church was right in the middle of the plantation. The church is still there. I went to school during the week and church on Sunday.

WP: You write about the relationship between the Cajuns, who took over after the Second World War a lot of the land which the blacks had been sharecropping for almost a hundred years, and the blacks who were forced to farm the least desirable land and who then were forced out entirely. The young blacks all moved away. Has that changed?

EJG: It has not. My people had been slaves on the place and they had become sharecroppers when the owner of the plantation turned it over to sharecroppers. But then the Cajuns became sharecroppers as well. They got the better land. They got better machinery, and they produced more, and a lot of the blacks moved out because they could not compete. And of course the Second World War not only took a lot of young blacks into the service, but many others escaped and went to the North to find work, leaving the older people there, and eventually the Cajuns had all the land in that general area. During the sixties, something else happened. Larger companies took over and leased this place; soy beans took over and oil wells took over, and the Cajuns were moved out as well. In *A Gathering of Old Men*, that's what it is all about. The ones who loved the land, worked the land, and then were kicked off the land.

WP: Has there been much ideological criticism pro or con of your novels?

EJG: By whom?

WP: By either the blacks or the whites.

EJG: I've been criticized, but not really. I don't think I'm taken seriously yet as a writer to a point where there can be long articles or comprehensive essays about me and my work. I have known people who have done masters on my work.

I have known people who have used me in their doctorate, but I'm not one of those people whose work is written about by the major critics. Every so often, something gets in one of the black oriented journals, like *Callaloo*, which is published at the University of Kentucky at Lexington. But I'm not taken so seriously that any books have yet been written about me.

WP: I think the problem may be be that *Miss Jane* was too popular and the others haven't been popular enough.

WP: That's quite possible. I won't mention the name of this particular person or the magazine, but when *Miss Jane* first came out, this particular person said to me, I haven't read your book, and I want to tell you why. After *Time* and *Newsweek* and *Life* gave you such great reviews, I knew that the book had to be a waste of time, and I will never read it.

WP: Which of your books would you say has gotten the best reviews? I know that *A Gathering of Old Men* got some splendid one. The one in *The New Yorker* I know was super.

EJG: I think *Miss Jane* got the best reviews out of all the books. Next was *A Gathering of Old Men* and the *Bloodline* stories. I had the lead review in *The Saturday Review of Literature* when *Bloodline* came out. I think Granville Hicks did it. It was a great review. I thank that's what turned a lot of people about the book and then later, people started anthologizing "The Sky is Gray" and it hasn't stopped yet.

WP: I wondered about the technique of having so many voices tell the story in *A Gathering of Old Men*. Were you thinking of Faulkner's *As I Lay Dying* when you were doing that?

EJG: I was not particularly thinking of Faulkner. I had done that in the last story in *Bloodline*, "Just Like a Tree," using multiple points of view. But Faulkner's *The Sound and the Fury* has had its influence on my work. I don't know that I would have ever been able to write from that multiple point of view had I not read Faulkner, but at the time I was writing it I was not thinking of Faulkner. The original writing of *A Gathering of Old Men* was done from a single point of view by Lou Dimes, who was the newspaper guy, Candy's boy friend. Then I realized that Lou could not see these old men gathering because he was in Baton Rouge—he could only hear about them—and it was then that I decided to make the change for two reasons: number one, I wanted to see the gathering, and number two, I wanted language. I wanted a little boy running down the street bragging about the way to hit a horse when you want it to run fast. I wanted a litany as Janey went through the house calling on God: Lord have mercy, Lord have mercy, Jesus, what now, what now. I wanted her looking out onto the back yard at the old lady, then looking out to the major on the porth. I wanted a rhythmic language throughout the book.

WP: When I talked to Madison Jones, he said that he felt that after his novel, *A Cry of Absence*, in 1961, which dealt with the destructive effects of white racism, he went through a fallow period because he felt that history had taken away his subject matter. Looking back on that period now, what do you think was the total effect of all that ferment on the creative writer?

EJG: I don't think that it had too great an effect on the subject I wanted to write about. (Pause.) It did add something to what I had in mind that I already wanted to write about. *Catherine Carmier* takes place in sixty-two. Before writing *Catherine*, I never knew that I wanted to deal with a broad period of time. I never knew what I was going to deal with, but after that one book, I realized that I wanted to say something else, and what I wanted to say was something before 1962. So it was then that I could write *Of Love and Dust*, and then after writing that book, I realized that I wanted to go further back. It was then or maybe a little before that I realized that I wanted to get those stories together. And then I wrote *Miss Jane Pittman* because I wanted to go further and further back. During the time I was writing *Miss Jane Pittman*, between sixty-eight and seventy, so much was going on in California as well as in the South. That was when Martin Luther King was killed, that was when Bobby Kennedy was killed, that was when all the demonstrations were going on on the campuses. All of these things were going on when I was writing this book. The civil rights movement, the demand by black, all these things added something to the black experience which I was trying to capture. It brought it up to the present. I could go as far back as 1862 in *Miss Jane* and bring the story up to 1962, but I can go beyond that now, because by the time I finished *Miss Jane*, other things were happening. So I could just continue to go on. Someone asked me why *Miss Jane* ended in 1962, I said, well, I didn't want to get involved with JFK's assassination—Miss Jane would have died just before that—but other stories could be affected by it. *In My Father's House* is post Martin Luther King, and I could write that book only because those things had happened during that time. It was really only a continuation of what I was trying to do all that time. I'm still talking about the plantation life, the old lady who lives out in the field, the small town, the racism in the small town in "The Sky is Gray," as another element in the civil rights movement. The little boy in "The Sky is Gray" cannot go into this place to have a glass of milk; this is what Phillip Martin is fighting for *In My Father's House*. It's just a continuation, a broadening, it did not change my philosophy.

WP: How did you get into teaching?

EJG: My books were not supporting me. I was being invited to give readings—I've read everywhere in this country—different institutions would ask me, would you like to come over for three weeks or something like that? For example, Denison University back in Granville, Ohio, asked, would you like to come by for six weeks, and I said sure, and eight or nine years later, they gave me an honorary doctorate. In May I'm going to pick up an honorary doctorate at Whittier, Nixon's old college; I taught there a quarter. I was at the University of Arkansas at Fayetteville for a week. I've been everywhere. I made absolutely nothing on *In My*

Father's House except for the advance they gave me. Well, I made a few bucks, but nothing that could pay me for the seven years I spent writing it. During one of those dry periods right after I published the book, I got a special delivery letter from the University of Southwestern Louisiana here in Lafayette asking if I would like to teach for one semester or four semesters, for a half year or two years, and I didn't want to. I said, I don't mind leaving San Francisco for a short period of time, I don't mind going out and giving a reading, but I don't want to leave for any long period of time. But I was as broke as I could possibly be, I was there with some budddies and my lady friend, and she said, well, I would try it if I were you, and they convinced me to do it, and I got in touch with the English department. I came down, and we met in Baton Rouge at the Hilton, and we talked and talked, and they told me what I would have and what they would pay and what they wanted me to do, and I agreed. I came down in eighty-one and spent a year, and they asked me if I would like to come back every year for one semester, and I said okay. At that same time, the University of Houston asked me to do the same thing, to teach one semester on alternate years, and I thought I could teach one semester at Houston on one year and one semester at USL on the next. I could write the rest of the time. In eighty-three, when I came here to teach my second year at USL, they gave me the key to this house. They said, this will be your home if you would like to have it, and we're offering you tenure. Good Lord, now,I have to call the people in Houston and tell them that I'm not coming back to Texas. This is how I got into teaching. I teach three hours and I have four hours for office hours. Usually, I spend more time in my office talking with students than I do in the classroom.

WP: I realize that you haven't been teaching that long, but have you had any outstanding students?

EJG: Well, I've had students who have already published a few things. One student my first year had I think two stories published in *The Southern Review*. That was Jude Roy. He writes about Cajun life. I've had other students who've had things published. One young lady has had poetry published. I don't do poetry, and I don't know anything about it at all. I have students who have potential, but I tell them I had potential too, but it took me ten years after I left college in order to get something going. Well, I published *Catherine Carmier* seven years after I got out of college. However, in 1964 no one heard of it. I think they printed fifteen-hundred copies and probably sold one-thousand, and five-hundred went on remainder.

WP: What did you do during those seven years?

EJG: I worked. I worked in the post office. I worked as a printer's helper. I washed dishes. I did all kinds of things. It was all part of my life.

WP: That kind of background was I think more typical of writers of an earlier period than of now.

EJG: Oh, yes, at that time I was offered a little teaching job, but I said no. I was staying away. I wanted to write and teaching would take everything that I have. I had heard enough about people trying to write and to teach at the same time. I had had teachers at San Francisco State who were writers, and of course Wallace Stegner at Stanford was a writer who wrote some good books while he was teaching, but all the awards that he received, the Pulitzer awards and the other awards, have been in the last ten years after leaving Stanford.

WP: What sort of reading do you like to do in your spare time?

EJG: I like to go back to the old things. I can read Hemingway and Faulkner at any time. I pick up Tolstoy, the romantic poets.

WP: Of the people I've talked to, Dostoevsky seems to be the particular favorite.

EJG: I don't know. People think that I should like Dostoevsky, and I've never liked Dostoevsky. (Laughs.) I think I got enough Dostoevsky when I read *Crime and Punishment* and *The Brothers Karamazov*. Dostoevsky took over, and he wore me out. I've always known what I wanted to say, and I wanted someone to show me how to say it, and Turgenev always showed me much more than Dostoevsky ever could. Turgenev's *Fathers and Children* or *Fathers and Sons* showed me much more than any book of Dostoevsky. Dostoevsky wrote so much of hunger, of deprivation and pain that people said, you've gone through that sort of thing, you should like Dostoevsky. He had a big influence on Richard Wright, on Ellison, and on the early black writers, but I've never ever thought of him as being a teacher. I was much more influenced by Flaubert, Maupassant, and especially Turgenev. *Fathers and Children* was a bible to me when I was writing *Catherine Carmier*. I read that book every day. For example, when Charlotte meets Jackson, it was the same as when Bazarov meets his parents. I didn't know how an older person could meet a young person. I didn't know what a young person would do during the time he was thinking about leaving, what he would do during that time he was not with a girl. But then I read how Bazarov went through the fields with a switch knocking the leaves off the weeds and popping tassels off flowers. So I made Jackson walk down to my favorite river and take these rocks and skim them across the water. This was the kind of thing I learned. When I mention Turgenev, I've been told that Turgenev was an aristocrat and wrote about the aristocracy, but I'm talking about form. James and Flaubert thought a hell of a lot of Turgenev, and form is what I'm interested in.

WP: Turgenev was interested in the different levels of society just as you are.

EJG: Oh yes, the younger, the questioning group, and the older traditional group.

WP: What current novelists are you interested in? Walker Percy seems to be the top dog now among the Southern novelists, most of whom have a kind of love-hate relationship with him because he's so famous.

EJG: I really don't have any favorite writers. I met Walker for the first time at the Southern Review literary conference. He read, I read, Eudora Welty read, Robert Penn Warren read. I really don't know his works that well. I don't read contemporary novels except when some one sends me one. If it's a collection of stories, I'll read some of them and put it down. Maybe I shouldn't be saying that on a tape like this since I am teaching, but I really don't look at myself as a teacher. I look at myself as a writer who sits in a classroom or sits in his office and says, these are the books I was brought up on. Maybe there are better ones being written today, and if there are, I hope that one of the professors would point them out to me. Up to now, I haven't given my students any assignments, but I think I will, starting next semester, because I want them to start reading. They haven't read anything. They don't know about the multiple point of view, the omniscient point of view, the single point of view; they don't know what the hell I'm talking about.

WP: The writers I've talked to read all sorts of things. Madison Jones reads the Bible and theology. Shirley Ann Grau reads newspapers. John William Corrington reads law books, Joyce and the classics.

EJG: Oh, I read newspapers.

WP: The point about her was that she said she read newspapers looking for material for stories.

EJG: No, I don't do that.

WP: James Baldwin is an interesting writer, but it seems to me that his fiction has been crippled by his feelings of hatred. I'm not talking about his essays, which are brilliant.

EJG: I agree with you.

WP: In spite of the fact that his books have sold a lot, I don't think he's an important writer of fiction.

EJG: I agree with you. I think probably his best book was his first book, *Go Tell It On the Mountain. Giovanni's Room* was okay. In *Another Country* you begin to see that the form is falling apart. I haven't read anything since *Another Country*. That was the last of the fiction I read of his.

WP: There is a good analysis of his fiction in an old book, *The Negro Novel in America*, by Robert Bone.

EJG: That's another book that was really criticized by a lot of the black critics. They thought that Bone had decided which were the good black novels and which were not.

WP: Is he black or white?

EJG: He's white. I met Bone in sixty-four at a conference just outside of Monterey, California. A red-headed guy who taught at Columbia, or the City College of New York, someplace like that. I saw him again at the Library of Congress, I think it was, in seventy-four, after *Miss Jane* was made into a film. After doing *The Negro Novel in America*, he also did *The Negro Short Story in America*. I admire his work. I think he's a damn good critic. I think he knows what he's talking about. He's dogmatic, but I think he's bright. He said, these are the books: Jean Toomer's *Cane*, Ellison's *Invisible Man*, Wright's *Native Son*, and a few others. And he said why he thought that these books were better than others.

WP: The writers that I've talked to have all had a love-hate relationship with teaching. They liked it for supporting them, but they felt that it cut into their time too deeply and took too much of their energy.

EJG: It does, it takes a lot of time and energy, but I've done seven books, if you consider the children's book *A Long Day in November* as one of them, and I think now, if I concentrate for the six or seven months away from my teaching— I'm not teaching this semester—I teach every fall—I think I should be able to get something done. I still try to write well when I write, and I still would like to write six or seven more books—I don't think it's possible—but I would like to do it, I dont't feel now that I have to put in those eight hours or those five hours five days a week twelve months of the year. I don't care about doing that any more. If I had a lot of money and absolutely nothing to do except write, I might put in three hours a day and work ten or eleven months out of the year. I think I still have time to write and to teach because I don't have to teach the entire year.

WP: Basically you write totally about Louisiana, although I realize that they are occasional excursions off to California or elsewhere. Is there any feeling that you wanted to come back to Louisiana to be closer to your subject matter?

EJG: No, no, I could write just as well in San Francisco about Louisiana as I can here in Lafayette. Everything I've had published has been written in San Francisco on a little table. Well, *A Gathering of Old Men* was written on a big table, but all the other books were written on a small table facing a wall. I would come to Louisiana and spend a week or two a couple times a year, and that was what I was doing, and I would see what I want to see. What I was writing about all this time was no longer there. That sharecropping place, the store, the houses, are not there. The river is there, but the banks are all built up now. I can see the past sitting in a place in San Francisco just as well as I can see it sitting in a place in Louisiana. I can see it better there because I don't have the distractions.

WP: How do you write? You said that you typed *Catherine*?

EJG: That was before I really knew what I was going to do. I really had written it out in long-hand and then I was picking it out on the typewriter. I still write in longhand.

WP: Do you type it or have someone else type it?

EJG: Oh, no, I type it myself because I'm constantly changing. I'm constantly changing, especially dialogue. Discriptive passages are difficult for me to do, so I'm constantly changing them from time to time.

WP: I think of you as an intensely dramatic writer. Have you thought about writing plays?

EJG: In Louisiana, the people moved westward; they went to California, to Los Angeles, San Francisco, that general area. Eastward of Louisiana—

Mississippi, Georgia, Alabama—people moved eastward, to Chicago, New York, Philly, in that direction— now, I think if I had gone east, I would have ended up as a playwright. I probably would have ended up in a big city where you don't have all the space you have out West. It would have been much more intense, and I think I would have ended up as a playwright, I think because of my use of dialogue, not because I like to describe big city feelings. I love outdoor space, places to run and play and do all kinds of things, and West is the place for open spaces and the novel.

I think if the movement of my people had been eastward, I would have become a playwright, and I think that, without false modesty, I could have been a pretty good one. I think I could have been a better playwright than I am a novelist, really. I think I would have concentrated on dialogue even more than I do now, and I think I would have concentrated more on keeping characters at a certain point after I had mastered technique. I did a little of it in college. I studied language arts with an emphasis toward creative writing. My minor was English lit, but my major was language arts. You have some playwriting and direction, speech, journalism, a little of all the language arts. I liked doing it, I liked writing little skits.

WP: You studied under Wallace Stegner who was a very famous creative writing teacher. What can a creative writing teacher teach a student, assuming of course that he has some talent?

EJG: I'm glad you added that, because you couldn't teach many football players out there how to do creative writing. The writer feels down at times: what am I doing, where am I going, am I doing anything at all? How do I get this right? A teacher can read your work. I think every great writer has had someone to bounce things off: Hemingway, Tolstoy, Flaubert. They didn't have to have writing classes, but they would say, what do you think of this? What do you think of that. What do you think of this comma? The teacher says, read such and such a writer. Stegner would never say what Tolstoy said, "Don't read that guy, he's dead", or Gertrude Stein would say, "Don't read him," and Hemingway would say, "I like reading him." A good teacher would never say, Don't read him." He would say, "Now, between these two, you might learn something if you read that. This passage here should be cut off. Build up this passage. I'm not going to tell you how to do it, because I'm not going to write your novel, but I'm going to tell you how it should be done. I'd suggest you read a certain writer because he does the same sort of thing." This is what I try to tell my students at my seminar here.

WP: Most writer today are published by several different publishers, but you've only been published by two, Dial and Knopf.

EJG: Well, Dial and Knopf, but the first one, *Catherine*, was published by Atheneum. It took me so long to write that book that they were not interested in me afterwards. Dial was. Dial was one of those publishing houses that would take a chance. They would not pay you very much money. About the only person they paid money to at that time was Norman Mailer. Baldwin and Mailer were Dial writers at that time.

WP: *Barbary Shore*? It wasn't *The Naked and the Dead*.

EJG: The later books, yeah. Dial offered me a small amount of money, but it was the only publishing house that would offer me any money at that time. I was trying to publish the *Bloodline* stories. I finished them before I finished *Of Love and Dust*, but no one wanted to publish a book of short stories by an unknown writer. Bill Decker, who was to be my editor at Dial, and Ed Doctorow, who was the editor in chief, said that, if I wrote a novel, they would give me a two book contract and publish the stories. These stories are the best thing around here, but you're unknown, so since I had written "Three Men,' I got the idea that I would continue that story. I wrote the first draft of *Of Love and Dust* in about three months and Doctorow wrote back, I like the first part of that novel, I like the secondpart, but the first part and the second part have nothing in common. You made the first part tragic and the second part comic. Make up your mind about how you want it done. He sent it back to me, and I looked it over and saw that he was right. So I made the second part tragic and sent it back to him. He said, you've improved it ninety-nine percent. I'm going to send it back to you and I want you to pass it through your typewriter and do anything you want to do and send it back to me and we'll publish it and publish the other. So he published the novel, and the stories the next year.

WP: Was Doctorow related to the novelist?

EJG: He was the novelist.

WP: How did you arrive at Knopf?

EJG: My agent, Dorothea Oppenheimer, felt, that after *Miss Jane Pittman*, Dial was not doing enough, the company was breaking up, Doctorow had gone, Bill Decker, who was my editor, had gone, I think the publisher had gone. The whole business was breaking up. Dorothea felt that *Miss Jane* should have been one of the top books, it should have won the Pulitzer or the National Book Award if there had been enough support and enough pressure. Quite a few people felt *Miss Jane* would win the Pulitzer. As a matter of fact, Wally Stegner beat me out with his book. He thought that I would win. Others thought I would win the National Book Award, but it went to Flannery O'Connor for her *Collected Stories*, posthumously of course. So my teacher beat me out for the Pulitzer and a dead woman beat me out for the National Book Award.

We could have gone to Farrar, Straus and Giroux, but they had turned us down originally, and we could not forgive them for that. But I'm very happy with Knopf, with my editor, Ash Greene and the rest of the people there.

WP: How many of your books are in print?

EJG: All of them, except *Catherine*, and the children's version of *A Long Day in November*. North Point still has copies of *Catherine* around, but they're not printing any more copies. *Bloodline*, *Of Love and Dust* and *In My Father's House* are all published by Norton library. *Miss Jane* is still printed by Bantam, and *A Gathering of Old Men* is printed by Vintage.

WP: How many translations have you had?

EJG: When we go back over to the conference room, I can show you the different translations. They've been translated into Japanese, into Chinese, German, Norwegian, Russian, Swiss. . .

WP: Did you get any money from the Russians?

EJG: No, I haven't gotten any money from the Russians yet. (Laughs.) I've got money from a lot of the others, but not from the Russians yet.

WP: I wonder how they handled the dialect.

EJG: I don't know how any of them handled the dialect. People who have read the German version say that they handled it pretty well. But I've had books published in about eight or nine different foreign countries. I think *A Gathering* is coming out in Portugal. Amazingly, none of the books have been translated into French yet. I know some people at the Sorbonne, but as of now nothing has been done.

WP: What is the relationship between intelligence in general and the ability to write novels?

EJG: Well, I think Joyce was the brightest guy around and I don't think he was the greatest novelist. What he did with language and style changed the world. I think Hemingway was a hell of a short story writer, but I don't think he was the greatest novelist during his time. You don't have to be the brightest person in the world. I don't think Faulkner could have dared touch Joyce as far as intelligence goes, but good Lord, compare what he has written. No, it's something else that makes that writer.

WP: Madison Jones said that Faulkner seemed to have a genius. He simply didn't seem aware of what he was doing.

EJG: Absolutely, I would agree. I think Faulkner the genius writer and Faulkner the man are two different people. He was not the brightest man in the world or he probably would not have said some of the things that he said in his interviews. When he sat down with that pencil and that little handwriting that he had when he wrote these things, he was possessed by demons who had taken over. I think he said that the characters always take over on page one-fourteen, or something. Hemingway criticized Faulkner for not rewriting carefully enough, but I think Faulkner did the best he could according to the way he rewrote. His handwriting showed that he was very patient, but if he had been a much more educated man, I think that he would have written in a different way. But it wouldn't necessarily have been better.

WP: A lot of twentieth-century writers have written a lot of criticism. Have you written any?

EJG: I can't. I could not give you a lecture on writing. I could not give you a lecture on my writing. I've never written an essay. I've written a couple little things, but they're pretty bad. As far as really deep analytical theories about my own stuff, let alone on Ellison or Baldwin or on the others, I can talk with someone who knows Baldwin, or Ellison, or Joyce, or Turgenev. I can sit around and talk with them at a party or in a classroom, but for me to stand up there and give an hour talk on these people or on my own stuff, there is no way that I can do it. I know Faulkner appeared at Virginia and several other universities, but I don't know that he ever lectured. Anthony Burgess and I were at Chapel Hill in 1969, and I got up and talked for fifteen or twenty minutes, and I sat down, and he got up, and put a hand in this coat pocket and a hand in this coat pocket, and he talked for about an hour and a half. (Laughs.) He started with Shakespeare and came down to this character who wrote something last month. Good Lord, I could never do that sort of thing.

WP: He is unquestionably a superb reader.

EJG: I used to see him in New York in the late sixties. My agent would give a party for me, and he and his wife would come by and have drinks.

WP: Could you say anything about your current project?

EJG: I don't usually talk about it. This is where you get all the ohs and the ahs when you're trying to say something about something that you really don't understand yet. The time of the novel would be when the executions were taking place in the parish seat in which the crime was commited. That would be until about the mid-fifties. The reason why I wanted that particular time was because I wanted the community in some way to be involved. A teacher who is on vacation has been asked by the prisoner's grandmother to visit this boy, this young man, on death row, and to make him know something about himself and life before he dies. The reason why she wants that is that, when the public defender who was trying to get him off appealed to the jury, he said that this man has no more intelligence than an animal. As a matter of fact, putting this "boy"—he uses the word "boy" all the time throughout his defense—in the electric chair would be like putting a hog in the electric chair. "None of you all around here would like to execute a hog, now would you." Still, he has an all white male jury, and he is sentenced to die. The godmother, or the grandmother—I haven't decided which she is going to be— says, okay, if he has to die, I don't want him to die as an animal. I want him to die as a man. She approaches the teacher, and the teacher says, "I don't want to have anything to do with it." He is the kind of teacher who existed up until the last twenty years when the only profession that blacks could get in the Southern part of the United States was teaching. And he is a guy who would rather not be here. He would rather be an artist or an writer or a playwright. He would like to be someone else in New York or Los Angeles or somewhere where he could study that and not teach, but he has an older person there that he is attached to, and he feels that he owes something to her, and that's the only reason why he's hanging around. He doesn't want to teach, he doesn't want to do anything, and teaching this class in this church school is just a way to earn a living so that he can get away some day.

He's just running in place. When this old lady approaches him about teaching this guy to be a human being, a man, at first he says no, but somehow she convinces him to do it, to accept the challenge of his life, to teach this guy who could die in a month or two, or six months. The reason I haven't decided how long is that I haven't talked to enough lawyers yet to know how long the process would be.

As a matter of fact, on Monday, I'm supposed to meet an older sheriff. Although he did not witness an execution, he said through someone else that he could have someone there with him who had gone through this sort of thing. I want to know exactly what the prison cells looked like in the forties and fifties. I want to know what kind of clothes the sprisoners wore, what kind of food they ate, what kind of exercise they took. I want to know if there were windows, I want to know all these sort of things. I talked to a former DA a couple of months ago, and he gave me some information I could use, but far from all the information I need. There are people here who are getting me contacts with people who know these things. In this story, I want the approach that Shaw uses in *Pygmalion*, also the Elephant Man type thing. Not physically, of course, but there is a kind of mask over the brain. The brain has not had the chance to get the light that would make him aware of all the things a man should possibly be aware of. What is a beach like? What is it like to have a vacation? What is it like to know a poem? What is it like to have a birthday, a day all your own with all the trimmings? What is the Constitution, and what is the Bill of Rights all about? Who was Frederick Douglass, or who was so-and- so? He never experienced any of that in his lifetime.

I'll be perfectly honest, as of right now, I don't know what that teacher is going to say when he walks into that room. (Laughs.) I have no idea at all. I do have questions: how far would a guard stand away from them while the teacher is there? What would they allow you to say to him? Could the teacher communicate with him if there's a guard there? How did the blacks communicate with each other during slavery while the guards were around? How can you make this young man here a true human being? is it right to do that, knowing that he could die a week after he realizes what a poem is all about. This is what I'll have to work out.

WP: Have you ever considered writing a novel set in San Francisco or some other place?

EJG: Yes, I've tried three San Francisco novels. I've even tried my army experience, but nothing worked out. I've got to get all that Louisiana experience out of me first, and I don't know how long that's going to take. I may never be able to do it. (1986)

Chapter 6
After the Confederate War: A Conversation with John William Corrington (1932-1988)

[The following interview was done in the Spring of 1985, some three and a half years before the death of John William Corrington, and was published in a slightly shorter form in *Louisiana Literature* for Fall, 1985.]

John William Corrington's first novel, *And Wait For the Night* (1964), takes place during the Confederate War and introduces the Sentell family, which was later to become the center of a projected—but unfortunately unfinished—trilogy. Corrington's fourth novel, *Shad Sentell*, published twenty years later, is set in modern times, and is chronologically the third volume of the Sentell trilogy. The projected second volume is discussed below. *The Upper Hand* (1967), Corrington's second novel, is the story of a young man who forsakes the priesthood in the middle of a mass for life among the derelicts of New Orleans. *The Bombardier* (1970) tells the interrelated stories of four pilots involved in the bombing of Dresden and, later, in the turmoil of the Democratic convention in Chicago in 1968.

In addition to his novels, Corrington published prolifically in other fields. During his lifetime he published a volume containing two novellas, *All My Trials* (1986), and three collections of stories: *The Lonesome Traveller And Other Stories* (1968); *The Actes and Monuments* (1978), and *The Southern Reporter* (1981). The stories are reprinted, along with an unpublished story, in *The Collected Stories of John William Corrington* (1990). Particularly notable among the later stories are several centered around the law and reflecting the author's experiences in the late seventies as a lawyer. Corrington also published essays and four collections of poetry. Strangely enough, however, he never published any fiction directly related to his broad experience in Hollywood and New York as a writer, with his wife Joyce, of movies and soap operas.

The interview took place in the author's large and comfortable house in uptown New Orleans. There were books on every side, mostly beautifully bound editions of the classics, but the author assured us that this was not his working library. Casually dressed, feet propped in front of him, smoking cigars, Corrington spoke rapidly and fluently. Afternoon slid into evening, and presently Corrington's wife, Joyce, joined us. A compelling mixture of toughness and femininity, she majored in science before joining her husband as a collaborator in life, on screenplays and, lately, on a violent and artistically successful series of crime novels set in New Orleans.

WP: Who were the writers who influenced you?

JWC: When I grew up I had Faulkner, Hemingway, Fitzgerald and Wolfe. These were the four great pillars, and there were any number of others. Later, of course, there was William Gaddis and *The Recognitions*. Then, quite late, there's Cormac McCarthy who's superb, and almost no one has heard of him. *Outer Dark* is one of the most striking pieces of pure prose I've ever read in my life. He's a writer's writer, but who knows it, and who cares? When I was twenty-three years old, I reviewed *The Recognitions* and said this is a finer novel than Joyce ever wrote, but no one paid any attention outside small circles. *The Recognitions* is a great book and Gaddis is only beginning to be recognized. With McCarthy, on the other hand, it's pure prose.

WP: He did a screenplay which I think is just about the best I've ever seen, called *The Gardener's Son*, which was done in 1977 for PBS, by Richard Pearce.

JWC: On one hand, I'm surprised McCarthy could reach out to that. On the other, I wouldn't think he'd want to. On the third hand, I guess he could use a few bucks just like the rest of us. (Laughs.)

WP: How did you first become interested in writing?

JWC: It was a fallback position. My first love and my last will always be music, and I wanted to be a professional musician. Unfortunately, I was born approximately fifteen or twenty years too late, and with a very small talent. My great ambition in life (and it still would be if there were a time machine) was to play lead trumpet in the Glenn Miller orchestra. That was the way I grew up. The pillars then were Tommy Dorsey, and Goodman, and Shaw, and Miller.

WP: And that interest shows in *The Bombardier*.

JWC: That's true. A graduate student somewhere in the future may discover that the recording session in the book regarding the Miller orchestra is done precisely as it occurred. One week before Pearl Harbor, they recorded, "It Happened in Hawaii." I had the RCA Victor-Bluebird discography, so what I did was to erase Chummy McGregor from the band and put my character in his place. And Chummy was so self-effacing that nobody would notice. But you got people like Paul Tanner, one of the trombonists, talking to my guy, and Fats Waller at that time was playing up on Forty-Second street. No one will recognize anything here except a literary creation, and yet it's damn close to a documentary.

WP: What does AMDG at the beginning of all your books stand for, dare one ask that?

JWC: It's something that I was taught when I was just learning to write, taught by the Jesuits to put at the head of all my papers, and it's the only thing that I carried away that I have any use for—that and the discipline they gave me. It stands for "Ad Majorem Dei Gloriam," "to the greater glory of God."

WP: What did you think of Thomas Wolfe when you were young?

JWC: I read Thomas Wolfe when I was seventeen, and it was an incredible experience. I read him again when I was about forty with great trepidation and found out that he stands up very well indeed—unless of course you've forgotten you were ever young. My wife wishes I would write more like Thomas Wolfe. I said, look, I'm not in that tradition. I'm in the Faulkner tradition. I invented the definition of the traditions. There's the Shakespeare tradition and the Dante tradition. In the Shakespeare tradition, the artist vanishes in his work. Obviously, writers like James Joyce are there; in the Dante tradition, the writer, pretty much in his own persona, is present. In Proust, both in the early drafts of *Remembrance* and in the final draft, the narrator is more or less Proust. That's also the Thomas Wolfe tradition, but it isn't mine. I'm not comfortable without a persona, but I love Wolfe very much. Also Faulkner, as soon as I was able to read him. Hemingway, of course. My generation, the boys who grew up in Shreveport then, were influenced by Hemingway, whether they read him or not. They were stoic to their core. I started reading the classics very early, and Marcus Aurelius had a great influence on me.

WP: You said in the note at the beginning of *And Wait For the Night*, that the book is not an historical novel. What is it?

JWC: You remember that I was walking into a traditon which at that point was *Forever Amber*, or *The Silver Chalice*, or something of that sort. What the note fundamentally meant was that as to that point in Southern history, 1865, the attitudes were fairly well maintained, and it wasn't "historical" in quotes in any sense except in Faulkner's sense that the past isn't dead, it isn't even past. In the 1950's and early sixties, the South still existed. As far down as my generation, there were still men and women who could tell you what Reconstruction was like. There were a very few Confederate veterans still alive. I think the last one, Walter Williams, died in Houston when I was in Rice University. I did not intend the book to be "history," nor did I believe it to be a piece of embalmed imagination.

WP: What about the influence of Faulkner? I think it's obviously there, but it's not like Shelby Foote, who was publishing his novels about the same time, whose novels sounded like Faulkner warmed over.

JWC: Well, I made one decision very early: you will never have a style. You will burnish the instrument, you will read every word of every significant writer, including translations, you will even learn a little bit of Greek to have some sense of language, and then you will serve the material with that instrument. You will bring the instrument to the material and you will determine who the narrator should be and how the characters will speak and so forth to the limit of your capacity. You will not take the material, as E. E. Cummings or Hemingway or even Faulkner did, and twist the material until it suits your instrument. In a sense, I think my arrogance was greater than that of a man who perfects a style. I was determined, and I hope it's true to this day, that if you were to read four novels without an author's name on them, you could say, those are all four terrific novels, these must be four interesting writers—that you would not identify them as the work of the same man. That is what I would hope. I don't know if it's true or not, but that was the hope. No novel would produce the instant recognition of, oh, Corrington.

WP: Your first novel, *And Wait For the Night* has a magnificent opening and a firm sense of structure, but's it's not clear to me how much personal experience went into it. How much personal experience, or family experience, or stories went into that book?

JWC: It was mainly imagination, enormous reading in the period. The book came out of my reading. I was in my middle twenties. At the Rice University bookstore, I casually picked up Hodding Carter's *The Angry Scar*. I had never really been all that conscious of being Southern until I read that book. It sounds ridiculous, but a hundred years later I was so god damned mad I could hardly breathe at what those Yankee scum had done to us. I told him before he died: Mr. Carter, you may not believe this, but *And Wait For the Night* came directly out of my reading your book. The material in *The Angry Scar* was more ferocious and awful than in my novel. The feeling, the whole sense, of what it meant to be a Southerner in the 1860's and seventies sprang from Carter's book on reconstruction. It is a masterpiece.

WP: I asked Madison Jones if he had ever considered writing a book about the Civil War, and he said no, that he didn't think people were still interested in the Civil War, but I told him that wasn't my impression of the people in Louisiana.

JWC: Well, there has been an enormous erosion of the sense of the South in the last twenty years or so. I can remember when Miller Williams and I used to go around on tour delivering a lecture on the roots of Southern literature when we still considered the Civil War to be alive and working. I fear that's not really true any longer. I think television has managed what Sherman's troops never could. We aren't the people that the Irish or the Israelis are. Finally, we always were Americans, a peculiar breed of Americans, true—but in the final analysis, don't ask Americans to keep any idea or passion or principle in mind for more than four years. They can't do it. The Vietnamese war was evidence of that. I knew what was going to happen. I told my wife in sixty-five: we'll never cut it, because those Asians can hold an idea in mind for two thousand years. We can't. Not even Southerners.

WP: Where did the idea for the structure of *And Wait For the Night* come from, with the opening sequence, and then the moving back in time to the siege, and then the moving forward again?

JWC: It just seemed the way to do it. It was not a conscious choice. It was not something where I said, well, let me see.... In fact, I am more likely to use a model today than I was then. But of course I know more now. (Laughs.) I recently finished a book which I think Arkansas Press is going to publish called *The Risi's Wife*. "Risi" is the Indian word for a seer with extraordinary powers from the time of Rig Veda. And the form is patterned after Conrad: if you know Conrad, you know this form. It's two lawyers discussing a case that one of them once had. It started as a divorce case and ended as a manifestation of Shiva, but it's done with cold, calculating determination to get the same kind of effects that Conrad was able to get out of Marlow's monologues in such works as "Heart of Darkness".

WP: Do you remember when you started thinking of the Sentells in terms of a group of stories, a couple of novels, or whatever?

JWC: I kind of had it in mind at the beginning, but didn't know where I wanted to go. As a matter of fact, I had a second novel in the series in mind almost immediately after *And Wait For the Night*, but I wasn't ready for it. In fact, it's going to be the next large book I write, I've got the first chapter done on that. The name of the book is *Under the Double Eagle*, and it's the story of E. M. Sentell, the second, the son of Major Sentell, the grandfather of Shad, in the 1880's and nineties, as a member of the Brotherhood of the Workers of the World. What he does with his associates from all over the world is to go around and kill plant own-ers and strike-breakers, and police and railroad detect ives. It's the K Squad of Brotherhood of Workers of the World—the kind of thing which did go on at Cripple Creek and the Westead Mill and places like that. They call it labor vio-lence, but that's not being very sophisticated because it amounts to incredible acts of terrorism by the owners against the workers and the workers against the own-ers. A kind of slow-motion civil war, if you will, after the Confederate War. It fig-ures that the son of a Confederate soldier might find a new focus for his anger. I love the old man as he appears in *Shad Sentell*. I thought he was a remarkable character. He was so unexpected, so totally out of the mould, with the battle between him and his son E. M. To me one of the most harrowing scenes in the book is the death of the old man. So I said to myself recently, you really know enough now. It would just have been a kind of silly, super-liberal, pro-labor novel if I had written it while I was in my twenties, but I think I can write something bet-ter now. And I love the title, *Under the Double Eagle*.

WP: You strike me as the most unreconstructed of all the Southern novel-ists I know anything about.

JWC: I consider that just about the greatest compliment anyone could give. I can think of no reason to be reconstructed. My country is the South—especially North Louisiana and East Texas. The antique values and ways of thinking are good enough for me.

WP: What did the reviewers think of *And Wait For the Night*?

JWC: It was very well reviewed except for one reviewer whose name I have probably repressed, who called it a Ku Klux Klan tract, and I said, if I ever meet this guy, and he's eight-five and I'm seventy-five, I'm going to punch him in the face and stomp him. The book is anything but that. But the most interesting review was by Granville Hicks, the chief reviewer for the *Saturday Review* for years. He gave the book a very good review, he said that this guy is a superb writer, but he has a bizarre fantasy that the South should have won the Civil War, and he went on with the usual F. O. Matthiessen type of crap. I met him some years later, and he had by then reviewed my second novel, *The Upper Hand*, very well indeed—he certainly liked my work—and he asked me how I could conceivably hold the position that the South should have won the Civil War. Well, Mr. Hicks, I said, about the same way that you held until recent events that Stalin was the glory of the Russian revolution. (Laughs.) And he damned near died. I guess that he thought folks had forgotten his support of the purge trials in the 30's. You've got to understand that at least my fantasy hasn't cost thirty million lives. My fantasy, if you choose to call it that, didn't cost anything. He was a very small old man, and I didn't want to say it, but I don't feel that you can let people like him walk around—what is the wonderful line, "Pray do not give yourself airs"? I think I did a good thing in the sense that Allen Tate used to call "knowledge carried to the heart." I think I got him right where he lived. I do not think he was a bad man, but he was prepared to say things and support things without realizing that, as Richard Weaver put it, ideas have consequences.

WP: I judge then that *And Wait For the Night* did not draw directly upon personal experience in the way that many first novels do.

JWC: No, it was marginal second generation experience from my grandfather and grandmother. What you say, I think, is the conventional generalization that the young man and his alter ego are fairly close, but I've never found myself as interesting as the world. This is why my wife and I endlessly argue about the foundations of epistemology. She maintains that the Cartesian, "I think, therefore I am," is the basis of all knowledge, and I say that I well remember things outside myself before I ever came to have an ego, and I'm not too fond of that ego even now. (Laughs.) I find that my ego is my most unpleasant trait and one that I would like to crush before I die. Later, I found that T. S. Eliot agreed with me, and that made me sort of feel good. He says that only one who has a personality knows what it means to want to escape it.

WP: *The Upper Hand* is certainly not what anybody would expect from reading *And Wait For the Night*.

JWC: So I'm succeeding. Not the same style, not even the subject matter—in other words not getting trapped in a box when you're thirty, or even fifty. If *The Risi's Wife* is published, I'll send you a copy, and you will not expect it. A good old boy from Shreveport, from Rapides Parish, actually, gets drafted, and as one of the lawyers tells the other one, by some misbegotten fate, they send him to the China-Burma-India theatre where he flew the hump. And everybody who flew the hump smoked the hemp, because when you got up in one of those damned C

47's, you are flying from Assam in Northern India across the Himalayas down into Northern China. Here's the problem: your ceiling is twenty-thousand feet and the mountains range up to twenty-nine and thirty-thousand feet. If you misread your compass and your map, you can fly down a four-hundred mile corridor into a sheer face of rock—and there's no turning back and there's no going up—you're dead. This makes for a very nervous bunch of guys. In a certain way, it was more terrifying than having to combat German fighters. The description of the Himalayas I'm very proud of, just the sheer awe of something that reduces mankind to the size of a gnat. We're going to have to go into deep space to encoun ter anything more humbling than that. Anyhow, he comes back and he has yoga powers he didn't even intend to get. Imagine yoga powers in Shreveport in 1947.

JWC: If *And Wait For the Night* belongs vaguely to the Faulk ner tradition, *The Upper Hand* seems to me to grow directly out of Nelson Algren.

JWC: I would not be surprised if Algren had a considerable influence upon me. I loved his work, especially *A Walk on the Wild Side.*

WP: I read *The Man With the Golden Arm* recently and then I read your book and I was very struck with the similarities.

JWC: That's funny. I thought *The Man With the Golden Arm* was a pretty awful book, but I thought *A Walk on the Wild Side* was an unacknowledged American masterpiece. I'm sure I had *Walk* in mind when I wrote *The Upper Hand.*

WP: He published *A Walk on the Wild Side* and then he quit publishing novels. Well, he did write another one just before he died.

JWC: This happens. It happened to Mailer, and it happened—a little before our time—to Scott Fitzgerald. He ends up writing *Esquire* stories. He ends by writing *The Crackup*, a confessional. He ends up writing everything except com- mercial jingles. Of course, it didn't start with him, but started well before him. This is a great American literary tradition. Of course, Faulkner stayed away from that sort of thing like the plague.

WP: Someone asked me to describe *The Upper Hand*, and I told him it was Nelson Algren out of Dante. Would you agree with that?

JWC: Yeah, Nelson always wore his Chicago on his shoulder. Remember the renaissance writer who said he used no Latin word which did not appear in Cicero. Well, Nelson used no word which did not appear in the *Chicago Tribune*. The more I read in history, philosophy and religion, the more determined I am to use everything I can, because what you want is the broadest possible human basis for your work—in the sense that Dante reached for it in *Commedia Divinia*. You've got to be very careful so that it doesn't become a kind of pastiche, but then that's up to one's digestive apparatus. I thought *The Upper Hand* also had over- tones of *Sanctuary*. The personal motivation behind *The Upper Hand* was precise- ly that of *Sanctuary*. I wanted to write a book that was lurid enough and strange enough and loathsome enough that it would get an enormous amount of attention in the Yankee press and make me some money.

WP: Did it do that?

JWC: No, but it became an underground classic in California. When I went out and taught at Berkeley, everybody said: he wrote *The Upper Hand*, heah, man. (Laughs.) Unlike Faulkner's *Sanctuary*, it didn't make a lot of money, but it was grisly, I did my very best. But you have to understand that grisly by 1965 standards wouldn't make an R today. You could probably make that movie as a PG. It was also, of course, a book in which I was experimenting with styles.

WP: As *The Upper Hand* opens, Christopher Nieman abandons the priesthood in the middle of a mass. Is your character related to James's Christopher Newman in *The American*?.

JWC: Yes, but that's another thing. If I went back and reread *The Upper Hand*, I could not tell you everything that's in it. There is a doctoral dissertation-worth of literary tags. For example, there is a section lifted out of *Goldfinger*—no,*From Russia With Love*—that describes Billy Bob Stoker getting his back rubbed down in a courtyard by Mary Ann Downey. There is another passage describing a girl they find drowned in the lake lifted out of *The Atheist's Tragedy*, by Cyril Tourneur.

WP: Huysmans?

JWC: Yeah, naturally, *La Bas, A Rebours*,—and Xenophon.

WP: What about Dr. Aorta? Did anybody comment on him in the reviews?

JWC: Not much, except to say that I was rather Dickensian in my naming of characters, but if I'm not mistaken, there was a Dick Tracy comic character by that name. But that was way back; we're talking about the 1940's. Oddly enough, the notion of a German Jew who became a doctor for the SS did not strike them as all that odd. I personally would be willing to bet my life that if you could check it out, you would probably find that there were a number of such characters. Human nature is constant and unbounded.

WP: I was thinking that if you published that today you would probably get some people after you with meat cleavers.

JWC: Strangely enough, not at all. As a matter of fact, if they had said anything to me, I would have said, if Walter Lippmann had been a native German and a medical doctor, he would have been Dr. Aorta. Lippmann is famous for being a noted Ameri can Jewish pundit who never once mentioned the holocaust in his writings. Never. He was horrified at being Jewish. This a man who was beneath human contempt in my estimation. He always knew what was best for everybody, but he didn't even care about his own people. In fact, the reason I remember that negative review of *And Wait For the Night* is that that was the only time when I was attacked on the grounds that my work represented some special pleading, or racial or religious bias.

WP: Mr. Christian Blackman works in a basement in a swamp which never dries up repairing vehicles of one kind or another and trying to live from day to day so that he can get enough dope to go on to the next day.

JWC: I liked him. I liked him as a person because, to me, he had more metaphysical dignity than anybody in the book. I think Christopher liked him a lot too because he had figured out the name of the game and he knew who the enemy was.

WP: He's also long suffering. (Laughs.) He expects the worst and just hopes to get through the night.

JWC: It's really funny. Some people have said they think that Toole, who wrote *A Confederacy of Dunces*, had read *The Upper Hand*, but I don't think that's possible, because the time doesn't work. His book was written well before *The Upper Hand*. But he has one black figure whom I liked and thought was a lot like Mr. Christian, except more puritanic.

WP: I am appalled by the fact that so many important American novels of the recent past are out of print.

JWC: I think that if there is anything the National Endowment for the Humanities should do, it should be to remedy that. That should be a subsidized progam. God, the Russians do it for non-entities. First of all, the collected complete works of the major American authors—and I think we could agree who belongs on that list. I'd include writers like Willa Cather, for example.

WP: I thought about writing the Library of America just to see if they were going to include her. She is the greatest unread American writer today. [The Library of America has to date, 1992, published the nearly complete novels and stories of Willa Cather in three volumes.]

JWC: But there are many such writers today....

WP: I meant of that period, of the first half of the century.

JWC: I agree. Even if such a program is reduced to the level of a bunch of scholars getting together and deciding who the great writers are, better that than nothing at all, and the works should be kept in print.

WP: They have to be kept in paperback because that's what graduate students and people generally read.

JWC: And not just novels. E. B. Tylor's *The Primitive Mind* is out of print. That book in 1872 established the concept of animism and a whole attitude toward the history of religions. I've been looking for the book for four years. If you're dealing with the classics, or the history of religions, what is out of print is more important than what is *in* print. And when it comes to fiction, forget it. I would hate to see, for example, what I could find of William Goyen. He's not anyone who particularly moves me, but he is an important writer, and you cannot find his work in print. The book industry is now a throwaway industry, just like movies, just like records.

WP: Were you interested in movies much when you were younger?

JWC: I viewed them as pure entertainment, something to have fun with, to live vicariously. I was John Wayne in *Flying Tigers*, and that kind of thing, but I never dreamed that anyone would consider them an art form, and I still find that astonishing. I have seen only one film that I would regard as art. Posssibly another two, but they're dubious.

WP: What?

JWC: *Breaker Morant*. It is absolutely the finest film I have ever seen. I've seen it three times and cried like a baby three times. If I saw it again, I'm sure that I would again. There is no flaw in it that I can detect. It has the one thing that film almost never has: austerity. The second I'd consider art would be, believe it or not, the television version of *The Godfather*, where they run it chronologically. *Godfather I* is in the middle. You start with Robert de Niro and you end with Marlon Brando. There is some magnificant stuff there. Finally, Leone's unedited *Once Upon a Time in America*.

WP: Most of the writers I've talked to, with the exception of Shirley Ann Grau, have had a love-hate relationship with Hollywood, and most of them have written screenplays.

JWC: My career in Hollywood has been remunerative but undistinguished. If somebody in Hollywood or in New York television calls me and says that he'll give me $100,000 a year if I swear never again to write for film or television, I'll say, you just got yourself a deal. In fact, I can be gotten for much less than that. I never wanted to do it, I do not presently want to do it, and next year I will not want to do it. But I can make more money on one crummy piece of TV than I can on five books. I did a lecture in Shreveport last year, and I said: you must understand the spiritual confusion of a man who has seen the best work he ever did go for peanuts, and the most banal crap his mind could conceive of paid for at the rate of $200,000 to $300,000 a year. But maybe I'm mistaken. Eliot said that Dante after all was an indifferent critic of Dante. It seems we're talking about a non-culture called America, but perhaps I'm part of that, and it's the films and TV—not the writing—that's worthwhile.

WP: What do you think about the idea of individuality in films? Could an intelligent person who didn't know anything about it know that *Breaker Morant*, *Tender Mercies* and *King David* were all the work of the same person?

JWC: *I* didn't know that. (Laughs.) That strikes me as astonishing. There's an old Louisiana proverb that one of our house keepers used to use. She said, you've got to remember that even a blind pig will stumble on an acorn now and then. This should be placed underneath the big sign up in the hills as you drive into Hollywood.

WP: Do you think of yourself as a visual person?

JWC: No, but Roger Corman does. That's how Jo and I got into film. Roger read *The Upper Hand* and called me and said, you have a cinematic imagination, and I said, I do? I believe it in this sense: When I'm writing, I'm taking dictation from real people speaking. I do see the place. It's not just words strung end to end. In fact, that was part of the process of perfecting the instrument. One reviewer recently said something that really amused me. He said about me what James Joyce said about himself. He said, Corrington can do anything with words. It's not true, obviously, but it's true enough. If I've got that kind of instrument, I am now free to listen to my people. I don't have to sit there for twenty minutes thinking, she says such, what does he say. Well, he could say this or that. I *know* what he's going to say. Since the internal flow doesn't break, the dialogue should have a certain perfection. With some writers you see these sheets scratched over and scratched over. I can show you an eighteen-hundred page manuscript, and I'll bet there are not five-hundred scratches in the eighteeen hundred pages. Because the instrument is there, I'm now free to do what a writer is *supposed* to do, which is to listen to his people talking and to be able to describe what they see, not because he's so creative, but because it's in his mind's eye.

WP: When I talked to Madison Jones, I commented on the fact that his novels have very firm structures, but he said he never knew what was going to happen, and he had to work it out very slowly and laboriously as he went along, but I judge that's not your experience.

JWC: Mostly I wait until it happens in my head. I have found out that I am perfectly capable of sitting down and writing twenty-five pages of crap, if it hasn't already happened inside. And I learned early on that that is frustrating, it is destruct ive, and it will drive you away from the typewriter or word processor or your own copyhand for five days, and you will feel ashamed of yourself—so don't do it. One of the things that Hemingway taught me was, don't end when you're worn out. End when you still have somewhere to go, and later, when you start again, pick that up. He was absolutely correct. In fact, he was usually right. The trick is to get it more or less done in your head before you go to writing. If I could write faster, I would have written a lot more. I've always had an immense facility at the verbal level. To my mind, if you haven't solved those verbal problems, you have no business trying to be a writer. Those are threshold problems that you must solve before you can come to grips with material, with characters. If anything you write is going to be worthy of what Faulkner called the sweat and anguish of writing, for God's sake, we have to assume that you're fully literate and that in your mind is a palette of all the great minds you have encountered and the things they did and the way they solved problems. Now, you dont' copy them, but all of their stuff digests, and when you face problems the solution just springs out of that accreted experience that now belongs to you.

WP: Well, you make it sound a hell of a lot easier than it is for most people.

JWC: I have a mythological mind. My first real sally into the world of rationality was law school, which I found exceedingly easy because all that was required was mere rationality and any fool can do that. The new way to talk about mythology is in terms of Zen Buddhism: I don't write, *it* does.

WP: *The Bombardier* was your third novel. It's very differernt from your other two.

JWC: Hooray.

WP: Were you as happy with it as you were with the first two?

JWC: In some ways, happier than with the *The Upper Hand*. There was an editor at the *Chicago Review*, Peter Michaelson, who was an extraordinarily intelligent young man. He published a lot of my poetry, and once we were together with him—Joyce and I were in Chicago, and he said, Corrington, good God, you will give the world for wit, and I said, Peter, I don't think so. But when I look back at *The Upper Hand* , and I see what he was talking about. I seem to have been a young man who had not thought about it but who instinctively knew that he could do almost anything with language and who was parading his erudition, which was exceedingly moderate, considering that what passed for erudition in the fifties and sixties would hardly have gotten you into a decent prep school in England in the 1920's. Nevertheless, with one eye you're ahead of the blind folks. I was parad ing it, and had a serious case of the cutes. For example, think of the overall chrystalline tone of *The Upper Hand*, the narrator's tone. It's as cold as Alpha Centauri. Only the characters bring it to life: Bennie Boondocks's first person, for example, the blue movie-maker who when the cops get after him hits the New York airport trying to get out of the state, says, I'll take the first flight anywhere. The lady says, well, our next flight is to New Orleans: "Do I need a passport?" (Laughs.) Bennie is a creation, Mr. Christian is a creation, Billy Bob Stoker is a creation. All this is very virtuoso. In *The Horse's Mouth*, Gulley Jimson says, "well, technique, style. It's like farting 'Annie Laurie' through a keyhole. Clever as hell, but what does it mean?" If I were a critic writing on my own work, that would be the epigraph for the chapter on *The Upper Hand*. It is too clever by half. It has a few things to say, but it's overburdened with the technique and the style and the cleverness. *The Bombardier* was a far more serious book. It sprang directly out of my having spent three months teaching at Berkeley.

WP: I had some problems with the unity of the book, with the idea that the characters weren't closely enough related.

JWC: I think when you burn collectively 135,000 people to death, that creates a certain connection. The problem of unity to my mind was fused in the raid on Dresden. (Laughs.) I thought that was precisely the unity of the book.

WP: Is it really true that those pilots carried those Norden bombsights around their necks?

JWC: As I've heard, only the optical unit, which was like a telescope. It dropped down into the rest of what was a fairly big and complicated machine, but the optical unit could be with drawn, just as you can take the telescopic sight of a rifle out of its mount. So I am told. I never saw one of them myself except in photographs.

WP: The novel is a massive act of the imagination. Where did all this information come from?

JWC: You know where the Glenn Miller stuff came from. I knew Germany pretty well. When I was there in fifty-eight, a lot of the scars of war were still there. You would see a beautiful new building and a huge vacant lot screened off by a fence, and when you looked behind it, you could see a broken baby carriage, a broken bicycle, and all the bombed buildings were still there.

WP: In the novel, Jacobs, one of the characters, helps to get Mailer's second novel, *Barbary Shore*, published.

JWC: I like that. I love to play with the interstices of history. In *And Wait For the Night*, when Grant was riding up the road to accept the surrender at Vicksburg, a Confederate sharp shooter aimed at him. Grant did in fact ride up that road at that time of day on that date. That a Confederate sharpshooter drew a bead on him and Sentell knocked his rifle away is not history, but it fits. In fact, in our most recent sale, Joyce and I have taken to writing mystery stories, filling in the interstices of history once more. Viking has just purchased the first two.

WP: Could I ask the names?

JWC: The first is called *So Small a Carnival*, the second *A Project Named Desire*. In the first one, a young reporter walks in a bar on St. Peter Street and finds thirteen people machine-gunned to death. He is from Shreveport and hates this damned place and he and a black captain of homicide manage to solve the mass murder in the bar—and they also discover the truth of the assassination of Senator Huey P. Long in 1935. This is playing the interstices of history. Harry Williams and I were good friends at LSU. I saw him almost every day when he was writing the Long biography, and he would tell me the things I wanted to know about, and all I did was to take the biographical information, which was massive, and fit my characters into it, so that if somebody says, this is totally imaginative, I will say, oh, no, it isn't. Sorry. We have the dates of the DeSoto hotel meeting when the assassination was planned. We know there were eyewitnesses to the fact that Dr. Weiss drew the short straw, etc., etc. This is in Harry's biography, which is definitive, and nobody is going to better it until the information which I'm sure he stored at LSU is released. He had a number of quotes in there listed as private communications because the people are still alive, and I don't think they too much want to be known.

WP: I think it's a great book, I read it and reviewed it when it came out, and I'm an admirer.

JWC: It's a very admirable book. He told me it was astonishing to him, having lived through and participated in Long's life as a writer and historian, the incredible capacity of the Northerners to turn a socialist into a fascist. It was a remarkable achievement of the *New York Times*, the *Washington Post*, and the North in general, to be able to turn a man who was, if anything, a little further to the left than I'd be confortable with into a proto-hitlerian. They say, ah, but look at the way he ran the state, but of course leftists don't run dictatorships, do they?

(Laughs.)

WP: I judge then that your opinion of *All the King's Men* would not be that great, at least from a political point of view.

JWC: The book was too easy.

WP: You think that Long was a more complicated man than Willie Stark?

JWC: Well, they picked the right actor. Willie is Broderick Crawford. but Long was no rednecked country boy in overalls. He was a hell of a lot of things, but he wasn't that. Huey was an incredibly intelligent, shrewd and able man who saw himself as a modern-day hero. And let's talk about the empirical reality that when you drive from Hammond to New Orleans, much of the roadway was built by Huey Long. In Evangeline Parish, all of it was built by him. Huey Long built bridges where there were no bridges, at Shreveport, across the Mississippi, the Huey P. Long bridge at New Orleans; wherever you go, this state was built under the regime of Huey Pierce Long. He built Charity Hospital, he put LSU on the map, he passed old age pensions. Maybe he ran a police state, but that is not quite the issue. I have great doubt if I could have lived in the state when he was governor, but at the same time the material benefits which he gave the people of Louisiana can not just be sloughed aside. And look at the history of Louisian politics after him. I have noted two men who were perhaps above the herd, Sam Jones and John McKeithen, but I doubt that anyone would suggest the present incumbent [Edwin Edwards] is a great gain over Huey in integrity or any thing else. And he's not as smart. Huey was never under indictment. And if he'd lived until 1980, he still wouldn't have been.

WP: When did you go to law school?

JWC: I quit teaching at Loyola and entered Tulane law school in 1972, graduated in seventy-five, and then practiced from seventy-five through seventy-eight, when we got a call to come do TV for about ten times what I was making at Loyola. It just seemed to me that common sense said that temporarily at least it was a step I ought to be taking. But I'm still a lawyer. I would not fail to pay my bar dues.

WP: I think that two or three of your short novels about lawyers are your best work. I think that one of the glories of American literature has always been its short novels.

JWC: I've always wondered why people didn't reprint *The Long March*, you know, get Styron when he could still write. That was a fine piece of work. Faulkner's *Old Man* part of *The Wild Palms*. I agree with you. The novella has been an enormously successful form, between eighty and 150 pages, something around there. But let me tell you something: commercial publishers will print Campbell Soup can labels before they'll publish those. Thank God for the university presses for those of us who just happen to love the form. Right now, I have three or four books that have to be considered novellas. Forget it, they're not going to be published commercially. One is called *All My Trials*, which is about a

Shreveport judge, whose wife dies and he retires hoping to go and read Berlioz's memoirs and to listen to symphonic music until the Lord comes for him too. But getting out of the world is not that easy. So things begin to happen. No commercial publisher will touch it. The University of Arkansas Press is looking at it. So what you get is a situation where, if what you want is a literary tradition, the kind that Horace Liveright and Edward Aswell, and Max Perkins and people of that sort kept going back in the twenties, it will now have to be the responsibility of the university presses. And that's all right with me—so long as you get the right kind of people reading the manuscripts. I think you need someone a little harder-edged than the usual academic committee.

WP: There used to be a lot of magazines that published stories and even short novels, but there're not many left anymore.

JWC: The reading public isn't there. I wonder if there will be a reading public of any sort in another twenty years. When I see young men and women look at me with stars in their eyes and say, "my God, you wrote *Boxcar Bertha*, that's the art form I want to practice," I tell them, I wrote it for thirty thousand bucks, I think it's crap, and their little hearts break. If that is art, what in the name of God do you call *Tom Jones*? It's like calling Walter Lippmann a great political philosopher. What the hell do you call Plato? (Laughs.) It's like calling contemporary rock and roll great art. We're facing a generation that doesn't realize that the stuff they're listening to is not in the same world with what we were looking at and listening to twenty years ago. Listen to Chuck Berry. It sounds like he just recorded it two hours ago. It still has a clarity, a cleanness of line, and the stuff you're listening to today sounds like somebody's breaking the guitar. Twenty years ago, Procal Harum, the Band, Creedence Clearwater were creating splendid American folk music, and today my son is listening to garbage. (Laughs.) Who knows? Maybe it's just my age.

WP: In your verbal facility, your interest in music, your love of James Joyce, your writing for films and television, and your Catholicism, the writer you most remind me of is Anthony Burgess.

JWC: I don't like his work at all. I remember *A Clockwork Orange* made me both uncomfortable and angry.

WP: He writes too much.

JWC: There's a funny thing about writing too much. *Shad Sentell* was in my mind for ten years during which I wrote only short stories. I was having an academic battle at Loyola part of the time, I had family problems part of the time, and I went to law school part of the time, but when I finally wrote it, it took me four months. It's two and a half times longer in the original version than in the poor, butchered version that was published. The original name of the book was *The Man Who Slept With Women*. The publisher looked at the first draft and claimed I'd written too much.

WP: I meant to ask you about the relationship between that story and the novel.

JWC: That was to be the name of the novel from day one. There is no more psychologically painful thing than to have a book in your mind and to write it and to have a publisher say, no, you can't use that title. But I hear that the Englishpaper back is reverting to the original title. As I said earlier, I still have to write the middle volume of the Sentell trilogy. The funny thing to me was that of all the reviews of *Shad Sentell*, some good, some bad, mostly treating it as a good old boy romp, no one recognized that the book is virtually scene by scene from line one to the end as a paraphrase of *Don Giovanni*.

WP: Did they say, this is too long a book?

JWC: Yes, they wanted to keep the price down. I tell you that the size of that book was dictated down to the last word that I was forced to cut from it in order to get the son of a bitch down to fifteen-ninety-five. At a dollar more, I could have had a hundred more pages, or fifty more pages. What you read was cut precisely for the price the book would sell at.

WP: I think of the book as a romance, a tale of high adventures, larger than life characters, that sort of thing.

JWC: I'd think a reader who was even semi-educated would say sooner or later, holy mackerel, this is *Don Giovanni*. Do you remember the scene where Sonny (who obviously is Leporello) goes through the book singing, and the young girl Cissie is saying, this man, I think, is my father, and here is this incredibly vulgar book in which he keeps not only the names and addresses of these women and where their husbands work and when they come home, and exact details, including ratings on how they conduct themselves in certain sexual activities.

WP: And numerical designations as to anatomical endowments and that sort of thing.

JWC: Precisely. The catalogue scene in *Shad* is *Don Giovanni*. Jo said, look, everybody doesn't know opera, and I said, you're right, I didn't know it until I was about forty years old. I should be less demanding. But damn it, it makes the novel move.

WP: I reviewed a book by Charles Willeford a few years ago called *Cockfighter*, and he wrote to me and we had a little correspondence, and he said, of course, you recognized that I based the book on *The Odyssey*, and of course I hadn't recognized that at all.

JWC: Since that had already been done, I thought I'd stay away from *The Odyssey*. (Laughs.) Of course, the whole point was that I didn't settle with the opera. I just realized that Shad in many ways had the same character as Don Giovanni which is to say a certain endearing character. In the end, you remember that Don Giovanni goes down like a trooper. He doesn't scream out for grace and mercy. You remember the passage at the end where E. M. Sentell says to Shad, give me your hand—"dammi la mano in pegno"—this parallels the scene with the statue right at the end of the opera where Don Giovanni is dragged into hell, and that was the way the novel was going to end with the explosion on the oil derrick, and Jo said, no, Don Giovanni was a Spanish count: he'd go to hell, Shad would figure a way out. And I said, you're absolutely right.

WP: Considering the kind of character he was, I fully expected him to return, and I would have been disappointed if he had not.

JWC: I said to her, you're perfectly right that all of the rednecks in the Western world have studied the Alamo carefully and decided that wasn't the best way to do it. I remember the greatest redneck line I ever hear was delivered at the beginning of *Patton*: It's not for you to go out there and die for your country; you want to make those other sonsabitches die for their country. (Laughs.) I saw it in Shreveport and the whole theater went up. They loved it. One Alamo every two hundred years is plenty. And when you add Appomattox on top of that, it's about time that that sort of stuff stops. Vietnam isn't offset by Grenada.

WP: I read in a *TLS* review that the Argentine victory was already the most written about episode in British history since World War II. Apparently, a small victory is a victory nonetheless.

JWC: By the way, the *TLS* review of *Shad* was incredible. It wasn't long, but the guy at the end says, the only way one can characterize this novel is: "Mark Twain with his pants down, or *Dallas* with its style up."

WP: How did it sell?

JWC: It was selling well enough until the publisher went out of business. He went into bankruptcy; I think he took chapter eleven. He owes me three thousand bucks.

WP: What happened to all the books he had? I assume he had some.

JWC: That's what I'm trying to find out. I said, look, I will be happy to take the money you owe me in books, but I'm slammed into the situation of being a creditor. I've been watching the Publishers Central Bureau to see if the book is being remaindered.

WP: Have there been any translations of your works?

JWC: You can believe this or not, but the first one is up coming. *Shad* has been purchased and is being translated into Dutch. I was offered a copy of the galleys to check to make sure that the Dutch translation was correct, but I told them I thought I'd pass on that.

WP: Madison Jones showed me a copy of a translation of *An Exile* into Japanese.

JWC: Did he find it an acceptable translation? (Laughs.) *The Actes and Monuments* is going to be translated into Spanish in Argentina, and they asked me if I would check the proofs on that, and I said, I can read scholarly Spanish, but not idiomatic Spanish and certainly not Argentinian idiomatic Spanish.

WP: So recognition seems to be coming?

JWC: It seems to be coming. The situation now with Viking is—I had always said, look, I can do better than Hammett or Chandler, I was a police reporter for two years in a very tough red neck town back when it was a very mean place, I know as much as they did, maybe more, I got better style and these books are finally not about real people. Oddly enough, the nearest to a real person always struck me as being Mike Hammer because the passions that he felt are much more clearly delineated by Mickey Spillane than in the other books. I said, it's a great American genre, the detective story, and I want to try one, and not only did it work, but when Viking bought it, the Senior Editor says, there's no re-writing to do. (1985)

Chapter 7
"The Language Instructs You": An Interview with Madison Jones

Madison Jones is a careful writer who has built a large reputation upon a comparatively small body of work. His first novel, *The Innocent* (1957), set in Tennessee during the 1930's, is the somber tale of the disintegration of a man who vows revenge when his hopes of building an empire around a magnificent stud horse come to grief. *Forest of the Night* (1960) is a frontier novel about a man who falls in love with a woman belonging to the legendary Harpes family. Although not an historical novel in the usually accepted sense, the book presents a vivid picture of frontier life. Jones's third novel and his longest, *A Buried Land* (1963), is a grim tale of retribution centered, like James Dickey's later *Deliverance*, around the flooding of vast areas of land in the name of progress. It is the story of a man who finds that even the waters of the vast dam cannot hide his guilty secret.

With his fourth novel, *An Exile* (1967), Jones became one of the South's important novelists. Published complete in *The Sewanee Review* before it appeared in book form, AN EXILE was widely admired and was filmed by John Frankenheimer under the title, *I Walk the Line* (1969). *A Cry of Absence* (1973) was hailed by Allen Tate and Andrew Lytle, among others, as a masterpiece. Set during the civil rights struggle of the 1960's, it is the story of a woman who defends the old ways without realizing the contrdictions they embody in her two sons, one of whom is involved in a racial murder.

Passage Through Gehenna (1978) is the first of Jones's novels to make his religious preoccupations the center of the plot. Judd Rivers, Jones's protagonist, must fight clear of the extremes of religious fanaticism and hatred of religion to achieve his own identity. It is Jones's most problematic novel and his most hopeful. *Season of the Strangler* (1982), although called a novel by the publisher, is actually a book of short stories set in a small Southern town in 1969 and unified by the fear of the serial killer who haunts the town and its citizens. Characters appear and disappear from one story to another; the strangler never appears, but he is present in every story.

My discussion with Madison Jones begins in his office on the top floor of a new building at Auburn University, where he is now contemplating retirement after lengthy service as Writer-in-Residence, and continues at his home. The contrast between the two places where Jones writes could hardly be more marked; the first is functional and cold, the second warm, filled with books, and lived in.

Jones answers my questions slowly and thoughtfully. His voice is so soft that I check the tape recorder from time to time to make sure that I am picking it up. The door and the window of his office are open and voices drift in from outside.

WP: How did you become interested in writing. I assume that Donald Davidson and the group at Vanderbilt had something to do with it.

MJ: I guess that insofar as anybody outside of myself had to do with it, it would be Donald Davidson. I really had very little idea of any such thing when I came to Vanderbilt. I had never had any academic inclinations at all really and wasn't even much of a student. I came to Vanderbilt and still wasn't much of a student and quit for a while. But I came back and finally I got the idea that I would like to write. Then I took courses under Davidson, and he gave me a lot of encouragement. That kicked me off really. He was the authority outside that told me I was good. It's like everything else.If you think you can do something well, you start to do it. I went to the University of Florida because Andrew Lytle was down there; that was his first, maybe his second year there, and I did a year under him, and then I couldn't get a job with an M.A., and so I stayed on and did the Ph.D. work. I never did the dissertation; I wrote *The Innocent* instead, but not while I was there. For the last two years I was in graduate school, I really didn't write at all. I didn't have much time.

WP: What field were you working on a Ph.D. in?

MJ: I had a dissertation subject that was sort of picked at random, Arnold Bennett. I was going to do the French influence on Arnold Bennett. I wasn't really equipped to do a dissertation like that. I didn't have enough French. But I didn't spend much time on it. Instead, I got seriously to work on *The Innocent* after I got out of graduate school. I wish I had submitted it for a dissertation. Later, they told me they would have taken it, but they didn't tell me at the time.

WP: *The Innocent* seems to be an unusual first novel, since it does not seem to be at least in any obvious way based on personal experience.

MJ: Well, it's the most personal of all my books in certain important ways. That's based on a place north of Nashville, about twenty-five miles north of Nashville, Cheatham County, Tennessee. Did you ever hear of Cheatham County? Ashland City? Anyway, it was a beautiful farm that my father owned, a very isolated place surrounded by high bluffs, and the book was, I think, I hope, a picture of the place. It was based on that actual place. The horse that is so central in the book was a horse my father owned. The colored family on the place, well they weren't really like those in the book, mostly, but they were based on those people. I lived up there for a couple of years by myself. There were two families on the place but not very close to the house I lived in. There were certain incidents such as, if you remember, when the hero Duncan Welsh goes to look for a sire for the mare, that old man who owned the horse, part Indian. He was a man I had met who lived back over across the Cumberland River. A great many things in the book are based on actual places and people. In a very vague sort of way, the isolation of the characters was partly mine. And so it was the most autobiographical in a literal sense of any of my novels. The killings and all of that sort of violent business in the book did not happen, but a great many things were paralleled by circumstances that I encountered in my career there.

WP: I think it's a very dark book. Do you think of it as naturalistic?

MJ: (Pause.) I guess so. You mean in the technical sense of extreme realism?

WP: In the influence of heredity and environment?

MJ: Yeah, yeah, I suppose so. I didn't think quite in those terms. I don't think most novelists do. I was just telling the story. If the story doesn't accrue a certain amount of meaning, I think I, and most novelists, lose interest. It's the action, the on-going action, that's always been the thing that seized my interest. Questions of whether something is naturalistic or surrealistic or anything else hardly have crossed my mind in the course of writing. I don't theorize about it.

WP: What about literarty influences? Faulkner of course was very big at that time. What about Robert Penn Warren's *Night Rider*, books like that?

MJ: I had of course read some Warren and some Faulkner, and I think they certainly did have some influence upon me. Conrad I think did. And most of all Dostoevsky. I don't know whether that was the deepest of the literary influences I had, but probably it was. Certainly by the time I had gotten to my second and third novels. By that time it certainly was, though if I had to name a writer who had the most lasting influence on me, it would be Moses. When I was a child my grandfather used to read the Bible stories to me. Those were the stories I knew best, the ones that made the biggest impression on me. That was likely the strongest literary influence I ever had. I think that the very early influences are the ones that really count.

WP: I think I can see the influence of Dostoevsky in almost all your novels in the process of working out the psychological processes of a character who has done something that he shouldn't have done.

MJ: That has been an abiding sort of interest of mine. It's there in Doestoevsky, of course, and I suppose a great part of my interest in Dostoevsky is simply that his preoccupations were, and are, also mine. I was very religiously raised, puritanically raised, and conscience and theological questions were big factors in my early life, and things like guilt were natural subjects for fiction. In this same line, of course, Hawthorne got to be important. Certain stories, for instance, "Young Goodman Brown," I always felt a strong kinship with.

WP: Did you do any research for *Forest of the Night*?

MJ: I did a little, I suppose you'd say superficial research. I read up on the fundamental matters. I had to know of course what sort of food did the pioneers eat, what sort of clothes did they wear, what the appurtenances of daily life were, and what ever. I read for those purposes and just as background. I didn't really feel that I needed or wanted to saturate myself in the life of the frontier. I always felt that, up there in Cheatham County where I lived in the late thirties, I was very close to the frontier even then. Some of the people I knew had been raised in the woods back over across from the Cumberland River. They were raised in log cabins where there were no electric lights or anything like that. I knew one such family very well and a man who told me a great deal about that life. As a child he had worn the old frontier style garment, a wampus, they called it. I always felt that I had the essence of what the frontier was like. I did some reading about it, but I didn't do thorough research.

WP: I assume it's actually true that they did cut the ears off of some criminals.

MJ: Oh, yes. That was very common. I had of course read about that. The Harpes, if you remember in *Forest of the Night*, are written about by several historians of the American frontier. There was a lot of that kind of thing, cutting off of ears and other physical dismemberment performed on criminals.

WP: What about the girl Judith? She's an interesting character. Where did she come from?

MJ: She's based on a woman who lived with the Harpes, who actually was a Knoxville preacher's daughter. The Harpe brothers themselves really are background—or maybe enveloping action—in the book. Well, they're used as kind of ghosts actually. There's not very much known about them. One of them was caught and executed; the other was supposed to have escaped, and nobody knew what became of him. The girl apparently did just return to civilization and marry somebody and live a respectable life, but she, along with a couple of other women, had belonged to the Harpes and was pretty often seen with them around through the Tennessee wilderness. The Natchez trace, etc. Of course, I used that in the book, and worked my hero against the ghostly background of the Harpes. So that much is factual. (Pause.) That's a book that in a way I should have written later. I've never been entirely satisfied with it, especially the last part. I think I rushed myself and went on and finished the book before I was prepared to finish it. I should have waited to see just how to bring off the last part. I think that the fact that there's sort of a skip in time about two-thirds of the way through signals the fact that there's something I skipped over that should have been there. I've always felt that if I had waited a while I could have made a much better book out of it as a whole, though I still like it. But I've always felt that of all the ideas I ever took up, that could have been the most fruitful for me.

WP: In spite of that, the scene where the girl comes back to Jonathan, the protagonist, and he realizes that apparently she really thinks he's Wiley Harpe, is extremely powerful.

MJ: I'm glad to hear that. That book's always had a place in my heart. I worked on it very hard. It embodies the Hawthornesque situations that always fascinated me, especially when I was younger. You know, the dark forest. Now that book approaches, what would you say, the surreal in some ways.

WP: Who published those two books? It wasn't listed in my paperbacks.

MJ: Harcourt, Brace.

WP: I think that your style is the main thing that has changed, not your preoccupations. It seems to me that your earlier books have a more violent style. You've moved toward an understated, more classical style. Is that your perception?

MJ: Yes. I think that in *Forest of the Night* I was aiming at a rich style, physically speaking. In details and elaborateness and rhythmical preoccupations, it's the book of mine which is most so. As I went on, I began to feel that it was a little too ornate, that things ought to be said more simply—and especially in the last ten years or so, I've simplified even further and moved toward understatement. In a book I'm working on, I have moved back to the first person simply because it relaxes my fiction more, my style more. I've definitely simplified my prose. I don't know what that means in metaphysical or psychological terms, but that's been my tendency, to go back to a simple conversationsal style. There's much more of the conversational style in *Season of the Strangler*. I got one very bad review of that book, and that was one of the points brought up, that it had no style. . .

WP: Stupid.

MJ: ...and he cited *A Cry of Absence* and said that one had style, but this one didn't because it was just like flat talk, and he gave examples and so on.

WP: I think the only thing wrong with *Season of the Strangler* was that it presented a marketing problem that the publishers weren't quite prepared to deal with. They didn't know how to sell it. They didn't know whether they were selling a novel or a book of short stories, and they always have been uncomfortable with books like that.

MJ: I made a strategic error, I think, with that book. In the first place, I never should have let them call it a novel, you know, on the jacket and so on. And I should have found some way in the introductory piece and in the epilogue, probably in the epilogue, to indicate that this figure of the strangler was not something that the reader ought to get to work on and find out what metaphysical or sociological role he was supposed to discover that was beyond what the individual stories have to say about fear and crisis and so on. Some readers were likely to be put off by saying: what does this strangler mean in himself? Maybe I put the readers to looking for something that's beyond what the individual stories have to say about fear and crisis.

WP: Did you ever consider putting the strangler in the book either overtly or covertly, hiding him there somewhere?

MJ: No, but I had an editor who did, the editor who accepted the book for Doubleday. I had shown him three or four stories—I wasn't at that time finished with the book—and those stories were ones that were more closely interrelated. Like the two about black people. He had the idea that they were all going to be more tightly interrelated than they are. He was full of plans for me, such as having the strangler coming in and out of the book and having a policeman, a detective, pursuing him through the stories, and so on. I nixed all that. He wanted me to make it into, I don't know what, a television series, I guess. He was thinking about that. Very recently, what started me thinking about this was that I sent a copy of it to Robert Penn Warren. I did so because he had written me about an essay I had written on his novels, and he said he admired my fiction and hadn't read this book. So I sent it to him. He had very nice things to say, but then he had a final thing to say. It was that he was not sure he understood the book as a whole. Meaning what I'm talking about, putting it all together in terms of the strangler and what the strangler means in terms of all the different stories. Uniting the whole book, every story, under a single thematic statement, like a novel.

WP: I think that your first books, particularly *Forest of the Night*, are very much like Warren, particularly *World Enough and Time*, but your later books are entirely different. I don't much believe in originality, but I think *Season of the Strangler* is just about as original as a book can be, and I think it's very unfortunate that it's not better known.

MJ: It got mightly little press. I was very much disappointed. I'm getting along in years, and to have it pretty much sit there after it had been published was not an encouraging development. It got some reviews. It got an awfully good one from the *Los Angeles Times*, of all places. But the big places in the east didn't respond at all. And that's where you've got to get on. For all our talk about the great Southern renaissance, the Southern revival, and all the just pride we take in Southern literary accomplishments over the last generation, we still sit and wait to see what the Yankees are going to say before we start liking anybody. And if the East doesn't praise somebody, you can be pretty sure he won't have any reputation in the South. That is still where it's at, I'm afraid.

WP: *A Buried Land* has the situation you often have in your novels, the working out of a crime or misdeed, but here you also have the metaphor—and which of course was not just metaphor but reality, that you have in Dickey's *Deliverance* or in the Elia Kazan film, *Wild River*—of the dam refugees.

MJ: That of course gave a chance to my Dostoevskian interests. Once again that took place in the same place, in that farm in Cheatham County I was telling you about. They didn't really have a big dam in that area. They did put a small dam on the Cumberland river along there, the the water did cover a little bit of property, just enough to suggest one of those giant developments you see on the Tennessee. That of all my books is probably the one that most delights the people of agrarian inclinations. Dan Young of Vanderbilt was through here about a week ago and read a paper here, a rather long paper that's to be published somewhere in Ohio, and he has a long section on that book. I'm sure that of my books that's the one that Dan most likes, because it's the one that most fulfills Donald Davidson's ideas about agrarian values and the consequences of burying the past. I still have agrarian interests, but at that time I was more ideologically persuaded and strong on the matter. That's the one that conservative and agrarian types like me best for. It was never my favorite because I was dealing with a main character who was pretty cold-blooded, and it was hard for me to feel much about him, and perhaps for that reason I remember the book in detail less well than any book I've written. When Dan read that paper here, he gave a rather thorough description of it, I was astonished to hear mention of significant parts I had no memory of, and I don't think that would be true of my other books. Not so much, anyway.

WP: I interviewed Shirley Ann Grau, and I can honestly say she hardly remembers some of her books. And of course Faulkner in his older years was an extremely poor critic of his own work. He didn't remember it.

MJ: He had an awful lot of it for one thing, and you get so often the sense of his having written it without quite knowing what he was doing anyway. You know how he gets going sometimes. You almost feel that he's ridden by his genius, and I suspect the intricacies of so much of Faulkner would redouble the difficulties of recalling.

WP: *An Exile* certainly is straightforward and gives the appearance of simplicity. I think *A Cry of Absence* gives that appearance too, but it only appears to be simple; it's actually a very complicated work artistically, the working out of the different points of view, the characters, and the contrasts between the characters.

MJ: I think *An Exile* is certainly the simplest. What gave me that idea was *Carmen*. It's certainly not very much like *Carmen*, of course, except for the archetypal situation of the good though flawed just man who meets the femme fatale. I translated it into that same Cheatham County locale and also into terms of past and present which have run throughout my work, but it is a simple plot. *A Cry of Absence*, if I remember correctly, was based on an anecdote that I wish I'd recorded. I don't remember it for sure now. I think that's my best book. It's the book that I feel, and felt, most deeply about, coming as it did out of the long ordeal of the sixties, and that was very intense as I'm sure you well know all over the South. Certainly it was as intense here as anywhere. We were right in the middle of a lot of it. I had a great emotional stake in it, and I'm glad I didn't write about it in the sixties when it was still at its greatest intensity. I wrote about it too late from the standpoint of its interest to the book buyer because there had been so many books that centered on racial conflict. But I waited until I had a little objectivity in the matter. It is still an important book to me because I had always thought of myself as writing about the South even though when you read a book like *Forest of the Night*, you might ask, what has that got to do with the South? I had always thought of myself, at least through the first five books as a defender of the South and of its ideas of itself, that sometimes took the form of attacking ideas that I felt were hostile to those that the South in my mind embodied. For instance, Jonathon Cannon in *Forest of the Night* is an enlightenment liberal who doesn't believe in essential evil. He goes forth into the wilderness where there's no dead hand of the past, where the Noble Savage is and everything is perfectible. It's the enlightenment vision of the nature of man as inherently good, and I meant the book as a sort of attack on this idea. Because I saw it as the essence of modern liberalism that was ravaging the natural traditional life of the South. This was a defense by attacking an opposite position. I thought of my books in this sort of a way then. Maybe I still do. *A Cry of Absence* was right in the middle of what I thought of even then, and think I was correct in thinking now, that the sixties were the South's last outcry, the last concrete expression of the South's fundamental difference, figured in terms of racial separation and so on. After that, there wasn't much of significance left to distinguish the South from the North. The sixties were the edge of the cliff, so to speak. I was very caught up the in whole business, and that book is the one that most contains my emotions, though I tried to objectify them as best I could.

WP: Garner, the preacher in *The Innocent*, who is a believer in social progress, struck me as being very up to date. The world seems to have come back round to him with all we hear about liberation theology and that sort of thing.

MJ: Yeah, yeah, I remember those arguments between Duncan Welsh and his brother in law Garner. Yeah, I guess so. It's the working out of the kind of idea Garner had to its final logical conclusion. Liberation theology is getting rid of the old cobwebs and old ghosts of the past, the supernaturalism and all the kinds of things that that point of view thinks simply make religion childish and oppressive. The opiate of Neanderthals.

WP: When rereading *A Cry of Absence*, I had the feeling that Handley was sort of a mirror image of Hester at times. Did you intend that?

MJ: No, but I've done that all the way through, not just in that book. It didn't start out to be so and until recent years never was entirely conscious. Those are doubles, doppelgangers, and I wasn't even aware of them for a long time. Maybe I had thought of it before, but Paul Binding, an Englishman, who wrote a book called *Separate Country*, published several years ago, and who went around and visited various Southern writers, pointed out the doppelganger theme in my books. I wasn't really conscious of it, but it's always been there; for instance Aaron was a doppelganger of Duncan Welsh, in *The Innocent*, and the Harpes are doppelgangers of Jonathan Cannon in *Forest of the Night*. I think I could probably locate it in *A Buried Land* too; it's been an important though essentially unconscious theme pretty well all the way through. I've got one in the book I'm working on now, but I'm much more conscious of it. It's still about the conflict of old and new, except that the old is not much in evidence in this book. It's represented simply by the last cry of an old lady who's got wise to the drug racketeers in town. The hero, a red necked boy in town, has a very dark doppelganger. I'm much more conscious of the theme now. I don't know how the book's going to come out, but I never do. I really *don't* know how my books are going to come out. I don't even know usually what I'm going to do after about fifty or one-hundred pages.

WP: In spite of that, your books have a very clear, a very firm, almost classical structure.

MJ: Well, I hope so, but it isn't because I pre-planned. I'm incapable of planning a book. I wish I was, because my procedure leads to all kinds of anxiety in writing a book. Am I going to be able to think what to do next? Somebody used the image of driving at night. You only can see as far as the headlights extend in the dark, and that's pretty well the way I write. It leads to all kinds of distress, because sometimes it doesn't work out. I started a novel which was intended to be a new version of *Forest of the Night*. I wanted to write it again and get it right. I started a couple of years ago, wrote about seventy-five or eighty pages and then got bored. It was something I'd already done. My boredom was what brought me to the point finally that I didn't know what to do. It's got to be something with obsessive power enough to keep your imagination working into the future. Anyway, I stopped that and put it away, and I started a second book. I wrote about sixty pages and thought, well, I can't go on with this. So, I translated it and gave lead roles to some minor figures and wrote a hundred more pages of that book that way, and though I was fairly interested, I just didn't see how I could go on with it, either. So I went back to the second one, and this time it came alive, after my having reworked it from this other point of view. At least it seems to me alive at this point. I'm very tentative about making claims because I've had this terrible experience of having one glorious week and then the next one saying, oh, my God, it was all an illusion, a terrible mistake. If I only could do what Henry James could do, sit down and outline the thing and even be in possession of individual scenes a hundred, two-hundred pages into an unwritten book. I can't begin to do that.

WP: That's astonishing. I think of your novels in terms of a very tight, classical structure, almost foreordained in some ways.

MJ: Well, I build them with great care. It's like building a building. I lay out a situation that I feel has enough complexity to carry an idea, but I invent directions for it to take as I go, and I try to have clearly enough in mind the psychological conditions that make inevitable the next development and not just let things happen unless they're very tightly related to what went before. When I'm successful, then there is the kind of organic relationship that I want there to be, but it's not because of pre-planning. I even have a hard time thinking about a book until I sit right there. I have to be looking at the page to do my fruitful thinking. I can think about it some from a distance, but it mostly comes from fooling with the language itself.

WP: In a sense, all of your books are historical novels. They're all set in the past.

MJ: At least a few years into the past. This one will be the least that way.

This one will be right up to date. I've always avoided being right up to date because I've never wanted to get caught up in topical types of situations which would cause the reader to bring the test of history, the test of present history, against them. That seems to me to limit imaginative re-creation, to be faced with the fact that say, this social problem prevails right now, and you're dealing with it, you're dealing with fixed fact that your imagination has got to accept rather than create. You push it away somewhere into the background. You take the reader's eye off it, you change the reader's feelings about it, he can't judge it, estimate it, guage it, against whatever actual situation prevails at the moment. He can't say, he didn't get that right, for instance, or that's not the way it really happens nowadays. But if you move it back, you have that kind of freedom to recreate at a distance which makes it possible to make it your own rather than a picture of literal present-day circumstances. I may have been a little excessive about this trying not to introduce current, real, close-to-hand situations and images. This new book is partly about drugs, which are used here to dramatize the loss of the self. For the first time, I think, I'm in the middle of material that's immediately contemporary, the narcotics business. I even use for the first time another book about the drug trade. A few years ago, down at Hurtsboro, Alabama, they caught a big DC 4 landing on a country airstrip carrying about fifteen or twenty thousand pounds of marijuana from Columbia. A fellow did a lot of research on it, and I am using his book to make pictures of something going on right under our noses that the old lady in my book is horrified by. This book is much closer to present history, something I've avoided in the past, but I think maybe a small reason for my lack of popularity has been that my books are not as much involved in the immediately identifiable as most books are.

WP: I think that in order to be really popular you have to publish a book every one or two or three years to keep your name constantly in front of the public. I realize of course that there are a few exceptions like Styron, or people like that, but there aren't many.

MJ: Well, of course, when William Styron publishes a book, it gets so much notice that it lasts a long time. I wish I had published more. It isn't because of laziness. Books got harder for me after *A Cry of Absence*, partly because I think that my theme had been pulled out from under me—you know, the South. That may be part of the reason. It becomes harder I think to write when you continue to feel not much of a sense of an audience.

WP: As you know, when Frankenheimer came to film *An Exile*, he was considered by many to be one of the most important active American film directors. Unfortunately, his films of the seventies and eighties did not bear out that judgment, but I still think, in certain respect, *I Walk the Line* is one of the better film versions of an American novel.

MJ: When I first saw it, I think I had the kind of response that most authors have when they see something they wrote put on the screen. It's just a totally different medium, but I to this day can't help but regret that he reduced it, or that the screen writer did, I suppose with his approval, to the purely sociological. The bad guy McCain, the father of Alma whom the sheriff falls for, is really not a bad guy. He just does what a poor man has got to do, he's got to step outside the law. So here the people of the movie are caught in a socio-economic conflict, and I don't like to think of my books as being based on conflicts of that kind. I like to think that they are based on much more universally human dilemmas and problems, and that they have application to the permanent in human experience. Poor and rich are important matters, but they are not the sole explanation of why people do bad and good things. And I certainly didn't want to see the book get reduced to that.

WP: Frankenheimer apparently doesn't like the film. I've read this story that whenever he sees Gregory Peck, he says, "I owe you one." Still, movie directors tend to see success and failure solely in terms of box office receipts. I think there is a lot to admire about the film. I think that was one of Peck's very best roles. The conflict between the flesh and his stern puritan rectitude make him perfect. And Tuesday Weld is marvelous.

MJ: I admit it had a lot of good things about it. And of course the woman who played the wife of the sheriff, Estelle Parsons, was awfully good. She was brilliant, I thought. I just wish that they had asked me to participate in writing the screen play. I would have fought hard to keep the idea that McCain was a vicious and evil person, even a devilish person, and not just a poor guy who has got to use his daughter.

WP: Have you written any screenplays?

MJ: Well, I wrote one for *A Cry of Absence*, but they never made it. It's still in existence. It belongs to Harold Cohen in Hollywood.

WP: Is there any chance that will ever get published? There are many screeplays by important writers that haven't been published.

MJ: He owns it, but I have the right to buy it back for $2500.00. I went to Palm Springs and stayed a while and wrote that screenplay. It's a good screenplay. I got a letter later from a guy at Paramount saying that it was a shame that they had not gone ahead at the time and mounted the picture, that Harold Cohen hadn't, but there were several things that kept it from being made. I think one of them was just the general fact that a lot of those racial movies had been made and most of them had been flops. This followed those. I understand that at one time Patricia Neal, a fine actress, signed up for the part but that because of problems they wouldn't insure her. And then I got a rather bad review in *Time* magazine about the time I was out in Palm Springs. That producer is a man of little faith, and I think the review among other things soured it for him. Two or three other people projected around with it, including the Fitzgerald boys, who did the Huston version of Flannery O'Connor's *Wise Blood*, and various other films.

WP: *Passage Through Gehenna*, when I read it, struck me as a critique of various fundamentalist religious attitudes. I thought that for the first time you were trying to come to grips with different points of view concerning the effects of the different fundamentalist religious groups. I realize of course that that had been at least a minor theme in all your earlier works.

MJ: I don't know. I don't think that was my intention. That's another one I'm a little bit fuzzy about. I worked so hard on that book. I wrote the first part and threw it away, then I started it differently, then started in another way, then went back to the first way, and rewrote it and took it on from there. So it took me a long time, between throwing things away and changing my mind. But I don't remember thinking of it as a critique of that sort. I don't know how successful that is, maybe because the woman, Lily, who owned the hardware store and who is the hero's femme fatale, may not be completely convincing. I think of the book as the story of a young man who, in his puritanical transport, is carried away by visions of beauty. I don't really know how to state the book. The woman Hannah, the woman who dies, is supposed to be something very hard to handle, a good woman, and she is destroyed by Lily, who is supposed to be Lilith, the first wife of Adam, who hates children. Judd is in rebellion against his faith. I'm going to have to sit down sometime and formulate in my mind exactly how to talk about this book. I'm not very good at talking about it.

WP: Judd, it seems to me, is the only one of your protagonists who, at the end of the book, seems to me to be on the right road. He's come through it, whatever it was. I thought of that as your most hopeful book.

MJ: Yeah, I think it is. I intended that he had learned what he should have learned out of experience.

WP: To be perfectly honest, it also seemed to me to be your most problematical book.

MJ: A good many people don't like it. Many do, though. It has its enthusiasts. I think maybe that if it's not too good a book, it was because I didn't know how to handle the Lilith figure.

WP: How did that come to be published by LSU Press?

MJ: Well, I had sent it—or rather my agent had—to a couple of houses, and at one point I thought it had been accepted, and it wasn't, and I got disgusted with fooling with it. So I wrote to LSU and asked them if they would be interested. At that time, they hadn't published any new fiction, and they said that they would, and so I sent it on to them and solved the problem.

WP: As you know, the publishing business is such now that writers who spend all their careers with one press are sort of vanishing birds.

MJ: I certainly have had a checkered career in that respect. Harcourt, Brace published my first two. Viking published my next two. Crown published my next one. LSU my next one. Doubleday my next one.

WP: Was David McDowell the editor at Crown when you were published there?

MJ: He was on *A Cry of Absence*. A good editor, too. I guess the best I ever had, the most attentive and the hardest working, not only in editing the book, but also in promoting it. He worked very hard promoting that book. I don't know why it didn't do better than it did. It did sell more than any of my other books in hardback, but it didn't really build up enough momentum to go on and do something. It sold about seventy-six hundred plus in hardback, which is pretty good for me.

WP: How many of your books have appeared in paperback?

MJ: Well, all of them except the LSU one. *An Exile* was in British Penguin paperback, and I've had a couple of Dutch translations and a Japanese translation of *An Exile*. (Pause.) I wish I'd written more books than I have. I'm a slow writer anyway, and then when I fall into uncertainties and have to keep discarding pieces.... But I think maybe the way I describe myself as writing has something to do with it. Since I can't see my way through ahead of the actual writing, so much of it is trial and error.

WP: You seem to have confined yourself mostly to longer fiction. Did you write short stories in your younger years?

MJ: A few, starting late in my Vanderbilt career and then at Florida in my first year there. I published a few of them. One of them was in Martha Foley's *Best American Short Stories*.

WP: Do you have enough for a book, or are they worth reprinting?

MJ: Two or three of them are. I didn't really write many. I never really thought of the short story as exactly my form. The pieces in *Season of the Strangler* are, I guess, short stories, but they work in a way like a novel by reference to a central situation, that is, by reference to the strangler and to the fear that he generates and the responses to it, which is kind of novelistic in method. But I never really got going on the short story as such.

WP: Have you written much criticism?

MJ: A little, not much. I've avoided doing it. I've rarely done it voluntarily. Usually, when I've written a piece of criticism, it's been because somebody asked me to present a paper at a meeting somewhere. I've twice written pieces of criticism simply because I wanted to. I wrote a little piece of criticism on three Hawthorne short stories many years ago that was published in *Studies in Short Fiction*, and then recently I wrote an essay on Flannery O'Connor's *A Good Man is Hard to Find* for *The Southern Review* last fall [1984]. I published two essays on Robert Penn Warren's fiction, but in both cases, it was because I was asked to do so. That was the one that I was in correspondence with Warren about. He wrote and thanked me for it.

WP: I think that he was a very important fiction writer up through 1950, through *World Enough and Time*, but that there was a sharp decline after that.

MJ: That's generally true, though I made a big point in this essay of the fact that I thought *The Cave* was good. I hadn't formerly thought so, but I reread it and thought very much better of it, and I spent a good part of the essay on it. I think he appreciated that fact, because a writer likes to see one of his novels that hasn't gotten much notice brought to light.

WP: If you don't mind, I'd like to go back to the religious business for a while which fascinates me. We have different opinions about religion. Walker Percy says that the South is "Christ haunted"; Shirley Ann Grau in the interview she did with me said that she can't see any religious influence in the South generally, at least in the current generation. Obviously, it's a question you've gone over and over again in your novels.

MJ: I've thought a lot about it. I was meant to be a religious man. I'm not very, but I'm fascinated by it, and I would say that I'm "Christ haunted," to use I think Flannery O'Connor's term. Yes, very much. I'm a fellow traveller. I read a lot of theology. It's one of my major interests. I just got through reading what I'm sure is one of the most marvellous works of all literature, which I had never read straight through before, the Gospel of Saint Matthew. A marvelous piece of work, quite aside from its religious value. Religious questions have engaged me all my life, even when I ceased—well, I still go to church a lot, mainly because of my wife, who's a Roman Catholic. I always go a lot, and I want to be a participant, but I can't quite believe it.

WP: That's your feeling about Roman Catholicism?

MJ: Protestantism too, for that matter. But if I ever get back my faith, I'll be a Roman Catholic. That would be my preference. I get furious at the fundamentalists, but I'd rather have them around than not have them.

WP: I don't know if I should say this or not, but I sort of felt that that's what you were working toward in *Passage Through Gehenna* and didn't know it.

MJ: You mean working toward believing it?

WP: No, working toward Roman Catholicism.

MJ: I hadn't really thought of it that way. I was raised in effect a fundamentalist, a Presbyterian, and my family were very pious people, clear back as far as I can remember, and I was very pious boy and at one time was even suspected of harboring notions of going into the ministry. That's the way I was when I was young. But I began to weaken. I was raised as a fundamentalist and a literalist. I no longer look at it in that literal way, but without the literalism, it seems to me you're in trouble, particularly when you start raising all the historical questions and so forth. Religion is to me a source of great fascination, and disturbance too. I'm not sure there isn't a literal hell, for instance. That's been my in-between position for a long time. I don't seem to make any progress.

WP: Did Donald Davidson write any fiction at all?

MJ: I don't believe he ever did. Outside of poetry and, you know the history of the Tennessee River, and literary criticism, and social criticism, the only thing I know he ever wrote was an opera, or an operetta, "Singin' Billy." It was performed in Nashville somewhere.

WP: Of course, Lytle has written distinguished fiction.

MJ: He wrote I think four novels. I don't know whether I acquired my deliberate habits of writing partly from Lytle's influence or not. He was very fond of careful construction andof perfecting each page as you went. None of this business of a draft and rewriting maybe ten drafts until you finish the book. I've never done that in my life. When I'm through with a book, I'm pretty well through. I've always tried to perfect each page as I went and not go on and say, "I'll fix that later." He always argued—and I either absorbed it from him or got reinforcement—that you can't put the second story on the first one until the first one is as near perfect as it can be made. The whole story has got to have its development step by step. You've got to find out from the language itself where it goes from here, because you've got the fullness of the thing only when you've perfected the language. You've learned from it what come next. Someone told me or I read it somewhere once that Ransom said that when writing poetry the language itself instructs you. This would be tied in with my idea and with Andrew's that through giving the fullest development to each paragraph, you are instructed in the nature of the next paragraph, and that if you leave it unfinished, you haven't got all the information, as it were, to go from step B to step C.

WP: How much teaching do you do?

MJ: In the Spring quarter, I taught one three-hour course. I'm now in the twilight of my career because I'm going to quit after this year. I'm teaching only about twelve to fifteen hours a year. Creative writing mainly, but also occasionally something else, usually now one of the British survey courses, or Southern lit, or Greek lit in translations.

WP: Have you had any students you would consider talented or promising?

MJ: Well, I've had a number of them that were promising. One boy who was a poet—not that I teach poetry—wrote me a letter thanking me for what I had done for him in a fiction class. I've had some others. The best one I ever had was a local boy named Wallace Watley. He had a piece in *The Southern Review*, Fall, 1984. He's tremendously talented, always was, but I never could do anything for him, he was so hard-headed. He couldn't stand criticism. It's taken him nearly twenty years to learn some things that I think I could have helped him get over within a brief time. Not that I think a creative writing teacher can do a very great deal for his students. But I always felt that I could have been of some use to Wallace, if he hadn't been so outraged at any criticism of what he wrote. But he was very talented, and still is.

WP: With the possible exception of Warren, all the Vanderbilt people seem to be better known as poets or as essayists, but what you seem to be saying is that the principles of writing, whether in poetry or short story or novel, are basically the same.

MJ: Yeah, I think they are very close. I'm sure there are differences I'm not aware of, but the great principle is the principle of economy in both disciplines, both modes: that is, working a piece of language until you have reduced it to a point where it makes words say more than they can say or would say without the close conjunction that you give them by reducing them to their essence. They speak things that they can't speak until they are squeezed together. The same thing applies in prose when you seek the sentence's ultimate expression. When you put it under enough pressure, it begins to say what you yourself hadn't quite thought of when you set out to write it. The same thing applies to a poet when he has an idea and keeps trying to say it in different ways. One stanza, I would think, without ever having experienced it as a poet, instructs him in what the next one should say, or more about what it should say. The compression is the thing, the distinctive thing, in fiction too. Words don't really speak their ultimate until they are put under the pressure of conjunction of other words. Maybe like nuts that have to be cracked. Is that at all clear?

WP: I think I understand it perfectly. (Pause.) What novelists are there around that you like or admire now?

MJ: The first one that comes to mind is James Wilcox.

WP: He's from Hammond, where I teach.

MJ: I'm reading his novel now.

WP: *Modern Baptists*?

MJ: No, the second one, *North Gladiola*. I think Wilcox is a brilliant writer. *North Gladiola* is a second novel, and I think that, as is often the case, people have more trouble with seond novels than with first ones. It was not entirely the case with me, but I think that it's a fairly common development. The second novel is very hard, especially if the first one was good. I feel that in this book he gets too mired in the possible comic situations that arise among the characters in the book, and that he never really develops a uniting theme for the whole, so that it seems simply to go on the same way and then stop. But I haven't read the first, so that I don't know whether that's a weakness that is going to be a constant in his career or not. He is such a brilliant young guy and has such a wonderful eye. His language is fine, and he has wisdom. This story has a whole lot to attract interest and admiration. He might turn out to be something.

WP: Anyone else?

MJ: There's a young fellow named Madison Smartt Bell. I haven't read his second novel, but I've read his first one. He's the son of some old friends of mine in Nashville. He's not quite twenty-eight, and he has published two novels. He sent me the first one, *The Washington Square Ensemble*, and then he sent me the second one, *Waiting For the End of the World*, but I haven't read it yet. The one that I read is not entirely coherent, but again it has a great deal of promise in its brilliant language and in its wonderful dramatic sense.

WP: Could you tell us something about your writing methods?

MJ: I'm not mechanically inclined, and I still don't know how to type, even though I now work on a typewriter. I wrote five novels without even trying to work on a typewriter, and the only reason I tried it then was that I was having a hard time with *Passage Through Gehenna* and just felt like that maybe some new way of doing would help. I thought, what if I tried working on a typewriter, would that make a difference? I started and I've done it ever since. Not that I can type faster than I can think what to put down. When I was younger, I thought that I couldn't possibly write on a typewriter, that it would mess me up, that I needed to be closer to it than that, so I wrote in pencil on a tablet. I wrote on a bed with my back against a couple of pillows. I wrote, and I erased, and I rewrote.

WP: Would you then type a second draft?

MJ: Yeah, I'd type it up after I wrote it. I'd usually finish a chapter and then I'd go back and type it before I'd start another chapter. But it was slow. It would take me two days to type a chapter. I'm really not much better now. I'm a terrible typist. I make a mistake in every line.

WP: Do you have a secretary or a student or somebody who types the final draft?

MJ: I have had that done, but I got shy of that because there were always things I saw that I wanted to change, and then if I had somebody type it for me, I'd have to go back and retype pieces of it and correct mistakes—and typists never know what to do with my spelling. I'm a terrible speller. The girl who typed my first novel didn't think she ever ought to interfere with anything I ever had typed on the page. She misspelled all the words just the way I did. But usually I pick them up when I read it and retype it. I see that "siege" is spelled "ie" and not "ei."

WP: Do you go to the movies much?

MJ: Almost never. I watch a lot of movies on TV.

WP: In reading a lot of books, you sort of have the idea of TV in the background, but that's not in your books. Is that because you came from an earlier period?

MJ: You mean, in the background in the sense of making references to them?

WP: Right. For example, there are a lot of references to them in Doris Betts's *The River to Pickle Beach*. There are references to them on almost every page.

MJ: I've always avoided that sort of thing. I've always had almost a superstitious feeling that once I started referring to current checkable matters—you know, putting the reader into a state of consciousness in which he could call me up on my factual accuracy—that I was moving into a area which limited my ability to create. I don't want the kind of limitations a historian has, and I've always avoided references to current matters, or even metaphors of that kind. I notice in reading Wilcox that he uses metaphors that refer to knowledge of, say, a certain picture show, or a present-day style of something, that a a reader has to be knowledgable about before he can get the import of the metaphor. He's got to have seen this picture show before that metaphor means anything to him, and I still don't like that feeling. The reader has got to know a lot of things, obviously, he's got to know a lot about the world, history, and religion, and all the things that a person ought to know about. But I never felt that I ought to hold him to knowing about current events, or current entertainment, or whatnot. This may be too rarefied a view, and I don't think that I hold to it as firmly as I used to, but I would never, probably still, use a metaphor that required the reader to have seen a popular picture show of the last two or three years.

WP: Have you ever considered writing a Civil War novel?

MJ: I have thought about it. Back during the civil rights crisis, I thought about doing one based on an incident in the Civil War when the Confederate Army massacred some Black troops. But I have enough trouble getting readers anyway, and it has just seemed to me that, at least since the centennial, the Civil War is not something I hear about much. I feel that I would just be creating more trouble for myself by writing about something that the readers aren't much interested in.

WP: Of course, Shelby Foote spent twenty-five years writing his narrative history of the Civil War, but I had the feeling that his novelistic career wasn't doing too well at that time.

MJ: He did a good thing, but I suspect that if he had written and published that now, it wouldn't be nearly as well received. It seems to me that there's just not any interest now, except among some Southerners.

WP: What do you think of Cormac McCarthy?

MJ: I read one book of his some years ago, *The Orchard Keeper*. He's a good writer, but I don't really read much new fiction. As I say, I'm more likely to read theological or philosophical works than fiction. I hear he's very violent.

WP: If you just look at them in the abstract, your books are violent too, if you just summarize the plots.

MJ: Yeah, I guess they are. Well, I have no apology for that. (Laughs.) I'm interested in violence. So often, I feel it's the only possible expression of my theme.

WP: You've been compared to Thomas Hardy. Do you read him?

MJ: I used to. I haven't tried reading him again in a good many years.

WP: I was wondering about the Arnold Bennett connection in your proposed dissertation.

MJ: I did admire *The Old Wives' Tale*, and I'm sure I still would. And he has one other really good one too, *Riceyman Steps*, a late novel, about a miser. That's a good one too. The rest go from mediocre to bad, I think. Generally, though, there are pretty good things in all of them.

WP: I think you're absolutely brilliant in dealing with red-necks. All of your novels have got those hard kind of ingrown, violent, careless people. What were the models for that? Were those based on people you knew?

MJ: I knew a lot of those people. A great deal of my most memorable experience came from Cheatham County life north of Nashville in the hills along the Cumberland River. I knew a lot of those country people. They worked on our farm, some of them, and around town, and so on, and I heard a great deal of talk.

There was one old man, the father of the wife of the man who was the foreman on the place. He was an old timer, and he had come to Ashland City, oh fifty years before, I think, on the run, from somewhere back in Cairo, Illinois. One day, he just sort of broke down and told me he had escaped from prison and killed a guard, he and another fellow, and he had lit out down the river, and that's how he had come to Ashland City. I was crazy about him. He was a wonderful old man, full of old tales. I knew him well, and a lot of others. There was a colored family on the place too. We hired various folks around the country, part-time and in some cases full-time, and then I knew various people around the community. It was a poor county, not really good farming land, most of it. It was poor and backward, and I felt pretty much at home with those people.

WP: In your novels, they often serve the role of tempter, that is, the protagonist maybe knows what he should do, but there is this voice saying, you know, I wouldn't put up with that. As a result the protagonist often chooses the wrong way, as in *The Innocent.*

MJ: Aaron McCool, in *The Innocent*, yeah. Those people are like any other people. There are good ones and bad ones, but it's close to the surface. There's not much sophistication to hide what they are, and they're easy to spot: you can almost tell the bad guys from looking at them. You can't do that so well with educated folk. Anyway, Aaron McCool was based very loosely upon a moonshiner I knew who lived, oh in rifle shot really, of my house. Moonshining was his life's work. He'd been to jail about twenty times, and he'd start right in again until they caught him. He had the house described in *The Innocent*. The wind blew through it. But he was a lot of fun. He was dangerous if he got drunk. I don't think he was to me, but to a person he was on unpleasant terms with. He wasn't the kind of vicious man Aaron was, but he gave me the archetype. I knew a lot of those people, and I heard talk about them. I'd spot some in town and ask questions about them to a man named Nell Hooper—Raynell was his real name—and Nell would know about them. I picked up a lot of knowledge of this kind and that in those years. (Laughs.) On this book that I'm writing now—you know I told you I wrote it and put it aside because I couldn't finish it—somebody wrote me from *The Chattahoochie Review* over in Atlanta and asked if I could give them something, and I said, well, I have something that I may or may not use, in this form anyway, if I use it at all. So I sent them the first chapter. It's about a red neck upbringing. *The Review* is published by De Kalb Community College. The April issue had a lot of good people in it, Fred Chappell and others.

WP: Do you keep the manuscripts of your books?

MJ: Unfortunately the manuscript of *The Innocent* burned up in my father's home when it burned nine or ten years ago. *Forest of the Night*, I don't know what happened to. I moved from one house to another, and it disappeared. It's gone; I can't find it. I still have *An Exile*. The Universtiy of Auburn has *A Buried Land*. I've never really thought about manuscripts. I've tended to be careless with them.

WP: One of the topics I always bring up in my interviews is the poor job the commercial publishers are doing in keeping books in print.

MJ: I lost out on *A Cry of Absence* because it went out of print in hardcover and then they ran out of paperbacks. I got calls and letters and inquiries wanting to know where people could get enough copies for classes. I had to tell them it was just not available, and interest just gradually faded away because people couldn't get hold of the book, and I guess now it's pretty well forgotten. I don't know what to do about it. That book is closest to my heart in terms of what I felt strongly about. I need one or two of my best books back in print for moral reasons, if for no other. It's so encouraging to get to work because you know somebody's going to read what you write. (1985)

Chapter 8
After the Lost Generation: A Conversation
with Vance Bourjaily

My interview with Vance Bourjaily begins with lunch at the Louisiana State University Faculty Club and, after a short ride, continues in the spacious but unpretentious living room of his home. After a long career of teaching creative writing at the University of Iowa, Vance Bourjaily is now director of the graduate program in creative writing at LSU. Bourjaily, now in his middle sixties, is a compact man who laughs easily and considers each question carefully before answering.

Although Bourjaily's first novel, *The End of My Life* (1947), was not a best seller, it was well reviewed, and the extended critical discussion of it in John W. Aldridge's now classic work, *After the Lost Generation,* established Bourjaily as an important novelist. *The Hound of Earth* (1955), was a controlled existential tale of a man on the run. *The Violated* (1958), *Confessions of a Spent Youth* (1960) and *The Man Who Knew Kennedy* (1967) were extensively and favorably reviewed and sold well. However, Bourjaily's later novels, *Brill Among the Ruins* (1970), *Now Playing at Canterbury* (1976), *A Game Men Play* (1980) and *The Great Fake Book* (1986) were less favorably reviewed and lacked the wide circulation of the earlier novels. Bourjaily has also written extensively about hunting and other male pastimes in *The Unnatural Enemy* (1963) and *Country Matters* (1973).

WP: You belong to the generation which came to maturity during the Second World War. Do you consider yourself in any sense a war novelist?

VB: Well, my first novel was a war novel and in most of the novels I have written I've felt some sort of a compulsion to tell what the characters were doing during the Second World War. What happened to those of us who turned twenty-one during the war was that it was probably a more crucial education experience than college. The war was where we went to college. That determined a lot of things in the way our lives went. Feeling that way about it that, when I'm working with a character around my age, I invest him with a World War II experience that has that kind of educational effect upon his life. I'm so aware of it that I deliberately try to get away from it. I think that in *Now Playing at Canterbury* I did manage pretty much to omit the Second World War as a factor in the characters' lives. (Laughs.) At least one of them has to talk about it. In any case, the Second World War was four very important years for us.

WP: What strikes me most about your treatment of the war is its obliqueness. Unlike *The Naked and the Dead* and other war novels which deal with the war directly, the war in your novels seems to be mostly a background.

VB: I think that's true, and I think it's because those four years were obviously not four years spent in continuous combat. They were four years of life experiences of various kinds during a good deal of which we were living in foreign countries having the experiences of late adolescence and young manhood by chance almost in those settings and making friends in those circumstances. The actual time spent in combat was relatively little. Between 1942 and 1946 I may have spent twenty days in combat situations.

WP: What were you in?

VB: That would have been the first part of the war when I was in the American Field Services driving an ambulance.

WP: That's what Hemingway did. That's what a writer is supposed to do, isn't it?

VB: That's what I thought at the time. (Laughs.) Later on in the war, I was in the infantry, but I wasn't in combat.

WP: A month or so ago, someone wrote in to Ann Landers complaining about somebody, her grandfather or somebody, who spent all his time talking about the Second World War, and every body agreed that he was an old fuddy-duddy; but then some man wrote in what I thought was a rather moving letter in which he said the Second World War was the most interesting and significant thing that had ever happened to him during his lifetime, and that nothing since then had made him feel so alive or interested in life.

VB: I'm sure a lot of people feel that way. You know it was in a funny way a good time. Obviously there were bad moments, but you were traveling—obviously not at your own expense. You were young, in very good physical condition. You probably had good friends. There were days and days and nights and nights of it full of high spirits and young male adventure. (Laughs.)

WP: What were the models for your first novel? It obviously has elements of Hemingway, but it's not like Hemingway. *The End of My Life* is a very original book.

VB: I'm glad to hear you say so. It's a book which was written without any knowledge of how to write a novel. I think there's a good deal of Hemingway and a good deal of Fitzgerald in it, but writing a first novel is really an act of innocence. You know nothing about the craft. There are just kind of voices in the air which you synthesize and out of which you almost automatically, almost instinctively, write a novel. After you've done the first one, you have to find out what it's all about. You begin to be a little more conscious, but there's a kind of unselfconsciousness about how I wrote that book. I just sat down and wrote it.

WP: How much editing did Maxwell Perkins do on that book? Is the story told in the Perkins biography accurate, that he suggested the first part to introduce the character of the girl?

VB: Yes, I was the biographer's source for that one.

WP: To me, the character of Skinner seems to bring back that time very clearly.

VB: I've always wondered about Skinner, whether Skinner unlike the characters in *The Naked and the Dead, The Gallery*, or some of the other good war novels, isn't too much a kind of representative Ivy League college boy.

WP: How much of that represented your own experience?

VB: Well, I was an Ivy League college boy. (Laughs.) Most of the people in the American Field Services were. At least, a good many of them were. We were from the eastern seaboard. I was raised in Virginia mostly, and in New York. I went to college at Bowdoin, which is a little Ivy League college.

WP: Sure, that's where Hawthorne went to school.

VB: Hawthorne went to school there, and so did Longfellow. They were classmates. Longfellow was apparently a very affluent kid who was popular and had a good time at college, and Hawthorne was a loner and a solitary person. The legend is that when he was at school, he spent a lot of time in the winter skating on the Androskoggin River. He would skate miles and miles up the river in the dark and back again.

WP: How did you become interested in writing?

VB: My mother and father were both newspaper people. They had a great deal of respect for the written word and they both were good journalists. My mother published a number of books. She was a popular novelist after she left newspaper work. Under her maiden name, Barbara Webb, she wrote *Misty Mountain* and several others, including *The Pedigree of Honey*, a title from Emily Dickinson— I'll get back to that. She wrote magazine serials and newspaper serials and what was then called "women's fiction." She had three sons, and I think that it was one of her personal ambitions that one of her sons would become a writer. Although what she wrote was popular fiction, she knew the difference between what she did and what was literature. She was a collector of Emily Dickinson editions; she used to lecture on Emily Dickinson. She read constantly and at a very high level. She was very fond of Conrad, and she was perfectly aware that the work she did was not literary, and I think that it was a dream of hers that one of her sons would amount to something as a literary writer. My father was less of a reader than my mother, but he also believed in the power of the written word. He published millions of words himself. During the last twenty years of his life he wrote canned editorials. Canned editorials were syndicated to small dailies that didn't have their own editorial writers, and he was very good at taking both sides of every issue so that his editorials were acceptable to whatever the paper's political views were. (Laughs.) He had forty or fifty papers and he wrote two or three editorials every day for about twenty years. He probably published a lot more words than I have.

WP: You were in college when the war started?

VB: I was in college at Bowdoin through the end of my sophomore year, then I joined the American Field Services. Like a lot of other people, I started back to college under the GI Bill of Rights.

WP: Some one is going to write a great book some day on the influence of the GI Bill on American literature.

VB: Well, there's a footnote to that, which is the influence of the wartime excess profits tax on American literature. The excess profits tax provided that anybody who had been in business before the war had to average his profits for ten years before the war, and any thing in excess of that would be taxed at ninety percent. Of course, American publishers had been in business ten years before the war, but the depression years hadn't been particularly profitable, and during the war there was a big boom in reading because of gas rationing and this and that. Also, a lot of books were distributed to the armed forces. And so the publishers made a lot of excess profits during the war. During the war there had been a four year period when young writers had not been coming along as writers because they were artillerymen or pilots. At the end of the war the publishers were very eager to sign up new writers and they had all this money that was only worth ten cents on the dollar from their standpoint, so that if you could spell your name the same way twice you could get a contract to write a book. The $700.00 that Scribers paid me as an advance on *The End of My Life* actually cost them seventy bucks. They were happy enough to do it.

WP: That book seems almost prophetic about what's going on in the Middle East.

VB: I get very sad about that. I almost can't read the papers about what's happening on the Gaza strip and that whole situation. It's almost personally tragic to me because I liked the time I spent in Lebanon. My father was born in Lebanon, as a matter of fact. It was a beautiful country, and it was a very stable country. It was the Switzerland of the Middle East, always neutral. It was the center of banking and commerce, and has lovely mountains and valleys. And to see it torn up the way it is now and to think of Beirut, which was a sophisticated, cosmopolitan city, as a place where one cannot live any more, is very sad to me.

WP: Your second novel *The Hound of Earth* seems to me the least characteristic of your novels.

VB: As I said, the first novel was written in innocence, and then I wrote an unpublished novel which I just couldn't work out. It still exists in manuscript at the Bowdoin Library. Anyway, it didn't work.

WP: Who edited the second book?

VB: After Max Perkins died, Burroughs Mitchell pretty much took over

Perkins' writers. Meanwhile, I had written a play that I was very pleased with. I wrote a couple of plays, and then I got into the editing of *Discovery*. *The End of My Life* had gone out of print. I hadn't published a second novel, and John W. Aldridge had published his book *After the Lost Generation* in which he said some very favorable things about my novel, which really revived me I guess as a novelist. It brought me some attention, and Aldridge and I became friends and talked one day about the success of Penguin New Writing, a vehicle for the young British writers prior to the Second World War. We wondered whether something like that couldn't be done. I took the idea to Pocket Books because the paperback format seemed like a good way to present a literary magazine, as Penguin had done, and Pocket Books said okay. Aldridge and I announced it and solicited manuscripts and did the first issue together. He dropped out after the first issue, and I did the next five, after which Pocket Books decided they didn't want to do it any longer. It lasted six issues.

WP: I read a manifesto you had in one of the issues. Have you written much criticism or non-fiction?

VB: Not very much. Occasionally, if somebody asked me to.

WP: Would there be enough for a volume at some point?

VB: I probably could get together my literary essays and reviews. I'm not sure that it would be worth doing. I had one in the *New York Times Book Review* in December, 1987. It's about jazz and fiction. But I don't really take myself to be a critic.

WP: An interest in jazz has run through your books almost from the very beginning to your last novel. Was jazz a characteristic interest of your generation?

VB: It was, I think, just before World War II and during the war. There were aficionados of jazz, of whom I was one, who felt as if we were the initiates who had a special knowledge of and enthusiasm for this particular kind of music, from which most people were excluded. It made us feel special. We collected records and recognized one another when we met by knowing who played trumpet with Tommy Dorsey on "Marie." (It happened to be Bunny Berrigan.) And I think that kind of jazz snobbery did eventually turn into a knowledge of and love for the music. I also learned to play. I have a cornet out in the shop. I play a little bit, but I got tired of the snobbery after a while. I guess that's why I bought the cornet. I thought I really shouldn't talk about this unless I could do it myself.

WP: *Confessions of a Spent Youth* is different from your other novels because it has an episodic structure. What were the models for that sort of book?

VB: The model was a book by Robert Graves called *Goodbye to All That*, in which he wrote autobiographically about himself, but using the techniques of fiction. I wanted to do it in a way almost as a correction to *The End of My Life*. I didn't mean to deny *The End of My Life*, but it seemed to me I understood that material in a different way ten years later. I quite deliberately went over the same ground seeing it less as something to make fiction of and more as something to try to tell the truth about. I don't know when it occurred to me that I should organize it topically the way I did, or why, but it did occur to me to do it as if it were a book of essays. An essay about one's experiences with drugs, an essay about one's experiences with religion, an essay about one's experiences with prostitutes. They're kind of mock essays in a way. Each one of the chapters of *Confessions* has a topic with which Quincy deals, and the rule of the book is that each successive essay may begin at whatever point in Quince's life the first experience under this topic heading took place, but it must end at a chronological point later than the preceding essay so that the book can move toward a conclusion. I really can't tell you at this point why I conceived that way of organizing the book. It just seemed like the way to do it. There is a particular voice in *Confessions*; it's my own voice. In *The End of My Life* and *The Violated*, I was developing and using a writer's voice. I tried to use a personal voice in *Confessions*. Probably, writing these mock essays helped me to establish the voice, and establishing the voice helped me to find the form. I think the prose in the *Confessions* is quite different from the prose in the other two books.

WP: How did you decide to center the main episode of *The Violated* around a young girl who decides to produce *Hamlet* in an abandoned house in Brooklyn?

VB: That was one of those amazing things that happens in life that people make fiction out of. I never saw that production of *Hamlet*, but it did take place. It took place in Mexaco City. In the early fifties, my wife and I and our little daughter lived in a suburb of Mexico City for two or three years. There was a little expatriate community of writers down there. Norman Mailer was there. Willard Motley was there. Budd Schulberg was there. At the time I got to Mexico City, people were talking about a children's production of *Hamlet* which had taken place just before we got there. The kids had put it on in a condemned house on Calle Insurgentes. I used to pass the house—a big run-down stucco place—when I rode downtown on the streetcar. It had "condemned" signs on it. We were told they had put on *Hamlet* and lit it with candles and that a fourteen-year old girl had played Hamlet, and that a fifteen-year old girl had played Hamlet's mother. Younger kids at their school had taken the other parts and rehearsed it in secret. I was fascinated with this event. I felt very deprived at not having seen it, but I very much wanted to know what it had been like, and I started asking people if they had seen the children's *Hamlet*. I remember one lady said, I saw it, and wasn't it cute. I thought, no, lady, it might have been anything in the world, but it sure wasn't cute if kids decide to do *Hamlet*, which is about parents and children, and parricide. The relationship between Hamlet and his mother is so antagonistic that, no. lady, there isn't anything cute about it. In any case, I had to discard her testimony. And I talked to a fellow who said, yeah, I saw it but I had a few drinks and a big supper, but it was dark in there, and I just slept through it. I can't tell you anything about it. And I talked to another guy who said, don't tell anybody, I was supposed to be there. (Laughs.) My wife thinks I was there. And finally I saw a strange young fellow who was a theater director who had come down from New York for another odd project which he directed, a bilingual production of *Peer Gynt* which was done outdoors in Chiculrapec Park. He was a very nice voluble homosexual director with a great deal of knowledge of theater. I thought, if he went to the children's *Hamlet*, I will finally learn what took place. And so I waited until the right moment and I said, "Listen"—pretending casualness—"I don't suppose you saw the children's *Hamlet* by any chance, did you?" (Laughs.) "Yes, I did," says he, and I got so excited. "Please," I said, "let's sit down. Do you want a drink?" And this very voluble generous and knowledgeable young man said, "It was wonderful, it was awful, it was so exciting, no, it was quite boring," and he said nothing except these dumb pairs of antithetical words for three or four minutes and stopped talking. I guess I realized at that point—or rather I realize now as an afterthought—that having been unable to see or learn about the children's *Hamlet*, I finally just had to create one for myself to see what it was like. I did see the little girl who played Hamlet at a cocktail party, but I never saw her face. I went to a cocktail part of affluent people in the expatriate community, and there she was. What I saw at this cocktail party was this shiny little blond head going out the door. I never got another look at her. The director who was unable to tell me about the children's *Hamlet* I used in the book. He's Ned Kildeer.

WP: Did they perform the whole play? In the novel, the performance is interrupted.

VB: I think they got through the whole thing. I'm not sure about that.

WP: Why did you leave Scribners?

VB: They did a poor job with *The Hound of Earth*. I was very fond of Burroughs Mitchell, as I said, but Burroughs and I were not a particularly successful combination as writer and editor. It just wasn't the right chemistry, I guess.

WP: You don't think that just had to do with the book?

VB: Well, Burroughs had been the editor of the second novel I spoke of, the one that wasn't published. We worked together on it; he'd write me about it, and I'd respond. Neither one of us could get a publishable novel from it. *The Hound of Earth* required very little editing. I just gave him what came out of my typewriter. It was like a bad marriage. We were just two guys that weren't meant to work together.

WP: Who was your editor at Dial?

VB: Jim Silberman. I stayed at Dial through a succession of more editors and publishers than I like to think about. I may not even be able to name all of them. Jim was the editor and George Joel was the publisher when they did *The Violated*. Jim was editor and Richard Baron was the publisher on *Confessions*. It isn't worth trying to name all the people, but they kept changing. I never had the same two people as editor and publisher twice. It got pretty confusing after a while.

WP: I don't know that I would want to use such a phrase as the "tragic view of life," but your novels often end with a sense of loss, a sense of waste, and you clearly are attracted to the darker forms of fiction.

VB: I think up until *Brill Among the Ruins* I would agree with you. Starting with *Brill*, but most particularly in *Now Playing at Canterbury*, I think I tended more to let people fulfill themselves. The people in *Now Playing at Canterbury* are by and large a reasonably happy bunch.

WP: I kept thinking in *Brill* about Bellow's *Henderson the Rain King*. Have you read that one?

VB: I hadn't read it before I wrote *Brill*. After *Brill*, somebody pointed out certain resemblances, so I quickly read *Henderson*, which immediately became my favorite of Bellow's books. As a matter of fact, I hadn't liked any of his books before *Henderson*. I still like *Henderson* a lot.

WP: That's his least characteristic book. He'd never been to Africa when he wrote that. It's just a big tall tale.

VB: That may be the reason I like it. (Laughs.) I think it's a book with a lot of energy and a lot of humor in it. I had a good time reading it, and I don't usually have a good time reading Bellow.

WP: *The Violated* is a dark book.

VB: It is a very dark book. I was concerned with the phenomenon in America of early promise. There are so many kids who look like geniuses who never amount to much. It's a book about unfulfulled lives. I'm not sure that my life experiences at the time I wrote it made me fully justified in taking that view of human lives. I guess I thought I was justified. It has certainly seemed to me since then that there is more fulfillment with more people than I thought. It's a kind of a change. I don't think that I've become or ever will become an optimistic writer, but my view of life is a little brighter than when I wrote *The Violated*.

WP: *The Man Who Knew Kennedy* is also a dark book.

VB: I have a real sense in that book that I did something prophetic. I think that with the assassination of John F. Kennedy, American history took a turn for the worse.

WP: In the statement at the beginning of the novel, you wrote that people in general were emphasizing the bright side of the Kennedy legend, while your book tended to take the other point of view. That's certainly not true now.

VB: What I'm talking about is not the dark side of the Kennedy legend, but it just seems to me that American life from the end of the Second World War throughout the Kennedy presidency was a time of hope. They were fairly bright years, certainly up to the time of his assassination. There was a real surge of hope in the Kennedy presidency. The country really seemed to be on track. We got off track there, and we still haven't recovered. The years since led to Vietnam, to Watergate, to a very retrogressive Reagan administration, or so I feel. The country got torn up by the Kennedy assassination, and we're still recovering.

WP: Is Dave Doremus in *The Man Who Knew Kennedy* a tragic character?

VB: Yeah, I suppose. I never thought of this before, but he was one of those gifted people with very great early promise whose life doesn't fulfill that promise. It's the discrepancy between early promise and mature achievement that is a good part of the American tragedy in the life of man like Scott Fitzgerald. But then as I've gone on living, I've seen other American lives which worked out a little better. I like to write about them too.

WP: One of the things that amazes me about your novels is how much you know about various trades, "their gear, their tackle and trim," about sailing, about archaeology, about horses, and so on.

VB: Most of those things are things I've know something about, at least enough so that I was pretty sure I wasn't talking through my hat. For example, about horses. In each case, I probably had to find out more. For example, in the farm we lived on in Iowa, we had some horses. My first wife was and is a very good horsewoman. Well, when Chink decides that he's going to take the shoes off the horses to load them on the ship, I went around and talked to blacksmiths. I'm not even sure that I used what I found out. The rule is when you write about something like that in fiction, you want to know about three times as much about it as you actually use.

WP: The Hemingway principle?

VB: Yeah. In the book I'm working on now, one of the characters is fishing for landlocked salmon. I know a lot about landlocked salmon by now. I've read everything I can get my hands on. I use very little of it in the book. I don't think it's going to matter very much to the reader that taxonomists think that the landlocked salmon and the Atlantic salmon are the same species, and that one is not a subspecies. I don't think that that's anything I need to impart, but I want to know it. (Laughs.)

WP: Have you ever done any archaeological work?

VB: It began when we lived in Mexico. I became a very intense amateur archaeologist. That was ten years before I wrote the novel. Once I had done it, I had in mind writing a novel with an archaeological background quite a while before I wrote *Brill*. But I went back to Mexico and did some more digging just to get it fresh in my mind. I had a little extra money from *The Man Who Knew Kennedy*, and so I got in touch with a guy with whom I had worked, a man named John Paddock, a very good Mexican archaeologist. I said, John, I got a couple of thousand bucks, and I want to back an expedition, and John said, all right. We did a little dig at a place called Caballo Blanco. You could do a lot for $2,000 in 1960.

WP: What about sailing?

VB: I had done some sailing and had taken a deep water sailboat trip from the Virgin Islands as a voluntary crew member, but there were terms and situations which I had to find out more about. I think it would be very difficult to write about something about which one had no experience whatsoever, basing fiction just on research. At the same time, I think there are a great many things which we can use that we already know a little about and can find out much more about before we try to use them.

WP: Was *The Man Who Knew Kennedy* your best selling book?

VB: Yes. It made more money than any of the others. *The Violated* actually sold more copies in paper. I think *The Violated* sold over a million in paper, and I'm not sure *The Man Who Knew Kennedy* did that well. I certainly made more money on *The Man Who Knew Kennedy*. It was a Literary Guild selection, the trade edition sold well, and we made a pretty good paperback sale. Until *A Game Men Play* all my books had paperback sales, except for the non-fiction books.

WP: Nowadays, mass market paperback sales for serious fiction have almost completely disappeared.

VB: Some important works are coming back into print. A firm called Carroll and Graf is bringing some important books back into print.

WP: I think *The Violated* and *The Man Who Knew Kennedy* are your best books, and I think they're both out of print.

VB: The only ones that have been in print recently are the Arbor House books, *Confessions of a Spent Youth* and *The End of My Life*, and they've just discontinued that line. It's the same kind of publishing story; the man who conceived that line, and whose heart was in it, left and went over to another firm. Who ever took over couldn't keep Arbor House enthusiastic about doing it, and a whole lot of books were remaindered.

WP: Your writing has gone against the main critical currents of the time. Your novels are in the traditon of realistic social fiction; they're basically in the Fitzgerald tradition, I would say. I don't think most critics are interested in that kind of writing these days.

VB: When you write a novel, there's really only one way to decide which of the thousands of novels you might write that you are going to write at this time. What you do is that you write the kind of novel that you yourself would want to read at that particular time.

WP: In the late forties and early fifties, when you began to publish, social fiction was still being written. Today most of the novels don't seem to be about anything.

VB: I think I might agree with that. I think that the novel might be an anachronism anyway. (Laughs.) We don't have the kind of audience for fiction that existed then. Whitman said that to have great writers you must have great audiences. I don't think we have great audiences today.

WP: You've had a long career as a teacher. Most of the novelists I've talked to have spent at least some time teaching, but they've all complained that teaching took so much of their energy that they didn't have any left to write.

VB: I can't say I feel that way. I've always arranged it so that my teaching took place in the afternoon. I remember talking with Vonnegut about this. Kurt said, "You write in the morning, and then what in the hell are you going to do in the afternoon? You might as well teach a class." (Laughs.) "You could go out and work on your patio or break the law." I also could quote Nabokov who said, "Should writers teach? What are you asking me? Should a writer work at a beautiful place like a campus with an excellent library?" I think that the answer is that there are some writers who are temperamentally suited to having some free time supported by the institutions for which they work. They support our creative work in the same way they support research. It's been a very productive relationship for me, by and large. I also think they're writers who would be driven nuts by the academic life. If you would say to me, "Should writers teach?" I couldn't answer it. If you would say, "Should Fitzgerald have taught?" I would say, "What could have been more wonderful for that poor bastard than to have gone back to Princeton as an honored man and been able to teach young men what he knew and to have the institution he loved support him as a writer. It would have been the perfect life for him." On the other hand, Hemingway would, I think, have found the whole situation intolerable. Some writers it suits, others it doesn't. In the various ways I've made a living, it certainly has agreed with me better than anything else.

WP: I think the fact that so many writers have been teachers has given the postwar American novel a self-conscious or bookish air.

VB: That may be, although it's remarkable the extent to which it seems almost an unrelated activity to what the scholars and critics in an English department are doing. It's not that we don't get along together and play poker and stuff like that.

WP: In many colleges, the creative writing teacher is often the low man on the totem pole.

VB: That's not true in Iowa, it isn't true at LSU, and it's not true at Arizona. Those are the three schools I've been at. What has happened is that the graduate writing programs are such a powerful tool for an English department in recruiting interesting graduate students that the people who run the English departments put a fairly high value on their writers. I'm able to bring LSU bright and interesting and gifted students of a special kind, people who want to write or who want to combine writing with scholarship who would not consider coming if the writing program weren't here. I think my colleagues, most of them, are quite aware of that and are quite supportive. I guess LSU probably started the MFA program three years ago as a way of getting new graduate students.

WP: You spent a long time on *Now Playing at Canterbury*.

VB: It was ten years from the time I wrote the first pieces of it to the time when I finished the book. However, in those ten years I published three other books. So, it wasn't ten years of continuous work. I'd put it aside and pick it up again. It took a while to figure out how to write it. Eventually, I decided I knew how to do it, so I went ahead and did it.

WP: The CIA background of *A Game Men Play* puts it in a different category from that of your other novels. It has elements of the thriller.

VB: I was thinking about writing the particular book you would like to read next if somebody else would write it. I enjoy thrillers when I read for pleasure. I think thrillers is the wrong word; I'm talking more about the detective novel tradition of Dashiell Hammett, Raymond Chandler and so on. I read most anything, but thrillers too, and I was particularly interested in the American tough guy character who exists in those books and in society and who it seems to me does not ordinarily become a character in what we call serious fiction. I was interested in creating one of those guys, but not in the present, but to give him a background, and an education and a family, to investigate how this particular American personality can come about. I was trying to give him some substance. I don't know whether it works or not.

WP: Was there any liberal criticism of that book?

VB: Yeah, I think there were some people who thought that the book was wrong politically. I didn't think that Chink Peters had any politics, to tell you the truth.

WP: That's what I would have thought.

VB: But there were those who disagreed.

WP: Have any of the reviews been helpful to you?

VB: I don't think it's really possible for a writer to be instructed by his critics. You know, you're grateful for good notices and resentful of bad. When I was a young man, I thought that reading reviews or criticism would teach me something about writing, but it doesn't, and it's not intended to. Criticism does not exist for the instruction of writers. It's just a kind of literature of its own. The only thing that instructs writers is reading other books. It's nice to get good reviews and it's a pain in the ass to get bad ones. (Laughs.) I'll admit that there are some reviews that make considerable commercial difference. Unfortunately, the only ones that you can say that about with any certainty are those in the *Times Book Review*. It's the one reviewing source that has any real influence. It's a shame. When I was a kid, there was the *Times*, there was the *Herald-Tribune* and there was the *Saturday Review of Literature*, and there were several other places, and I think all of those places and the weekly newsmagazines, *Time* and *Newsweek*, could sell books. *The New Yorker* could sell books. But it isn't true anymore.

WP: What is the function of the creative writing teacher?

VB: There are all kinds of ways to answer that question. One of the aspects of that is that in publishing today editors no longer have a teaching function. Editors are so busy overseeing the promotion and design and selling of the book that they no longer spend time with young writers in the way a man like Maxwell Perkins did. Something had come along to take the place of an editor who could work patiently with a talented kid to the point where a publishable book came out. Since that no longer happens in publishing, what we do in the universities is very much like what editors once did. The other thing that happens in these writing programs which seems to be of value is that through the exposure of his work to a group of his peers, through group criticism meetings, the writer has an experience which is like that of publication. A story is dittoed; fifteen or twenty people read it and they sit down and talk about it, so it's like being published and reviewed. Finally, the writing programs supply something like what traditionally happened in European countries when the gifted young man or woman from the provinces went to the capitol, went to Paris, went to London, and on arriving found out at what cafe or what coffee house writers gathered whom he or she had read, and started hanging out there. Made himself useful, ran errands, read proofs, carried packages, and hoped that eventually the master would be willing to read a piece of work and talk about it. Whether or not the particular criticism offered was any-thing a writer could use would have to be analyzed on a case by case basis. In any case that kind of gathering of people with the same passion for a certain kind of creative work is the traditional way in which painters always learn, and sculptors always learn. I'm not sure if that's true in music; I suppose that something like it happens. What these university writing program supply is a kind of studio train-ing. It's some thing fairly new, about forty years old. By now a lot of the people who are publishing have been through these programs, so I guess they work.

WP: Have you ever been tempted to write screenplays?

VB: I wrote one years ago. It was supposed to be for Lena Horne, but it was never used. That's a very familiar story. Many screenplays are written, and few screenplays are produced. (Pause.) But I respect films. I remember once telling my son, if I had it to do over again, I might prefer making films to being a novelist because you reach out and touch so many more people.

WP: Your books have a way of circling around a story that I find very interesting. They sometimes have this two-part structure, like in *Brill*, or in *A Game Men Play*, where you have all this business going on in the background that you don't know about. The book begins with Chink getting a telephone call, and you know that there's a lot going on in the past, but you don't know what that is. Or even in *The Violated*, where you know that you're eventually going to get around to this little girl putting on *Hamlet*. It's a kind of gradual revelation, but it's not really a suspense technique.

VB: It's a way of structuring a novel. I'm pretty much aware of what you're talking about, and in the book on which I'm now working, I'm trying to avoid doing that. I want to write a straightforward chronological book, which all takes place in its own present without moving into the past at all. I want to see if I can do it.

WP: What are the models for that technique of gradual revelation? I haven't been able to come up with much.

VB: The models? (Pause.) I suppose *Gatsby* is a book like that. If I thought about that question a lot, I think I could answer it for you. I might be able to cite Conrad, but I'd have to be careful about picking my examples.

WP: I'm going to have to look up my review of *The Man Who Knew Kennedy*. I mentioned Fitzgerald in my review, and I remember in an interview that you did on public television at the time, you mentioned Fitzgerald. He seems to be more constantly in the background of your novels than any other writer.

VB: I think certainly in the early books, yeah. I admired Tolstoy very much for a time when I was writing *The Violated*. I would say of the people who were alive and publishing during my lifetime, probably Nabokov. I think that he taught me that you could do anything you want with a book's structure. When you read a book like *Pale Fire*, in which the story is buried in the footnotes to a poem, you realize that there are no limits to the way you can put a novel together. That was a very important lesson for me.

WP: It would be difficult to argue that you have much in common with Nabokov.

VB: Nope. I don't have much in common with him, but I have tremendous respect for him.

WP: We heard you read from a story called "The Duchess," which you said was one of three intended for a book.

VB: "The Duchess" and "The Amish Farmer," which are the two I've done, are stories which take place in the classroom. They are first person stories told by a character called Vance who is a teacher of graduate students in fiction writing. In "The Amish Farmer," he tells them a story, and in "The Duchess," a colleague is dying. I think the reason I'm doing these is that I don't have any intention of writing a book about writing, but I think I know a few things that are worth writing down, and so I'm sort of incorporating them into these stories. There may be several more stories; there'll be at least one more. Since I did that reading, I've gotten into writing what will be I believe a very short book that's quite unrelated to those stories. I'm trying to get it done this spring.

WP: You have a liking for interpolated bits of drawing, graffiti, kilroy-type characters and the like which seems to me in a writer whom I would think of as almost totally realistic to violate the different levels of reality. In Nabokov, I'd say, that's what I expect, but in reading Bourjaily that's not what I expect.

VB: I hope I don't do it every time. (Laughs.) That story I read at the Gallery does have a drawing at the end. It may be a very bad impulse. It may be the same impulse that causes poets to write a poem that will make a kind of picture to try to do something visual that enhances their words. Probably it is a mistake. Probably it does change the level of reality and makes the reader aware that he's reading at a time when he shouldn't be aware of it. In *The Great Fake Book* I intended to do a lot more of that, but the publisher did not do typographically what I wanted him to do. I wanted the letters to be done in typewriter face.

WP: I think that old newspaper man is a wonderful creation. He sends the protagonist what is in effect a political questionnaire before he will have anything to do with him. Was he based on a real model?

VB: I don't know who I had in mind. He was easy to write. I always knew what he was going to say and sound like, but I wouldn't say he was based on the city editor of the *San Francisco Chronicle* or anything like that. There may have been a little of my father in him, I'm not sure, but if so I certainly didn't think about it at the time.

WP: Do you do your first draft in longhand?

VB: No, I type everything. I find word processors very alarming. It seems like there is some kind of physical work that you avoid when you use a word processor that I'd better not avoid.

WP: Which of your contemporaries interest you?

VB: I've been rereading James Jones with a good deal of interest. I recently read *Whistle* for the first time and *The Thin Red Line* for the first time. Jones is an extremely interesting writer. When he gets away from the war, he's in trouble, but *Whistle* is fascinating. The obsession with oral sex in that book is really odd.

WP: Because they are very much tied to the temper of the times, your early novels have already become historical objects in the way that all novels do sooner or later. The blurb on my paperback copy of *Confessions* promised sensational sexual revelations.

VB: I don't think I'll ever exceed or want to exceed the orgy sequence in *Now Playing at Canterbury*. (Laughs.) I think that's where I said everything I want to say about sex.

WP: How do you like New Orleans jazz?

VB: The newest kind of jazz leaves me cold, the unmelodic stuff they're playing now. A lot of the jazz they're playing in New Orleans now is kind of by rote. It's not very creative. It not like they're improvising and doing much with it, so that while it's pleasant, it's more like background music than something you listen to with intensity. There are exceptions, of course. I think that most musicians will have to develop something out of rock and roll that has the same place that jazz has for me. Bill Haley and the Comets may be a great jazz band for all I know. At some point I just stopped hearing it. It's no longer the people's music. I think that some of the rock music of the last thirty years will have the same position that Louis Armstrong and Jack Teagarden had for the people of my generation. It's got to be close to popular.

WP: Where are your manuscripts?

VB: The University of Iowa has one of them. Bowdoin has the rest. They bring a fair price these days. It used to be that you could give a manuscript to a library and get it appraised and take the appraisal value off your tax. That was nice. Then the IRS stopped that and now libraries pretty much pay cash for them. (Pause.) There are many unhappy things about publishing these days. In order for an editor to impove himself or herself he has to change jobs, to change publishers. And so the person that you worked with very happily on one book has gone to another publishing house. Sometimes people can arrange to follow their editors if they wish, but more often they can't. As I said I stayed with Dial through four or five or six different editors and finally came up with one who was just disasterously bad. He was the editor of *A Game Men Play*. At which point I left Dial Press and Dial went out of business, and then I found myself hunting a publisher when I had a new book coming. But we all yearn for those days when we could have a long permanent relationship with an editor and a publishing house. There was a kind of security and stability which just isn't there now. (Pause.) But there is such an obvious vacuum that I think some one is going to fill it. Small publishing houses are starting to reprint books and university presses are starting to get into the act. Most of my books are out of print, but I'm fairly optimistic, that whichever ones deserve to be read will become available. Somehow. (1988)

Chapter 9
North of the Lake: A Conversation
with James Wilcox

My interview with James Wilcox takes place in his parents's house in Hammond. The novelist's mother greets me pleasantly at the door, introduces me to her son, and retreats into the recesses of the house, leaving me alone with the novelist in the living room. Athough I have known the Wilcox family for years—the novelist's father was long-time head of the Music department at Southeastern Louisiana University and later Dean—I have never met James, who went away to Yale about the time I came to Hammond to teach at Southeastern.

The darkly handsome novelist, now in his early forties, is the youngest novelist I have interviewed. In four novels, published at two-year intervals, he has built a solid reputation as one of the best of the current generation of Southern writers. Wilcox's first novel, *Modern Baptists* (1983), established both his reputation and fictional territory, small Louisiana towns bounded on the South by Lake Pontchartrain and on the North and West by the Mississippi state line. Later novels, *North Gladiola* (1985), *Miss Undine's Living Room* (1987) and *Sort of Rich* (1989), expanded Wilcox's characteristic subject matter and style. Widely praised by critics, the novels have attracted a constantly increasing readership in paperback.

After the customary and repeated check of my tape recorder, I begin the interview.

WP: The first question I ask is always a standard one. Do you consider yourself a Southern writer and do you think there is a Southern literary tradition?

JW: The same question came up in a panel discussion I took part in at the Tennessee Williams Festival in New Orleans, whether there is such a creature as a Southern writer these days. I don't think there is as much a sense of regionalism as there was, say, twenty or thirty years ago. There have been radical changes. Of course I'm a Southern writer, in the sense that I grew up in a Southern town, here in Hammond, and that no impression after that is as vivid or as strong. A good part of creative work, after all, is recovering the energy and joy of childhood, but my idea of a Southern town is mitigated by the fact that Hammond is not your typical Southern town. With a University here I was exposed to so many different influences that you wouldn't get in a more Faulknerian town. I don't have the agrarian background that people tend to associate with Southern writers, and my parents themselves were not born here. This maybe lends a slightly different slant to my view of the South.

WP: Do you thank that going away to a Northern school rather than staying in the South and going to a Southern school had any effect on your writing?

JW: Yes, I think that it broadened my view, gave me a new perspective. It was a real culture shock when I left Hammond in 1967 and went up to Yale. I was completely miserable up there for two or three years, a fish out of water. In general, people seemed so much more aggressive, curt, even rude. I finally got adjusted to the idea that that was just the way they spoke and behaved. They had a different social system that I was excluded from, so naturally I ended up with a violent case of homesickness.

WP: Did you go to Hammond High?

JW: I went to Southeastern High, which doesn't exist any more. There were first-rate teachers there, truly dedicated, like Philip Mouw, Velmarae Dunn, and Kathryn Meyers, who prepared me well for Yale.

WP: When did you first become interested in writing?

JW: I can remember writing plays when I was eight years old. I even wrote a very pretentious prologue to a massive Bildungsroman when I was ten years old—just a prologue, of course, no novel. In Cub Scouts I began a screenplay for a horror film that I hoped would be shot with my father's Kodak. I was fascinated by monsters then.

WP: What did you major in in college?

JW: English, with a minor in psychology.

WP: And did you take writing courses?

JW: During my sophomore year, I took a course with John Palmer who used to be associated with the *Southern Review*, I believe, along with Albert Erskine, and Robert Penn Warren. In the late sixties, Palmer was the editor of *The Yale Review* and was the dean of my college, Silliman. During the first semester, we wrote a theme a day around five hundred words long. It was a wonderful discipline, having to crank out a story everyday whether you felt like it or not. We wrote fewer but longer stories. After that I submitted my work to Robert Penn Warren and was accepted during my junior year for his writing seminar. We met once a week in a class with about twelve people, and there were private conferences with him on the stories we had written. Then during my senior year Mr. Warren agreed to be my tutor for a senior honors project I did, which was writing a novel. And so I wrote my first novel.

WP: Whatever happened to it?

JW: Well, it's crammed away in a suitcase somewhere. I hope it's lost forever. It's dreadful, shockingly bad, but I'm glad that I wrote it. The discipline of turning out 350 pages in the midst of other school assignments gave me a sense of accomplishment.

WP: What was Warren like as a teacher?

JW: In class we were assigned readings from *Understanding Fiction*. His comments were always fascinating, often quite funny, too. In the story conferences we would analyze line by line what I had written. Every word had to be meaningful, working toward the overall aim of the story. He would help you explore what the real point of your story was, and how you might be subverting yourself unintentionally through careless phrasing. He made you extremely aware.

WP: Warren was the most self-conscious writer in the world.

JW: He did believe in craftsmanship, in making form and meaning reflect one another. He had no use at all for self-indulgent writers, the unbridled stream-of-consciousness outpourings. He insisted that you know what you're doing, even if you are surprised by what your subconscious dredges up in the process.

WP: I thought he was a great novelist up to *World Enough and Time*, and after that I thought there was a very rapid decline.

JW: His poetry continued to be profoundly moving, but even his later novels sold well.

WP: What's your attitude toward teaching creative writing?

JW: I think it can be a catalyst for a student, maybe not right at that time, but later. There are certain things you can learn, I think, about the craft of fiction. You can't help someone who has no talent become a good writer, but I think you can help people discover what their range is and what their voice can be and give them technical ideas about what to avoid. In one sense it's a negative experience, saying what doesn't work. It's teaching someone to edit themselves. Most people are probably not mature enough in college to do work that is serious and good. At that age I wrote many stories, a novel, a play, none of which are publishable. But the very fact of having had that discipline and training and learning to be objective about my work paid off in the long run.

Then for seven years I was an editor and got very little of my own writing done, certainly nothing publishable. Maybe it was a time of lying fallow. I became absorbed in other writers's work and got a feeling for the economics of publishing—a distressing feeling, I might add.

WP: Vance Bourjaily told me that he thought the function of the creative writing teacher was to take the place of the old time editor like Maxwell Perkins who basically doesn't exist any more.

JW: Yes, I think that's true. Publishing was undergoing a sea change just about the time I came aboard. The fine old houses were being gobbled up by conglomerates. In August of 1971 I had an appointment to meet Bennett Cerf for a job interview at Random House, but he died just before the scheduled time. Of course, he had already sold Random House to RCA by then—and that was when you started getting a different idea of what publishing is all about. Gulf and Western bought Simon and Schuster; on and on it went. I felt the pressures in my job changing from worrying about getting a certain manuscript in its best form to knowing that the only way I was going to get ahead was to sign up a certain number of books that would make a good profit.

WP: Who were some of the writers you worked with?

JW: I started in 1971 at Random House as an editorial assistant to Albert Erskine. In the beginning I helped with authors that he was working with at that time. One of them was Eudora Welty. I helped him write the flap copy on *The Optimist's Daughter*.

WP: (Interrupts.) I think that's her best book.

JW: It's wonderful. It even mentions Hammond [Louisiana] in it. She comes up on the train from New Orleans and describes the Casa de Fresa, which has since been torn down. [The Casa de Fresa was a luxurious, but old-fashioned resort hotel of the type fashionable at the turn of the century.] Erskine was also publishing posthumous John O'Hara, *The Ewings* and some stories. Also, I did a word index of all the doubtful spellings in *Flags in the Dust*, Faulkner's original version of *Sartoris*. It was quite an experience, working from Faulkner's own typescript and manuscript; he wrote in Sanskrit, it seemed, so difficult to decipher. As Erskine's assistant I also worked with James Michener on *Centennial*. Michener is extraordinarily generous, and for my work on that novel he gave me a trip to Paris.

WP: Was Knopf a part of Random House at that time?

JW: Yes, it was owned by Random House. We had the same staff for sales, but the editorial departments were on different floors. Robert Gottlieb was the head of Knopf at that time. Now, of course, he's at *The New Yorker*. James Silberman was the editor-in-chief at Random House then. He went on to become the founder and publisher of Summit Books, which has been very successful. Jason Epstein took over after Silberman left. I lived under his reign for one year.

WP: Did you work with any Southern writers?

JW: No, I didn't. After learning the ropes, I was assigned some writers. I ended up with a motley crew, for instance, Dr. David Reubin, who wrote *Everything You Ever Wanted to Know About Sex... But Were Afraid to Ask*. I didn't work on that, but I edited another book that became a bestseller, *The Save Your Life Diet*, one of the first books recommending bran for good health. At the same time, I was assigned by Silberman to work with Hunter Thompson. Do you know him?

WP: Sure, I think he's starting to make a little comeback now after being out of the public consciousness for ten or fifteen years.

JW: Strangely enough for these Yuppie days, he is. Gonzo journalism was very popular in the Nixon years. He created a wild anarchic persona, which was not easy to distinguish from his real self. He was putting together a collection of his pieces, *The Great Shark Hunt*, but when I left for Doubleday, he took the book to Summit, which made sense, since Silberman was his editor.

WP: What did you edit at Doubleday?

JW: I was only there a year, which is how long it takes to start calling the cast of thousands by their right names. It's a huge company. I did sign up a novel and a book of nonfiction by Michael Mewshaw, a brilliant and very funny writer. It was around this time, just before turning thirty, that I thought I had to give writing. The responsibilities of editing were taking up all my time. I would have to get up at 5:30 a.m. to read manuscripts, and there were always publishing parties in the evenings. I had lunch every day for a year with either an agent or an author. The pressure was relentless and I knew I would never be able to write under these conditions—write well, that is.

WP: Since you worked for a publisher, I thought you might have some ideas on why so many good novels are out of print.

JW: I think that is a shame. Part of the problem is that a good many people simply don't know how to read fiction. Their idea of a good novel is barely disguised autobiography, the more bare, the better. Is it any wonder, with this plague of celebrities, that Joan Collins should enter the fray herself? Of course, the folks who buy Yuppie fiction would consider Ms. Collins totally uncool—but it's the same principle at work exactly. Maybe, though, to some degree this trend has peaked. A few good writers are beginning to be reprinted. Cormac McCarthy is one.

WP: I think he's the great unknown American writer. He's enormously admired by many of the novelists I've talked to.

JW: He was one of Albert Erskine's authors, and so I got a chance to meet him, and put in a comma in one of his manuscripts. He's a perfectionist and as far as I can recall, needed almost no editing. That's because he was merciless on himself, editing out hundred of pages before turning anything in. The only thing I can remember Erskine catching him on were some flower that he had blooming in the wrong season in *Suttree*. Erskine was a devoted gardener and kept his lawn in Westport in stunning order. No flower blossomed before its time.

WP: In certain ways McCarthy can clearly be seen as carrying on the Southern tradition, particularly in the influence of Faulkner. Do you have any sense of representing a Southern tradition?

JW: I didn't write my first novel out of a need to continue a Southern tradition: rather, I felt myself going against the grain. I think *Modern Baptists* is crossbred with my admiration for English novelists. I enjoy the early George Orwell novels—for instance *A Clergyman's Daughter*—early H. G. Wells, *Kipps*, *The History of Mr. Polly*—which were written before Orwell and Wells started to solve the world's problems. Muriel Spark's early works, particularly *The Comforters*, *The Bachelors*, and *The Ballad of Peckham Rye*, hold great appeal to me, the wry distance she keeps from her characters. I've always admired E. M. Forster, too, particulary *Howard's End*. Many folks may not think he's a great novelist, but I do. I got interested in him in Warren's seminar. Forster's deft touch, rarely portentous, is enchanting. There's an intimacy and distance at the same time, a lucid style tackling complex problems of race, environmentalism (before it was known as such) and the vagaries of love. His quiet humor deflates so much hype. How I wish he could have written a line or two on Malcolm Forbes's birthday party.

WP: Of course, Forster was much highly regarded forty or fifty years ago than he is now, but I think his reputation will revive.

JW: I hope so. Earlier I went through a Faulkner phase, but then the English won out. Trollope became an important influence, though his virtuous characters can be horribly trying. And I remain unhappy with *Doctor Thorne*, which is so repetitious I nearly screamed.

WP: A friend of mine told me to ask you about the humours novels. You know, Smollett and the rest.

JW: Smollett is too heavy-handed for me, and I find the violence a little repulsive, not so funny. It doesn't grab me the way Trollope does. The humor in Trollope is much more satisfying. Actually, I've always shied away from the notion of a comic novel. If someone tells me, "This is going to be funny," it seems like an aggressive act. My immediate instinct is to say, "Oh yeah?" It's programming you and it can actually prejudice a reader.

WP: That pretty much answers the next question I wanted to ask: Do you think of yourself as a comic novelist?

JW: No. I know I end up that way, but I certainly don't start out that way.

WP: But aren't you getting that reputation, and aren't the publishers sort of using that as a crutch to peddle your books?

JW: Yes, they do, but why, I don't know, since they're always telling me that comic novels are twenty times harder to sell than the regular Brand X. From the beginning, I never sat down to write anything funny. I don't think in that way. First of all, I don't like most, quote, "comic" novels. A lot of Kingsley Amis I find labored. I'm not wild about that tradition. The first story I wrote was not meant to be comic, although there's a furtive amusement there, I guess. The same with the novel. I didn't sit down to write a comic novel. I'll admit that people do end up saying that it is. But I'm not a very amusing guy in person. I don't tell jokes, and I've never come up with a single bon mot at a dinner party. For me people are funniest when they are most serious about themselves.

WP: Well, it's something you're going to have to get used to, since most people are going to regard your books as hilarious.

JW: Well, I'm not trying to sit down every day to write something that's funny. This seems to emerge as a side effect of what I'm doing.

WP: You said you wrote a novel while you were in college and then fifteen years later you published *Modern Baptists*. Are there any unfinished or unpublished manuscripts between those two?

JW: There were abortive attempts at novels and stories, but nothing more than a hundred pages or so. On weekends I'd some times sit down and write, but nothing ever got completed.

WP: *Modern Baptists* was published by Dial, but your later novels were published by Harper. Why did you change publishers?

JW: Shortly after *Modern Baptists* was in galleys, Dial was eaten up by Doubleday and later disbanded. My editor was let go.

WP: Who was that?

JW: His name was Richard Kot, a superb editor. He was accepted by Harvard, Yale, and Stanford law schools, but decided bravely to devote himself to publishing. He went over to Harper and Row, so I was able to continue with him.

WP: Did you feel that *Modern Baptists* was adequately promoted?

JW: Well, of course, it was a strange feeling to know that the publishing house was going under just as your first novel is coming out. I was given a very small advance, and the first printing was 2500 copies. After Rick left, I was a foster child with an editor who was not wild about the book. He did tell me later he liked the other books but didn't particularly like *Modern Baptists*. (Pause.) There is a great deal of chance in publishing, good and bad luck. It can be discouraging. When I first began to write, I had to forget most of what I had seen in seven years of publishing.

WP: As you know, there are a great many unpublished novels floating around college campuses, and there is a kind of conspiracy theory which holds that what gets published depends upon your contacts. Did your experience as an editor help you to get published?

JW: Quite the opposite. When I began writing I considered it a strike against me that I had been an editor. I thought everyone would hate me for quitting my job and trying to write, so I chose people who didn't know me. And I didn't let on that I had been an editor. After I had written half of *Modern Baptists*, I needed some money to keep going and sent the book to an agent. Could he sell it on the basis of what I had written? I wondered. I had published a couple of stories in *The New Yorker*, and I thought that might help. On my birthday came the answer. The agent told me that not only would he not represent me, but that he thought no editor in New York would ever buy the book—and never darken his door again. So I got quite a crushing blow. I was going to give up, but I showed it to a friend of mine from school, and asked him if he thought I should throw in the towel. He read it and thought it was worth finishing it. So I did. Then I sent it, completed, to an agent who didn't like the agent who had rejected me. And she liked the book and didn't get discouraged when it was rejected by five or six editors.

WP: Have you ever considered a book of stories? Short stories seem to be selling pretty well right now.

JW: They are. I haven't been writing many recently. Many? None, actually! It takes me quite a while to write a story, and there's no guarantee that it's going to be accepted. It's frustrating to put in six weeks' work, and then have nothing come of it. So I've stuck to novels.

WP: Since 1983 you've been producing a novel every two years. For these days that's a remarkable output.

JW: I've done it by giving up everything else, by concentrating solely on writing. I haven't been teaching. The most I did was some part-time work. I was typing labels for a lawyer and at one time I was reading film scripts for United Artists.

WP: The writers I've talked to have a love-hate relationship with teachers. Some people think it wears them out too much, while other appreciate the money it brings in. But I don't know of anyone who would like to do it if he had any choice.

JW: You mean if they didn't have to.

WP: Right.

JW: Well, as you mentioned earlier, editing is a type of teaching. I know that after a day of editing I had no energy left over for writing. Editing takes the same resources for me as writing. In fact, writing is almost synonymous with revising. I spend most of my time editing what I've written.

WP: Kurt Vonnegut presents another point of view. He says that if you write in the morning, you need to have something to do in the afternoon.

JW: I drink tea in the afternoon.

WP: You said that the first printing of *Modern Baptists* was 2500 copies. How well did it sell after that?

JW: It sold respectably well, I suppose. Dial did four printings. That was because it ended up with a review by Anne Tyler on the front page of the *Times*. That was just a fluke. I don't know how that happened. I'm sure it would have been sunk without that review. Penguin brought it out later as a paperback and the Literary Guild took it on, though not in a big main selection way.

WP: Another thing that connects you with the Southern tradition is the underlying religious preoccupations in your novels.

JW: Yes, that's very real. I've always taken religion quite seriously, no matter how funny it may seem. I was raised with a Catholic mother and a Protestant father, a Methodist father. In Pre-Vatican Two days, when I was a child, I was given holy cards by the nuns with prayers for the conversion of my father to the one true church. That didn't go over too big with him.

WP: It didn't work either, did it?

JW: No, but I haven't given up on him yet. I think all that nonsense made me much more aware of religion than if I had come from a family that went to the same church every Sunday. In high school, I was the organist at the Methodist church. I felt a little strange about doing that because I still hadn't gotten over the notion that it was sinful or disreputable to be in a Protestant church. I had divided loyalties, and it made me intensely curious about what was going on. I still am. I read all I can on theology, from Barth and Bonhoeffer to Tillich, David Tracey, Rosemary Ruether. And I'm particularly fascinated by Norman O. Brown (yes, lots of people dismiss him now) and his *Life Against Death*. What a book that is.

WP: You say that you used to be an organist, and I know that your family has always been intensely musical, and of course you used some of that as a background in *North Gladiola*. Do you see any sort of correspondences between your family interest in music and your interest in writing?

JW: I'm not sure if there is any direct correspondence. But the indirect are certainly there. Practicing and performing from the first grade on did instill a certain self-discipline that made it easier, later, to sit down in front of a typewriter and struggle to get the words in tune. I played both the piano and cello, the cello with the Baton Rouge Symphony for four years in high school. My father and mother always made sure I practiced at least an hour a day, often more before a contest or recital. Playing music does give you some sense of form, structure. Themes stated, elaborated upon, repeated, the gradual build toward a climax, the sense of an sending, all this must somehow sink in on some level of consciousness. In any case, I still play the piano. In fact, not long ago at a book signing and reception in Connecticut, I played Chopin and Schubert—on a sticky baby grand that refused to repeat the Gb above middle C. And of course I was playing the Gb Impromptu of Schubert's, which has only about five thousand Gb's. By the way, I recently learned Ravel's "Gaspard de la Nuit," where Miss Undine (in her French guise of Ondine) crops up amid a welter of demisemiquavers. I'd like to add—and this has nothing to do with music—that *Miss Undine's Living Room* grew in part from a admiration of Rene Girard's *Deceit, Desire, and the Novel*.

WP: Have there been any high notes, so to speak, in your sales? Are your books selling better?

JW: I think a slight progression, though nothing tremendous from one book to the next. For one week *Miss Undine* was number thirteen on the Doubleday Bookstore bestseller list. I think that was the week Doubleday sold only thirteen books nationswide.

WP: I think it's a tremendous advantage to publish a book as often as possible. I think the big reason for Updike's largely undeserved reputation, at least in my opinion, is the fact that he publishes a book every two weeks.

JW: Exactly, and Joyce Carol Oates every week.

WP: I don't mean that you have to publish that often, but you need to publish with some reglarity. Anne Tyler, for example, publishes one every two years or so.

JW: You're right, *Breathing Lessons* was her eleventh book, and she has concentrated, I think, solely on writing. Maybe her example is helpful to me. People always ask me, what do you really do for a living? I wish I could say I'm a brain surgeon who writes on the side. As it is, I squeak by as best I can with advances and an occasional movie option. And in 1986 I got a Guggenheim, which helped.

WP: Reynolds Price went to school in England, and what was probably his first significant publication was in *Encounter*. Have you had any English periodical publications or reviews?

JW: All my books have been published in England by Secker and Warburg. My editor just died recently. Barley Alison was unforgettable, a woman who had known Evelyn Waugh, all the greats, and had written me very funny letters. She had a black eye when I met her, the result of an improbable but true encounter with a fireman's axe. My books have been reviewed in the *Times Literary Supplement*, the London *Times*, the *Guardian*, and all sorts of papers I never heard of before. I even got a letter once from a lady on the isle of Jersey. It made me think what a shame it was that a cow and a state have been named after this place, which otherwise might have sounded more romantic.

WP: How would you feel about working for the movies?

JW: When I first started writing, I worked with a friend on an original script. We sold it to Columbia, pre Coca-Cola, of course. (Why does everyone get fired the minute they buy something of mine?) I've never done a script since then. It's a different process, and it uses a whole different sense of construction. I have great admiration for film scripts which are well written. It's very difficult to bring off. I was asked to do the screenplay for *Modern Baptists*, but I really wanted to get on and write novels. For some reason that's in my blood now.

WP: I think everybody wants to write scripts now because secretly they think it doesn't take any talent.

JW: (Emphatically.) But it does. And an awful lot of of hard work, as well. It can be terribly exhausting. We had meetings with Columbia, and they kept coming back with suggestions that had nothing to do with what we had in mind. I got discouraged and was secretly relieved when the project was put out of its misery. I was happy to get back to writing short stories again, to be able to write about a Volkswagen and not fear that some executive would make me turn it into a flying Volkswagen.

WP: You seem to have avoided many of the problems that haunt beginning novelists. Your first novel was not autobiographical, and your second novel was published without any delay, and it was successful. Did you have any feeling after the good press that *Modern Baptists* got that it might be a difficult act to follow?

JW: In a way, although what I did was to just get right to work. I try to treat writing as a job and get a little bit done each day. What the reviewers do with the final product is not my job to worry about. Any worrying I do is strictly moonlighting. Reviewers used to frighten me until I started doing a few reviews myself for the *Times Book Review*. Then I became somewhat frightened of myself and wished myself on an alternate earth where there were no such creatures as book reviewers.

WP: I've done a lot of book reviewing and my policy was that, if I didn't like a book, I wouldn't review it. If the guy was a real trash master like Harold Robbins, I figured that he would get what he deserved, but if he was a poor devil who'd spent ten years writing a bad book, I thought he ought to be left alone.

JW: That's a good policy. In any case, I try not to think about reviewers. If I do, then I realize that I do wish the mean ones would just leave me alone. But if they leave you alone, that's not good either. Then you're ignored. So there's no getting away from it. You're trapped like a rat either way.

WP: Do you plot your novels out carefully before you start or do you just have a general idea of where you're going?

JW: I have a good idea of the characters and of a very specific opening situation. I never write a first draft straight through, and I don't have a plot outline. I write fifteen or twenty pages and then I go back and revise. Then I might go ahead for ten pages and then go back and look at the whole thing again, and then maybe venture twenty pages beyond that.

WP: Do you write in longhand, or on a typewriter, or on a word processor, or what?

JW: I've written everything on a typewriter. I do so many major revisions that I'm not sure a word processor would help much. I like to see a real piece of paper, real ink. So I'm happy enough with a typewriter. I try to get a very clean manuscript by the time I turn it in to my agent.

WP: I believed in *Sort of Rich* all the way through, but one thing I didn't believe was where the woman threw the painting at the nutria. I didn't believe that that painting would sink.

JW: Even with a heavy metal frame...?

WP: That mother is going to float, no matter what happens.

JW: Oh, gosh. (Laughs.) I've never actually thrown a painting into the water. But now I must.

WP: Do you have people, especially here in Hammond, who ask you about the basis for the characters in your novels? Or ask whether the Chinese restaurant in your novel is based on one in Hammond?

JW: Actually I haven't had many questions like that. Perhaps if the Trey Yuen started serving hot dogs, I would. I don't get characters from anyone I know in Hammond. A lot of my characters grow out of things I've observed out of the corner of my eye when I've gone to the mall or sat in Morrison's. I look at what people wear, their gestures, and overhear snatches of their very amazing conversations. Although I keep a journal, I don't use it when I sit down to write. Maybe the very process of writing down these two or three exchanges plants a seed for something more full-blown in the imagination.

WP: I wasn't thinking of the dialogue or even the characters as much as the America of shopping malls and beauty parlors and karate studios next to each other. You seem to me to have caught that strangeness better than any other contemporary writer I can think of.

JW: I think that being away helped me in that respect. So many of the changes took place while I was away at Yale. It was like a nature film on public television with a desert blooming in time lapse photography, everything speeded up. I wasn't here to see it happen gradually. Every time I came back in the late sixties, there seemed to be another mall, and new fancy motel. To me it was amazing. I was used to the way Hammond was when I grew up in the fifties, so that if a karate shop opened up or a unisex hair salon, it stood out because it went against what I remem bered.

WP: Do you think that your novels have become more assured, that there has been a progression?

JW: I hope so. There are things I don't like in the earlier books, that I think are overdone. I was definitely doing some thing in the fourth book, *Sort of Rich*, that I felt was different. I thought I could be quieter, more focused. I thought that I could let myself do things that I was maybe afraid to do earlier.

WP: I don't try to outguess the writer, unless of course I'm reading a mystery story, but I was genuinely surprised when, two-thirds of the way through that novel, you killed off one of the main characters.

JW: Hm. Well, it was a risk. I tried to drop hints all the way through, even on the first page. They live on a dead end. He does have heart tremors. He doesn't think they're serious, but I think a reader can pick up on this. The very fact that Gretchen finds out they're using furniture from a funeral parlor may give something away.

WP: Some people I've talked to seem to see something of *A Confederacy of Dunces* in your books, especially the first one, *Modern Baptists*.

JW: I've heard that, and maybe that's the reason I've never read that book. I'm probably the only person in the country that hasn't. Some people have told me also that the resemblance is extremely superficial, they aren't at all alike. Whatever the case, the story of his publication is distressing, to say the least.

WP: I felt that the cover art of the paperback edition of *Modern Baptists* deliberately aped *A Confederacy of Dunces*.

JW: I never saw the cover of *Confederacy*, so I couldn't say. All I know is that I've always been heartily repelled by the Penguin cover. Poor Mr. Pickens is far too fat and oleaginous, and Tula Springs looks like Dodge City with its wooden sidewalks. And for the life of me I can't figure out how the po-boy shop is named something that was cut out of every draft but a very early one that never left my apartment. Penguin must have hired a cat burglar.

WP: What contemporary writers do you particularly admire? Have you ever read Alison Lurie?

JW: I loved her book, *Foreign Affairs*. This is the one where the diminutive heroine is in a fury because of a vile review in *The Atlantic*. (Laughs.) That killed me. (Pauses.) To jump back to 1908, there's Arnold Bennett's *The Old Wives' Tale*, which transfixed me in a strange way. And Walker Percy. I wrote my first and only fan letter to a writer to him—when I finished *The Last Gentleman* while I was at Yale.

WP: What about Peter De Vries?

JW: I haven't read him but I have been compared to him.

WP: It's a reasonable comparison.

JW: Perhaps, but I think I tend to avoid people that I'm compared to. I don't read books about small Southern towns. Maybe there's a bit of superstition there. Besides Muriel Spark's earlier works, I also have a mild addiction to Barbara Pym. I keep on rereading her and I gave two lectures on her for an MFA program in North Carolina. Of course, I do get put out with her when she gets too cosy and dim, which is often.

WP: Still and all, I have the distinct feeling that you're a lot more of a Southern writer than you might think you are.

JW: I definitely am based here.

WP: What about Flannery O'Connor?

JW: I absolutely love her, but I have a running battle with her novels, particularly *The Violent Bear It Away*. I'm not sure that her spiritual concerns are brought across at all well in this. There seems to be an obsessive-compulsive strain, baptism becomes a magic rite. It reminds me of the very worst perversions of Catholic doctrine, where so much emphasis is placed on the correct performance of ritual, the Pope Pius XII time when it was wrong, I think, to bite the wafer. The writing seems so labored, whereas in the stories, "A Circle in the Fire," "A Good Man is Hard to Find," "Revelation," there is a tremendous energy and joy. I love their easy tone, and I find them hilarious. She is the writer who inspires me the most. I've always felt a real kinship. My mother heard her speak, by the way, at St. Albert's [the Catholic student center at Southeastern Louisiana University]. It was my mother who got me reading her way back before I could understand what she was talking about. Even then she cast a spell.

WP: Do you feel closer to her than to Faulkner?

JW: Yes, his writing is so baroque. When I look back at some of his books and see what he got away with, I'm amazed. You have to give yourself over to it totally or it can look quite mannered. Faulkner has such a different sensibility, and sometimes I can't help thinking he's being murky and grand just for the sake of seeming profound. Of course, he is a giant, but I feel much closer to O'Connor's style of writing.

WP: I think that's a generational difference more than anything else.

JW: You're probably right. I'm not too wild about the other side of the coin either, Hemingway.

WP: I don't think there are many friends of Hemingway left anymore.

JW: There are some. They tend to live out West, I think.

WP: It's hard to believe.

JW: Cheever to me is much more interesting, his stories, that is.

WP: How do you feel about the wolf pack, including some of his relatives, who seem happy digging up a lot of dirt about him to sell books?

JW: A chilling precedent. I hope my parents don't get any ideas after I'm gone. I must remember to swallow the key to my journals. In any case, he's a wonderfully inventive writer. I'm not sure, though, why his novels seem so leaden. As for *Home Before Dark*, it was a revelation to me how difficult his life was. I had always imagined his path as smooth and assured.

WP: You were talking about Faulkner as baroque. Were you referring to his style?

JW: Yes, and baroque in painterly, not musical terms. What else can you say about such passages as [picks up *The Unvanquished*, which happens, conveniently, to be at hand] "that ponderable though passing recalcitrance of topography" or "the pattern of recapitulant mimic furious victory"? I gravitate more naturally to the understatement of O'Connor.

WP: Faulkner uses that some, but it's more of a comic device.

JW: Yes. I suppose I just have some genetic inability to appreciate lush prose. Strangely enough, I'm also allergic to minimalists.

WP: One the things that I find interesting is your move to make women characters the main focus of your novels. When I was in school, one of the commonplaces about American literature was the inability of male American novelists—Henry James was always given as an exception—to create convincing women characters.

JW: I don't like to make a big point about this issue, although I do have furtive thoughts about why some writers don't try to fully imagine women characters. As for me, I never like to write about anything close to home—me, that is. The imagination seems to become sharper, more focused, when dealing with the Other. I have trouble reading a lot of contemporary first-person narratives. They seem more like memoirs and tend toward self-indulgence. The "I" is usually the noble victim of unfeeling parents or spouses or ex-spouses. There's an awful lot of self-justification going on. Trying to imagine what life is like for the opposite sex, for an unglamorous, not particularly likable member of that sex, will, maybe this can stir things in the subconscious that would otherwise never come to light. I may be wrong, but this seems to be what fiction is all about, a process of discovery. If you want to get Jungian about it, didn't he say that men have to contend with their animus? The soul, the psyche, is after all, in this system, of the opposite sex.

WP: Do you think you'll ever live here?

JW: I don't really know. Everytime I visit, it's harder to leave. I know this sounds strange, but right now I don't have enough money to move back here. In New York I live very frugally, without a car. Of course, I put up with a lot of aggravation there. But being uncomfortable somehow stimulates my creative juices. I'm afraid I might be too happy in Hammond to write.

WP: Probably the thing that ties you most closely to the Southern tradition is that humor which is an outgrowth of character which used to be a part of the local color tradition. I don't know that anyone would ever call you a local color writer, but I see that incongruity as part of life in the South. There are so many strange things jumbled together and so many different levels of culture and sophistication.

JW: I just hope it works. Maybe it comes from growing up without much television. Dad was strict about limiting our time in front of the TV. My brother and I used to get up at 5 a.m. on Saturdays to sneak a look at Porky Pig. And then we had to give even Porky Pig up for Lent. But we had teachers and friends who relished telling stories. There's already a generation of writers who have no sense of an oral tradition, who derive all their metaphors from TV. They think they are being terribly up-to-date, but the sad truth is that they will probably sound very dated soon enought. Television culture is merciless, and nothing looks more ridiculous than someone trying to be hip five or ten years ago. Who can help smiling at the old Sonny and Cher in their ridiculous bell bottoms? And yet some writers now are staking their entire future on these bell bottoms. (1989)

Chapter 10
In Place of a Conversation
with Walker Percy

> At a table for four with his elegantly dressed sister-in-law was a noncrazy,
> a famous writer who lived in Covington. I suddenly remembered that when we
> were twelve years old, the writer's older daughter and I had planned to petition the
> pope for early entrance to the Carmelites, a religious order famous for its romantic
> iron grilles and nervous breakdowns among the novices. I caught myself smiling
> at nobody in the mirrored wall, and stopped.
>
> —Sheila Bosworth, *Almost Innocent.*

On Sunday, June 19, 1966, *The Nashville Tennessean* published my review
of Walker Percy's novel, *The Last Gentleman*, on the book page, "Under the
Green Lamp, With Floy W. Beatty." The review, accompanied by a photograph by
James W. Guillot of the author playing with a cat, read as follows:

The Last Gentleman. By Walker Percy. Farrar, Straus and Giroux. $5.95.

With the publication of this second novel Walker Percy joins the small
group of really distinguished Southern novelists.

The Moviegoer, which won the National Book Award for fiction, made
excellent use of New Orleans locales and developed several interesting characters,
but its theme struck me as being relatively abstract and undramatized. *The
Moviegoer* gave the impression of having been written by a man who knew what
he wanted to say but who had not yet developed fictional techniques adequate to
convey the full force of his vision.

The Last Gentleman is the odyssey of a young man in trouble. The hero,
Will Barrett, a Southerner by birth and a gentleman by inclination, is a personable
young man who suffers from mental blackouts and who regularly sees a psychia-
trist.

In an attempt to escape his sense of impending doom, Will has retreated to the alien wastes of New York where, after duly completing a prescribed course, he has become a maintenance engineer for a large department store. (His actual field is humidity control.)

Through a fantastic series of events—Mr. Percy openly admits that life is often mysterious—Will becomes involved with a family of well-to-do Southerners named Vaught. The father, who runs an automobile dealership of impeccable vulgarity, invites Will to go South with the family as a companion for his son Jamie, who is dying of leukemia. Will agrees, partly because he is at loose ends and partly because he has become enamored of Kitty, Jamie's sister.

Completing the Vaught menagerie is the ambivalent Rita, who fights Will tooth and nail for possession of Kitty. Rita is the divorced wife of Sutter Vaught, a brilliant doctor who has frittered away his career in drink, despair and alienation.

And gradually they move south, this widely disparate crew, through Alabama and Louisiana and then west to New Mexico, encountering along the way almost every possible variety of homo sapiens from wild-eyed liberals to KKK members. Mr. Percy's mordant wit and satirical skills have never shown to better advantage than they do during the long central portion of the novel.

Sutter Vaught, a kind of modern-day Raskolnikov who wishes to sample every form of experience, dominates the second half of the novel. And the final confrontation, in which the engineer figures as an active if somewhat unwilling participant, takes place at Jamie's death and involves Sutter, his sister Val, a nun, and a somewhat reluctant priest.

Without revealing any more of the plot of Mr. Percy's novel, I would like to list what seems to me to be its manifold blessings. The tone is wry and ironic, and Mr. Percy spreads his satiric fire with fine impartiality. Lacking academic training in creative writing, Mr. Percy has fortunately escaped the influence of Faulkner, which has swallowed so many young writers alive and digested them without a trace.

Mr. Percy's greatest glory, however, is his ability to create lifelike characters and to involve them in significant actions. Sutter Vaught is one of the memorable creations of recent fiction, not only because he is an autonomous character in his own right, but because he is the heir of the speculations of Dostoevsky, of Gide, and of Camus.

Mr. Percy's frame of reference is the widest possible—he, has, however, little to say of the poor whites who have been the staple of so much Southern fiction—and he reminds the reader more often of the continental masters than of, say, Wolfe and Warren.

And yet the whole attitude, the whole point of view of *The Last Gentleman* is shaped by its author's background and by the attitudes and feelings peculiar to the South.

Mr. Percy first became seriously interested in writing through the influence of his uncle, William Alexander Percy, the author of *Lanterns on the Levee*, and I am sure that he will take it as the highest possible praise when I say that his new novel is worthy of a place beside that distinguished autobiography, and that a great many of those qualities of humanity, of nobleness, and of moral concern have survived, in however changed a fashion,the arduous transition from the old South to the new.

I was much more certain of my opinions in those days, and I am now appalled by the sureness of many of my pronouncements, especially by my blithe rejection of the influence of Faulkner on Percy's first two novels. I had recently finished a dissertation in the literature of the English renaissance, and I was spending a lot of time reading and reviewing books, mostly novels, for the *Tennessean* and *The Southern Observer*. Mrs. Floy W. Beatty, the widow of Richmond Beatty, a distinguished scholar at Vanderbilt and co-editor of what was at the time the most widely used anthology of American literature, *The Norton Anthology of American Literature,* had seen one of my reviews and had asked me to write for the *Tennessean*.

Although I had missed *The Moviegoer* when it first appeared, I read it as soon as it appeared in paperback—Popular Library, New York, Ned L. Pines, President—and learned that Percy lived in Covington, Louisiana. I remember looking for Covington on a map and trying to imagine what the place must be like.

In 1965 my wife and I came South to teach at Southeastern Louisiana University, then Southeastern Louisiana College, at Hammond, Louisiana, some twenty-two miles from Covington. After *The Last Gentleman* appeared, I wrote to Percy, enclosing a copy of my review, and asked him for an interview. I received a courteous reply, suggesting Saturday afternoon, to my mind an unfortunate choice because Muhammad Ali was fighting on television that afternoon, but I gladly accepted, and in spite of the fact that I was unfamiliar with Covington, I had no difficulty finding Percy's house.

I was not then the high-tech person I have since become, and I have often regretted that I did not take a tape recorder with me. I remember the long conversation with Percy as one of the most pleasant afternoons of my life. I remember that we sat in his back yard on the bayou and that Percy's beautiful young daughter played happily by herself, only occasionally interrupting her father. I probably expected an alligator to appear at any moment and carry one of us away, but I concealed my fear.

I remember telling Percy that my wife and I had both received terminal degrees and had been hired to teach at Southeastern. He rather surprised me by saying, "Well then you're set for life." I did not feel set for life, but it is true that at that time college English teachers were scarce and there were many jobs available. I told him that I planned to publish my interview in *The Southern Observer*, and he said that he had never heard of the magazine. No matter, I said, few other people had either.

We began by talking briefly about Percy's start in writing. What the novelist told me about his life has since become well known. He said that, after the death of his parents, he had been raised by his uncle, William Alexander Percy—I am certain that is how he described him—and that he had eventually gotten an M.D. degree. He had done more than one-hundred autopsies on tuberclosis cadavers at Bellevue and in the process had contracted tuberculosis. During his extended convalescence, he had turned his attention to novel writing and, after writing two unsuccessful novels, he had eventually gotten *The Moviegoer* published. He said that learning to write novels is a difficult proposition and that you need an independent income of some sort while you were learning the process. Percy told me the story, which has since become a classic literary anecdote, of how *The Moviegoer* received the National Book Award. With the decline in prestige of the Pulitzer, the National Book Award had become the most prestigious American literary award. Apparently the sponsoring organization or the judges had sent a letter to the leading publishers asking that they supply books from their lists for consideration. Because of incompetence or negligence, Alfred A. Knopf, the publisher of both *Lanterns on the Levee* and *The Moviegoer*, did not send a copy of Percy's novel to the judges for consideration.

Jean Stafford, one of the judges of the award for 1961—the others were the novelist Herbert Gold and the cultural critic Lewis Gannett—was married to A. J. Liebling, newspaperman, gourmet, boxing connoisseur, enlightened critic of the press, and student of Louisiana politics. Liebling, who was at that time writing his classic account of Uncle Earl Long's last campaign, *The Earl of Louisiana*, saw a copy of *The Moviegoer* in a book store, bought it, took it home to his wife, and told her that it was a book that the judges ought to consider. The rest is, as they say, history. *The Moviegoer* received the National Book Award, and Percy left Knopf for Farrar, Straus and Giroux, who published him for the remainder of his life.

Our nearly two-hour conversation was almost totally literary, an outpouring of enthusiasms and reservations. Aside from literature, the only subject I remember talking about briefly was movies, about which Percy was enthusiastic, but I soon discovered that he was not, at least according to my standards, an omnivorous moviegoer, although he did watch a lot of old movies on televison, and that our interests in movies were quite different. The early to mid sixties were a great period for movies, especially for foreign films, and the French and the Italians set new standards for artistic excellence, but I do not think that Percy was primarily interested in movies as works of art: he was interested in the way they reflected the impersonality of modern life and what they told us about the nature of fame. He was, so to speak, interested in the movie as a transaction.

We talked about Percy's liking for Dostoevsky, Kierkegaard, Sartre and the existentialists. He liked my review of his novel and my, as it seemed to him, correct identification of the chief influences. I remember mentioning "Stavrogin's

Confession" from *The Possessed* as a possible influence for certain aspects of Sutter's journal, and while he may not have assented, he did not deny the possiblity.

We talked about the influence of Faulkner, and I said, tactlessly as it seems to me now, that Faulkner had swallowed a number of contemporary Southern novelists alive, and I mentioned Shelby Foote as an example. (I was so naive that I do not think it ever occurred to me that Percy might actually *know* some of the people we were talking about.) At the time I thought that Percy had escaped Faulkner's influence because he had started wrting at a later period when Faulkner's influence was on the wane, but that is probably an untenable position in view of the fact that Percy was already middle-aged before he took up the writing of novels, and the publication of Percy's juvenilia may show his first novelistic attempts at least partly as efforts to "get out from under Faulkner." At any rate, the question is still open.

We talked at some length about Henry James. Percy said that, while it might be possible to read Faulkner and survive, no writer could read Henry James to any extent without being strongly influenced by him. James, he said, would swallow you alive. We discussed the beautiful plum-colored New York edition of James's collected works, which had just been reprinted without the beautiful photographs of Alvin Langdon Coburn, and Percy told me that he had a copy of the original edition. We commiserated about the humid Louisiana weather, and Pecy seemed amused by the fact that the silverfish were eating on his edition of James: I was appalled.[1]

I remember recommending the English novelist Gabriel Fielding (*The Birthday King, Through Streets Broad and Narrow, Brotherly Love*), whom Percy had not read. Like Percy, Fielding was an MD, a convert to Catholicism, and a novelist interested in dissecting the malaise of the times. I do not know if Percy ever read Fielding or not. We also talked about Graham Greene, for whom Percy expressed admiration. We discussed *The Comedians*, which had just appeared, and lamented its lack of originality. "We've heard it all before," Percy said, meaning, of course, that the novel contained nothing that Greene had not done better in his earlier novels. A quarter of a century later, however, the criticism seems misplaced, and *The Comedians* looks like Greene's last major novel.

Percy talked about the difficulty of novel writing in general and the particular difficulty of writing philosophical novels, which combine a train or events or incidents with the interior lives of the characters. The American novel, so rich in character and incident, seemed to him almost totally deficient in philosophy. I remember expressing the idea, then much more common than it is now, that the American novel, except for Henry James, is deficient in convincing women characters and that *The Last Gentleman* is a notable exception. The idea pleased him, and I still believe it to be true. We both spoke admiringly of Saul Bellow's *The Adventures of Augie March* as an example of the exuberant and extroverted novel and wondered why Bellow did not write more in that vein. (In retrospect, *Augie* and wondered why Bellow did not write more in that vein. (In retrospect, *Augie March* seems so strange a work among Bellow's other novels that it might almost have arrived from another planet.) We marveled over the paradox that the novels and stories of I. B. Singer set in Poland before the holocaust seemed more realistic and convincing than the ones set in the present, which seemed to us almost totally lacking in conviction.

Percy said that it takes a lot of time to become a novelist, but that it takes intelligence and effort as well, and suggested that I should be interested. And I think that I might well have been if I could ever have stopped reading long enough to write so ambitious a project as a novel.

We talked about the reception of *The Moviegoer*, and Percy said that he was disappointed that the novel had not been more widely reviewed. When I asked him if he had learned anything about writing from the reviews, he replied in the negative. Percy seemed concerned that readers might not understand important points about the novel which were not explicitly stated, and as I prepared to leave he asked me two questions about the novel. The first question was if I thought the two women in the novel were involved in a lesbian relationship. I answered yes. The second concerned my interpretation of the ending of the novel. The question, although not explicitly stated, concerned whether Sutter was going to carry out his threat to commit suicide. I answered no.

I remember the bayou and the afternoon sunlight and the beautiful girl playing happily by herself for the most part and only occasionally interrupting her father, but most of all I remember the novelist at ease, with that quality of alert repose we have seen so often in him and which I thought of always in cinematic terms. The photographs of Buster Keaton, before his face became ruined, had often a similar look.

Some days after my interview, I sent Percy a package of books, including a novel or two by Georges Simenon, whom I admired greatly and whom we had discussed. I also included the second novel of a much praised young Southern writer. Back came a note from Percy. He said the book read as if William Faulkner had come back from the grave and had decided that he had "left out fucking" and had better write about it.

My interview, alas, was neither written nor published. *The Southern Observer* went out of business, and I dropped the project. I did write an essay, "The Novels of Walker Percy: A Qualified Affirmation," and sent it off to a literary quarterly, but a famous editor sent it back to me with a letter so savage that I destroyed both the essay and the rejection.

As time passed and as Percy became more famous, people kept telling me that he was a hermit and I kept defending him. He was merely a man who wanted to be left alone to do his work. People wanted him to review books for their book club, to talk to their social group or to write a short notice for this or that. I knew that he must perforce refuse most of these requests, and I did not want to add to his burden.

In April 1978, the Southern Literary Festival was held at my school, Southeastern Louisiana University, under the direction of Professor Tim Gautreaux. Participants included three novelists—Percy, John W. Corrington, Jr. (*The Actes and Monuments*), Guy Owen (*The Ballad of the Flim-Flam Man*)—and one poet, Miller Williams (*A Circle of Stone*). Percy made the main address and received $900.00 for his appearance, more than any other participant. He talked to students about writing in the afternoon and made the feature presentation that night, at which he read from his most recent novel *Lancelot* and discussed it. After the reading he appeared briefly and convivially at a reception at our house. I remember that he complimented me nicely upon my library. He also autographed a copy of *Lanterns on the Levee*—"From the nephew of the author"—and remarked that he had never seen a wartime edition of the book printed by Knopf on thin paper like the one I had.

Earlier that day, a number of people from the English department had lunched with the novelist at a Hammond restaurant. I was located some two seats away from Percy, and I spoke to him only occasionally, but I did comment on an item that had recently appeared concerning the novelist and critic, John Gardner, an advocate of "moral fiction." When Percy's most recent novel *Lancelot* had appeared some months earlier, Gardner had savagely and, I think, unfairly, reviewed it on the front page of the *New York Times Book Review*. Now, according to an item that had appeared in *Time* or *Newsweek*, a scholar in the field had shown Gardner's biography of the English poet Geoffrey Chaucer, recently published by Knopf, to have been widely plagiarized. When I repeated this story rather gleefully to Percy, he considered it carefully and soberly and said questioning, "You act as if that's supposed to cheer me up." I did not respond, although I thought that it certainly should have cheered him up, unless he was a saint, which he certainly was not, although he may eventually become one. But the answer was typical of Percy: he could accept nothing at face value without careful consideration, at least so far as his own motives were concerned, and the automatic responses that so many of us make were closed to him.

In 1971 my friend Frank Jackman of the History department at Southeastern had recommended me for a teaching position at St. Joseph Seminary College, run by the Benedictine monks at St. Benedict, Louisiana, outside of Covington. I taught one class of English there every semester and in the process began a slow but powerful turning toward Catholicism. During the 1982-83 academic year, Percy taught a one-semester class there in American fiction—standard stuff, Updike, Bellow and so on—and I saw him once or twice late in the afternoon. I remember telling him that I had converted to Catholicism. He did not congratulate me, but he gave the statement careful consideration and accepted it. "I didn't know that," he said.

Percy gave the commencement address at the seminary in May of 1983.

My wife and Mrs. Percy talked about Eudora Welty and sat in the audience of per-haps one-hundred. I sat on the stage, but because of the poor acoustics in the audi-torium, I did not hear much of the address. Percy stood with his legs apart, as solidly rooted to the floor as a Millet peasant is rooted to the ground, and defended the church and the priesthood against attackers. The essay has since been printed in *Signposts in a Strange Land*, and a facsimile of the manuscript, typed on a man-ual typewriter with corrections in longhand, is on display in the college library.

In the early 1980's I began researching and publishing a series of essays on filmmaking in Louisiana during the silent period. When the first of these, "Filmmaking in Louisiana During the Silent Period: *The Lone Wolf*," was pub-lished in *Regional Dimensions* in 1983—the periodical actually appeared in early 1984—I sent Percy a copy along with a copy of *Heroes' Twilight*, a small book I had written on the film director, Sam Peckinpah (*The Wild Bunch*, *Ride the High Country*). I knew that Percy was unlikely to share my high opinion of Peckinpah's extremely violent films, and the note he sent me about the Peckinpah book was courteous but noncommital. The next day, however, I received an enthusiastic card praising the Louisiana essay and asking rhetorically if anyone could doubt that movies were the art form of the century.

Shortly after Percy's last novel, *The Thanatos Syndrome*, appeared in 1987, my friend, Bill Dowie, who had written several essays on Percy, and I drove to Covington for a book signing party. Seated comfortably on the porch of the "Kumquat," a bookstore owned by his daughter, the novelist seemed perfectly at ease. I remember that the generally harsh afternoon sunlight of Louisiana seemed subdued that day and played gently on the edges of the shadows of the porch. He signed my copy, "From old friend Walker Percy." That was the last time I saw him.

Walker Percy seems to me to have suffered from a profound melancholy. I believe that he developed his analytical facilities and became a novelist in an attempt to come to grips with a constitutional propensity for sad refection. Percy's novels reflect both his tendency toward a profound mistrust of motives and a cer-tain grayness of outlook. This is not meant as a clinical judgment but merely as a statement of motivation. The question with Percy, as with many of us, is not whether the bomb is going to destroy us, but whether we are going to get through the night. Enveloped in a melancholy twilight, the novelist records, with a greater or lesser objectivity, man's final days.[2]

[1] James is such a poweful artistic presence that the idea of his swallowing up a writer's personality is a common one. After writing this introduction I came across a passage by Amy Clampitt citing William Gass's advice about imitating James: "A very poor model to follow. . . He will swallow you up. . . . Just run as fast in the other direction as you can" (*Predecessors, Et Cetera*, Ann Arbor: University of Michigan Press, 1991, p. 63).

[2] Without using the term depression in a clinical sense, I find myself in agreement with the analysis of Percy given by Bertram Wyatt-Brown. See Wyatt-Brown's "A Family Tradition of Letters: The Female Percys and the Brontean Mode," *In Joy and Sorrow*, ed. Carol Bleser (New York, 1991), pp.176-177.